Feltnes

Stephanie
Springgay

Duke University Press
Durham and London
2022

Research-Creation,
Socially Engaged Art, and
Affective Pedagogies

Printed in the United States of America on acid-free paper ∞
Project editor: Lisa Lawley
Designed by Courtney Leigh Richardson
Typeset in Whitman and Quicksand by Westchester Publishing Services

Library of Congress Cataloging-in-Publication Data
Names: Springgay, Stephanie, author.
Title: Feltness : research-creation, socially engaged art, and affective
pedagogies / Stephanie Springgay.
Description: Durham : Duke University Press, 2022. | Includes bibliographical
references and index.
Identifiers: LCCN 2022006104 (print) | LCCN 2022006105 (ebook) |
ISBN 9781478016267 (hardcover) | ISBN 9781478018902 (paperback) |
ISBN 9781478023531 (ebook)
Subjects: LCSH: Affective education–United States. | Affective education–
Social aspects–United States. | Arts in education–United States. | Affect
(Psychology) in art. | Feminist theory. | BISAC: EDUCATION / Arts in
Education | EDUCATION / Teaching / Methods & Strategies
Classification: LCC LB1072.S685 2022 (print) | LCC LB1072 (ebook) |
DDC 370.15/34–dc23/eng/20220421
LC record available at https://lccn.loc.gov/2022006104
LC ebook record available at https://lccn.loc.gov/2022006105

Cover art: Hand-lettering by Courtney Leigh Richardson,
photo by Jim O'Sullivan.

Duke University Press gratefully acknowledges the Social Sciences and
Humanities Research Council of Canada, which provided funds toward the
publication of this book.

For all the artists,
students, and
teachers who make
this work possible

Writing this book could not be possible without the love and support of my family and friends, as well as the vibrant arts and academic communities that I am a part of. I am especially grateful to the many students, teachers, and artists with whom I have had the pleasure of working over the past decade, especially Shannon Gerard, Hannah Jickling, Reed Reed, Rodrigo Hernandez-Gomez, Sarah Febbraro, and Hazel Myer. I am immensely grateful to my graduate student research assistants and collaborators extraordinaire: Aubyn O'Grady, Zofia Zaliwska, Julie Smitka, Andrea Vela Alarcón, Arden Hagerdon, Sarah Truman, James Miles, and Lee Cameron. You are colleagues and mentors, and you have always pushed my thinking to places I could never have gone on my own. This book is as much yours as it is mine.

The research-creation projects and the writing of this book would not be possible without Rita Irwin, who created a speculative, experimental, and collaborative space at the University of British Columbia in the early 2000s. You seeded the possibilities to do research differently. I am forever grateful for your mentorship and love and the enormous permissions you made for your students to intervene into the neoliberal logics of academic work. Among the many people I met in Vancouver, Leah Decter has been a constant companion in my research-creation endeavors, and I'm so glad that we can continue to think and work together. Nancy Nisbet is Vancouver kin who has been part of this journey through research-creation and radical pedagogy. Allison Moore's steadfast friendship (and our Zoom coffee conversations during the pandemic) has sustained me in more ways than she knows. Allison and I began our artistic careers together in Toronto in the early 1990s long before either of us had ventured into academia. We came together at a time in the arts community when feminist collectives were flourishing as an important site for reimagining artistic practice as research. And while she no longer go-go dances in my kitchen, Linda Knight's arts-based research continues to inspire my thinking-making-doing. Jess Dobkin has been a collaborator and coconspirator, and I am moved by her generosity and plushy pink trickster performances; one always needs a Lady-Jane latrine-vitrine as a counter-archive. Natalie Loveless's encouragement got me through some challenging moments in the writing process. Her research-creation theorizing and practice has been so foundational to the work I do; to me she is the research-creation whisperer. Jorge Lucero is my interlocutor in art as pedagogy. I am indebted to your *Conceptual Art as Teacher* practice. To all those whose names I can't cite here, do note that you are part of the pages (that I hope will become worn) and the life lived doing this work.

While the research-creation events described in these pages took place before I joined McMaster University, the book itself was written during my first year as director of the School of the Arts. I am so inspired by the creative energy of my colleagues in the school, and I am lucky to work in such an environment. This book was possible in an impossible year because of the work we will do in the present future together. I could not have survived the first year in a new position without my fierce feminist colleagues Susie O'Brien, Christina Baade, Melinda Gough, Chandrima Chakraborty, Christine Quail, and Catherine Anderson. Your mentorship and queer feminist care are incalculable.

I want to thank Elizabeth Ault and her team at Duke University Press for the encouragement and support to put this book out into the world. I met Elizabeth at the affect theory conference, and, to all those who were gathered together there by Gregg Seigworth, you are held in the highest regards. All the feels and felts go out to you. I am grateful to the anonymous reviewers for their capacious readings of the manuscript and their insightful suggestions to make the work stronger. Thank you to the Social Sciences and Humanities Research Council of Canada for funding the research-creation events. The photographs included here were taken by me, by the artists, or by the graduate students working on the various projects. Special thanks to Julie Smitka and Andrea Vela Alarcón for editing and managing additional photoshoots.

Finally, on a personal note, 2021 has been a year of immense pain, heartbreak, and loss, but within that space of crisis extra special thanks go to my mother Barbara and to Maurya and Liam for the meals made, loads of laundry completed, and your radical imaginings of a better and more just future. Your intellectual curiosity, creativity, and rage are felted into these pages.

Feltness

On How to
Practice Intimacy

Thirty-five elementary school students stand on the banks of the Don River in Toronto, Canada, a major waterway through the city that empties into Lake Ontario that lies only a short walk from their public school. They giggle and cheer as the artists Hannah Jickling and Reed Reed, as part of the *Upside Down and Backwards* residency, arrive in a red canoe filled with brightly colored wooden stakes measuring approximately three feet long and six inches wide. The students had painted these color bars in their classroom days prior. Each student created a bar of pure color (hue) and tints (adding white) in two-inch strips. While math, color theory, and paint mixing know-how were combined in the lesson, its main objective was to queer and interrupt settler colonial Canadian landscape art that often romanticizes nature as wild and untouched. Scholars like Myra Hird (2017) and Nicholas Mirzoeff (2016) argue that Western Enlightenment aesthetics is characterized by dominant narratives of beauty, rationality, and control. This is illustrated in the paintings by the Group of Seven Canadian landscape painters from the 1920s. Their iconic images of wind-swept White Pines, isolated karst rocks, and pristine waterways still permeate the Canadian national identity. The Group of Seven paintings, along with other landscape art that depicts Canada as a heroic and barren land available for human conquest, dominate elementary school art education. These landscape paintings, which tell a false story of *terra nullius*, are used to craft a narrative of Canada as a place of wild beauty—which is not the students' lived experience as racialized newcomers who live in the dense urban surround. Jickling and Reed introduced the students to contemporary art that looks critically at the Canadian landscape and offers counter-images: Jin-me Yoon's photographs that place her Korean community, family, and self in a landscape painting by the Group of Seven artist Lawren Harris; work by the artists Elinor Whidden, Terrance Houle (Kainai Nation), and Trevor Freeman, who manipulate the icon of the canoe to place it in landscapes very different from those swept by the great northern winds; and work by the Cree artist Kent Monkman, which reenacts iconic landscape paintings but tells the story of Indigenous genocide.

After the fanfare of Reed and Jickling's arrival, the canoe pulls up onto the shore and the color bars are unloaded onto the sand. Working in small groups, the students are encouraged to arrange their bars by staking them in the sand and shoreline and to use digital cameras to photograph various arrangements and combinations, including their own bodies in the photographs. The color bars have also been reproduced on vinyl paper and used to cover juice boxes handed out to the students for a snack. These kid-oriented color bars are also arranged (once emptied) in colorful compositions in the sand. As a counter-action, the multiple color bar configurations, called *Endless Paintings*, and the students' bodies are inserted into the Canadian landscape, disrupting the whiteness of typical landscape art. As a culmination of the event, the students and the artists arrange all of the wooden color bars in the sand at the edge of the water in a rainbow sequence facing a large metal bridge. The students gather on the bridge to view the rainbow color bars and their watery reflection. In the first weeks of the residency, the students had been shown a landscape painting of the Don River from the vantage point of that same bridge. In countering conventional landscape painting, the students' rainbow compositions create reflective interferences that queer the nature-culture divide (Springgay and Truman 2019a).

This book is concerned with socially engaged art as research-creation that germinates a radical pedagogy of "feltness." Feltness, as I will articulate throughout the book, invokes intimate pedagogies of touching, of transcorporeal, affective force. Each chapter is attuned to a number of research-creation events that were collaboratively coproduced among researchers, artists, students, and teachers over a decade as part of *The Pedagogical Impulse*, including residencies such as *Upside Down and Backwards*. Documentation of the research-creation events along with additional publications, living archives, and resources can be found at http://www.thepedagogicalimpulse.com.

Research-creation is a geographically distinct term that shapes the Canadian landscape of artistic research, placing emphasis on the coimbrication of creative practices and academic research. As *research-creation* is the term used by our major funding body, the Social Sciences and Humanities Research Council of Canada (SSHRC), it therefore must also be recognized as constructed within increasingly neoliberal institutional models of knowledge mobilization (Loveless 2019; Manning and Massumi 2014; Truman 2020).[1] While the definitions and practices of research-creation are diverse and varied, my specific interests are in its relationship to feminist, antiracist, anti-ableist, and anticolonial education. As Natalie Loveless (2019) contends, research-creation is a transdisciplinary practice that challenges conventional modes of knowledge and value in the university. Research-creation, for me, has become a question of how to work ethically and in *intimate relation* with diverse publics. As a white settler scholar working in TKaronto (Toronto) on Turtle Island (Canada) I recognize my privileged position within the arts and the academy. From this perspective, my research-creation theorizing and practice aims to critically reflect on and confront historical and ongoing enactments of settler colonialism and transatlantic slavery and the ways in which the arts and the university are complicit in such logics. I began my academic career at a time when artistic research was flourishing in the academy, rendering permissible alternative methods of research even before terms such as *research-creation* made such work legible. My privileges as a white artist-scholar allowed me to navigate the arts and alternative research practices with (some) ease. I recognize that the whiteness of research-creation has erased (and continues to erase) other forms of cultural production. While I situate my research-creation within socially engaged art and the Pedagogical Turn, I am also mindful of these colonial spaces and practices and the problematic savior narratives that are carried out within these fields.[2] (I return to these complexities later in this introduction.) That said, I find socially engaged art as research-creation compelling particularly for what it might do, the kinds of speculative worldings it makes possible.

The research-creation projects that make up the material of this book take up questions and matters regarding socially engaged art, research-creation, and radical pedagogy in postsecondary institutions as well as in elementary and secondary schools in North America. This book not only enlarges urgent conversations and theoretical frameworks for doing research-creation but contextualizes these arguments with examples from diverse socially engaged projects coproduced by students and teachers. Each chapter therefore makes an important connection between research-creation, socially engaged art, and radical pedagogy in different contexts, revealing how children, youth, and adults negotiate learning that disrupts and defamiliarizes schools and institutions, knowledge systems, values, and the legibility of art and research. The various examples in the book explore the *how* of research-creation as an ethics and politics committed to queer, feminist, antiracist, and anticolonial intimate practices. The *how* of research-creation resonates with Félix Guattari's (1995) ethico-aesthetic paradigm. In the final chapter of *Chaosmosis: An Ethico-aesthetic Paradigm*, he asks: "How do you make a class operate like a work of art?" (133). Guattari's provocation leads us to consider the artist-pedagogue. Departing from the view that art is work done by an artist to predictable materials, or that the classroom is capable of being shaped by a teacher, a *classroom as a work of art* renders art and pedagogy in an ever-evolving entanglement of mutating coemergence and co-composition. As an experimenter, the artist-pedagogue does not mold students into a work of art, as if the students simply become raw materials separate from the pedagogical event. Rather, artist-teacher-student-classroom become a creative assemblage replete with the potential to open itself to future creative instances. If a classroom operates as a work of art—not as an object manipulated from the outside but as a spatiotemporal site of cocreation—it becomes enmeshed and enlivened with potential future worldings. In opposition to dogmatic models of education, Guattari's words conjure possibilities of learning that are inventive, artful, and open. Subsequently, it asks questions about what a radical pedagogy of the future might become.

One of the motivating factors that led to *The Pedagogical Impulse* were questions that I had regarding what has been called the "Educational Turn": as curators and artists were using educational forms and pedagogical methods in their art practices, they were often doing so outside of public schooling and at a remove from students, teachers, and meaningful pedagogical theories. In this book I engage with some of the critical conversations on the Educational Turn and begin the work of thinking through the *how* of radical pedagogy. Specifically, I want to shift radical from defined as the avant-garde toward *pedagogy* as relational, transcorporeal, and affective, or what I have called feltness. In theorizing feltness, I bring this to bear on research-creation, radical pedagogy, and questions of collaboration.

The Pedagogical Impulse

Since the 1990s, under the auspices of the "Educational" or "Pedagogical Turn," artists and curators have produced a wide variety of artist projects, exhibitions, curatorial initiatives, alternative schools, discursive events, and published texts to counter neoliberal and capitalist models of education. These educational art and curatorial practices were in part a response to severe funding cuts in the arts and higher education and to the corporatization of the university (Allen 2011; Bishop 2012; Graham 2010; Holert 2020; Rogoff 2008). Some of these initiatives took place outside of formal institutions, for example in parks or shop fronts, while others set out to establish alternative pedagogical models within galleries and other institutional venues including art fairs such as Documenta. In some instances, educational forms such as the seminar or workshop were co-opted as modes of knowledge production and exchange, privileging the discursive as an art form (Podesva 2007). In other iterations, alternative models of education were developed as a counter-rhetoric against a formal education that was increasingly complicit with neoliberalism. Despite the diverse range of educational projects, in many cases they relied on art's instrumentalization of education, often absorbing the processes of knowledge production that they sought to disrupt. Through mimicry the Educational Turn perpetuated the norms of education under a rubric of alternative schooling. Debates were waged about whether these educational initiatives were artistic works and about the terms by which they could be evaluated; on the merits of antagonism versus conviviality (Bishop 2012; Kester 2004); or on the nature of collaboration and cooperation that such projects engendered (Finkelpearl 2013; Jackson 2011; Kester 2004). Claire Bishop acutely argued that because educational projects went "unseen" (they had no formal art audience), or had no concrete termination period (the work did not seem to end in some cases), they could not be adequately evaluated and critically analyzed on the basis of their aesthetics—in other words, aesthetics had been compromised and instrumentalized (see Bishop 2012; Bishop 2013; Bruguera 2020). I re-turn to these challenges about the role and place of audiences in chapter 1, and I suggest that such questions continue to privilege particular colonial values and tastes.

Notwithstanding these critical deliberations, few conversations occurred that interrogated what was meant by *pedagogy* in these instances. As Irit Rogoff (2008) argued, knowledge production, learning, and pedagogy were being used interchangeably and without any real inquiry into how education was being deployed, theorized, or for that matter altered. Pablo Helguera (2010) similarly contended that most pedagogical projects relied on historical, limited, and superficial understandings of current educational theories and praxes. When discussions about pedagogy were entertained, references were limited to Paulo Freire, John Dewey, and Jacques Rancière, neglecting the vast scholarship on curriculum and pedagogy that has occurred for more than a hundred years. My contention is that the majority of education-as-art projects only gestured at education and did not actually transform processes of learning, and that the pedagogical work undertaken was often undertheorized, short-term, and focused on spectacular modes of presentation.

As Janna Graham, Valeria Graziano, and Susan Kelly (2016) assert, few of the initiatives under the auspices of the Educational Turn made connections to the institutional struggles that teachers and students were experiencing or mobilizing against. They argue that pedagogical projects rarely intervened in the corporatization of higher education, or in the increasing debt that students and artists were facing. While many of these educational projects used the language of the alternative art school, or of experimental and inventive pedagogy, they too often simply mirrored neoliberal norms of education and failed to account for the kinds of educational reforms and radical pedagogies that already existed inside and outside of schools. Graham (2010) has also argued that, when artists and curators are perceived to be in a better position to imagine alternative arts education, while the teacher becomes merely a trope in the bureaucracy of schooling, the Educational Turn risks reifying the avant-garde. To reorient the Educational Turn, Graham, Graziano, and Kelly (2016) insist, we must learn from the histories that have informed radical pedagogy and art education, including social movements and ethics of resistance. These genealogies, they contend, locate art and pedagogy in wider practices of care, decolonization, feminism, and antiracism that are needed to "contest the anxiety, debt, precarity and isolation produced at the hands of current neoliberal educational reform" (Graham, Graziano, and Kelly 2016, 35). This is what Guattari (1995) meant when he proposed that a classroom behave like a work of art. Radical pedagogy becomes a practice committed to working transversally, to resisting disciplinary categories and hierarchies, and to an ethics and politics of relationality. Transversality cuts diagonally through dualisms and emphasizes processes of becoming that connect previously unexplored topographies. For Guattari (1984), transversality's radical potential was affective and collective.

My own research regarding socially engaged art and pedagogical art practices problematizes, questions, and examines the complex emergences of *radical pedagogy as feltness*. How are artists, in collaboration with students and teachers, understanding and materializing radical pedagogy? What is radical pedagogy and how might it create different future worldings? I found it curious that while there was a desire and need to alter the forms of the pedagogical encounter to be more relational and social justice oriented, much socially engaged art was happening *outside* of the classrooms of public education, and rarely in consultation and collaboration with students, teachers, and scholars of education. As educational forms were proliferating in contemporary art, they continued to take place apart from classroom spaces and therefore made no impact on art education, teacher education, or student learning. Arts education in schools remained on the periphery of contemporary art, in part because of perceived values associated with community-based art or school art (see Reed et al. 2012). To me this represented a missed opportunity to think deeply and intimately about what radical pedagogy could become and how it could offer strategies for enduring and changing precarious worlds. For education to significantly change, the Pedagogical Turn needed to move *into* the classroom (while at the same time disrupting it), to the site of its production, and at the same time become more accountable to diverse educational scholarship and theories.

Feltness: Research-Creation, Socially Engaged Art, and Affective Pedagogies enters into conversations about the transversal nature of research-creation and radical pedagogy. It proposes that the future of radical pedagogy is conditioned by what I call feltness, a practice of intimacy. In an era of increasing neoliberal reforms, the corporatization of the university and of education more generally, and the reliance on impact factors and numerical measurements to assess the value of research and pedagogy, I posit intimacy as a necessary source of disruption. The book is oriented around three concepts-practices-theories: *feltness*, *research-creation*, and *radical pedagogy*. Chapters take up these concepts-practices-theories through a series of research-creation projects and events in school contexts, along with analyses and historical archival research into the radical art and pedagogy of the 1960s and 1970s. Each chapter extends and unravels its own transversally connected theme to make way for diverse stories about my ongoing research-creation practice. The stories subtly reveal the relationships between the speculative ideation of grant proposals and initial research questions and the practice of research-creation as pliable, in flux, and context-responsive. These stories act like way-finding, or navigational, nodes within a messy and complex research landscape and situate my accountability to feminist, anti-oppressive, and anticolonial practices.

Entangling feltness, research-creation, and radical pedagogy, I produce a story that matters (Haraway 2016) about the impact of socially engaged art in school contexts. The book aims to offer theoretical and exemplary enactments of research-creation as intimate, contribute significantly to debates on, and practices within the Pedagogical Turn, and attune to the various ways radical pedagogy emerges in different educational contexts.

Feltness and Touching Encounters

Feltness has various entry points, including the textile process of hand-felting; affect theory and feelings; the material and embodied experience of being in the world; queer-feminist theories of touching encounters; and feminist materialist conceptualizations of more-than-human entanglements. Intimacy conjures radical relatedness, reciprocity, and care.

A starting place for the concept of feltness is my art practice of hand-felting sheep's wool or human hair (Springgay 2008; Springgay 2019).[3] Felt is a non-woven fabric composed of interlocked fibers. It is produced by matting, fusing, condensing, and pressing fibers together. The agitation of fibers in the presence of heat and moisture causes the wool fibers to interlock, preventing the fiber from returning to its original position; felting is irreversible. There is a myth that felt was first discovered by a monk who lined his shoes with wool, and another by a couple copulating on a pile of fleece; both stories convey the necessity of friction, in and through touch.

Wool felt is resilient and retains its strength and properties for a long time. Felt can be produced industrially and is used as a fire retardant and insulator, as well as a craft material. The process of wet hand-felting is an activity that is skin-based and tactile. Rubbing woolly fibers between palm and fingers is itself an intimate practice that touches. Feltness recognizes bodily, fleshy, tactile, intense, frictional becomings.

It is important to acknowledge that felt is part of the legacies of settler colonialism in Canada, as the fur trade profited from beaver pelts that were used to make felted beaver hats. From the late sixteenth century to the mid-nineteenth century, beaver hats were an essential part of men's fashion in Europe, and eventually in Canada as well. By the seventeenth century, beaver had been depleted in Europe, but the North American fur trade provided a new source. The Hudson's Bay Company was founded in 1670 to source and procure the much-needed pelts. It is not the focus of this introduction to detail this history, but at the same time it is crucial to account for felt's role in the violent dispossession of Indigenous peoples, the exploitation of Turtle Island, and the role that capitalism plays in anti-Indigenous and anti-Black racism.

Its history notwithstanding, felt has been a rich material source for feminist textile arts practices that explore social and political issues. Felt making, like other textile arts, was traditionally associated with women, craft, and the domestic sphere, devaluing it within the hierarchy of the arts (Parker 1984). Since the 1960s, many contemporary artists have turned to fiber and textile arts as a social and political statement, subverting its associations with domesticity and craft while asserting the politics of gender (Black and Burisch 2021). Artists who incorporate felting include Maria Hupfield (Anishinaabe), who meticulously constructs everyday objects out of gray industrial felt—a suit, mitts, boots, a canoe, an Anishinaabe jingle spiral—that can be displayed or worn by the artist and activated in live performances. While the gray felt conjures a neutral aesthetic, the objects reference Anishinaabe experiences and stories. Leah Decter uses wet and needle felting to create garments, objects, and spatial installations. Her work contends with histories and contemporary issues related to settler colonialism and settler and Indigenous relations. My own felting practice is shaped by feminist and queer contemporary textile arts and examines the labor of craft, durational performance, and body knowledges.

Deleuze and Guattari (1987, 485) call felt an "anti-fabric," made by the agitation or entanglement of fibers. It has no warp and weft, and it "is in no way homogeneous: it is nevertheless smooth, and contrasts point by point with the space of fabric (it is in principle infinite, open, and unlimited in every direction . . .)" (475). When felt is formed, the individual coils of wool are no longer individual but become an aggregate of the whole. The fulling process makes the individual fibers indistinguishable even upon close inspection. Deleuze and Guattari use felt as a model for smooth space, space which could be defined as full of potential. They write: "Smooth space is filled by events of haecceities, far more than by formed and perceived things. It is a space of affects, more than one of properties. . . . It is an intensive rather than an extensive space, one of distances, not of measures and properties" (479). This is in contrast to striated space that is gridded, linear, and metric. In this instance, feltness as radical pedagogy works in opposition to and ruptures neoliberal and capitalist structures of education and learning.

The commingling that felt performs enacts what Stacy Alaimo (2010; 2016) calls transcorporeality. Transcorporeality recognizes entangled and touching relations between bodies, things, and environments. Transcorporeality "emerges from a sense of fleshy permeability," eroding a human-centric understanding of the world (Alaimo 2016, 78). Or as Karen Barad (2007, 384) argues, "We need to take account of the entangled materialization of which we are a part." Connecting felt with theories of touch and transcorporeality becomes a way to open up and reconfigure different bodily imaginaries, both human and nonhuman, that are radically immanent and intensive; as an assemblage of forces and flows that open research-creation to helices and trans connections (Springgay and Truman 2017).

I also understand feltness as feeling, sensuousness, and affect—and I enjoy the messy leakages between different affect theories. Sara Ahmed (2004) describes affects through the language of "stickiness" and "circulation," contending that they matter because they move and, in moving, constitute dynamic economies between things. Movement and rhythm inflect affect and connect, disrupt, and invert life. Affects are the atmospheres generated by particular compositions between bodies. Attuning ourselves to the affective atmospheres around us asks us to be more deliberate about creating the kinds of worlds in which we want to live. An interest in the affective and in the materiality of all things seeks to rupture human exceptionalism, animacy, and agency while understanding the circulations and exchanges between entities as inscribed in relations of power.

Felting disturbs, intensifies, and provokes a heightened sense of the potentiality of the present. It is a proposition that remains open; it is infused with experimentation, emergence, and undoings. Felting invokes the intimacy of touch. Touch reminds us that gestures are incomplete and "that to reach toward an other is never more (or less) than the act of reaching, for an other cannot be discovered as such" (Manning 2007, 9) and that in touch is the ongoing unfolding of difference. This is what Donna Haraway refers to as *becoming with*, a mode of ethical touching; we are always imbricated in all that we touch and that touches us. Touch and its conjunctive intimacies, including the possibilities of "non-innocent knottings" (Haraway 2016, 29) and violent entanglements, becomes a powerful means by which to create and invent new ways of making a difference in the world.

In felting, wool fibers commingle and enmesh and evoke what Barad (2012) refers to as a queer self-touching. When we touch ourselves, she writes, we encounter an uncanny sense of the stranger or otherness within the self. Using quantum theory to shape a theory of self-touching, Barad explains how a particle touches itself, and then how that touching subsequently touches itself, releasing an infinite chain of touching touches. She writes: "Every level of touch, then, is itself touched by all possible others" (212). This radically queers any notion of difference and identity. Self-touching, she argues, "is an encounter with the infinite alterity of the self" (213). In touching, or felting for that matter, "each individual always already includes all possible intra-actions with 'itself' through all the virtual Others, including those that are noncontemporaneous with 'itself.' That is, every finite being is always already threaded through with an infinite alterity diffracted through being and time" (213).

Intimacy is conventionally described as closeness, affinity, attachment, and familiarity. As feltness—relationality and reciprocity—intimacy becomes a mode of invention and creation that proliferates indeterminately and affectively. This is an ethics of care that is "uncomfortable and perplexing" and that does not place human mastery at the center (Alaimo 2010, 17). In articulating research-creation as a practice of intimacy, I am holding space to be touched by the thinking-making-doing of research-creation, as well as the bodies (human and nonhuman) that co-compose the research encounter.

As a practice of intimacy, research-creation recognizes that everything is in relation, indeterminate, and constantly forming. However, it is crucial that we ask complex questions about what it means to be in relation; to be intimate: *How are relations composed and sustained over time? How are all bodies in relation being accounted for, attuned to, and offered something for their contribution to or labor of being in relation?* Opening space for the production of intimacy demands that we are response-able to the formation of relations. Intimacy stems from an awareness of the efforts it takes to cultivate relatedness in difference.

Research-Creation: What Does a Practice Do?

The Pedagogical Impulse has been funded by two Social Science and Humanities Research Council of Canada (SSHRC) research-creation grants. The first grant prioritized questions about socially engaged art with children and youth in K–12 classrooms in Toronto, Canada. I curated a series of artist residencies in public schools, developed curricular materials for classroom teachers, and explored pressing issues about doing socially engaged art with children in a series of socially engaged discursive events called the *living archive*.

Some of the residencies lasted only a few weeks, while others unfolded over a full school term. The artists did not approach the residencies with preestablished art projects in mind that would represent some aspect of the curriculum, nor a set of technical skills they wanted the students to master. Rather, what emerged in each classroom context was co-composed between teachers, artists, and students through class discussions, small experimental creative activities, artistic interventions, slideshows of contemporary art, research-driven assignments, and student interests and inquiries. Artists were paired with a classroom teacher and their students, and together they determined a starting concept for the residency and the socially engaged projects. This concept sometimes came from the school curriculum and sometimes from student interests or questions. For example, in chapter 1, I discuss two socially engaged projects that emerged from the concept of *trade*, which appears in the grade-six social studies curriculum. Artists were paid CARFAC fees and provided with a stipend for materials.[4] Teachers were provided half-day or full-day paid leave on a regular basis for meetings with the artists, research team, or any other activity outside of class time.[5] Research assistants (graduate students) were also funded through the grants and were paid wages for their contributions to the project. I offer more on the importance of feminist collaboration later in the introduction.[6]

I refer to all of the various events in a residency as both research-creation events and socially engaged art as radical pedagogy. The residencies were photodocumented by my research team, and in some instances students took control of the cameras.[7] Selected images were curated for the research website, and some have been chosen for the color insert in this book. The practice of research-creation produces different kinds of documentation. Some images are more ethnographic in nature and capture the activities and processes of student engagement. Other images document student research-creation work, while others represent artists' artworks included in the research-creation events.

Recorded conversations with the artists and teachers took place at regular intervals throughout the residency, and members of the research team kept detailed field journals. The combination of artistic practice and more conventional ethnographic practices is crucial to my orientation and practice of doing research-creation. Recorded conversations and field notes are used not to substantiate the artistic research, nor to give weight or value to it as empirical evidence. Incorporating methods of observation is as much a part of artistic practices as of ethnographic practices. In fact, Loveless (2019) argues that research-creation is a hybrid transdiscipline. This requires that we let go of disciplinary boundaries that insist on tidy categories such as art, education, social science. Rather, as a *hybrid* or what I would call *oblique* practice, research-creation cuts across the disciplinary specificity and generates something else altogether (Truman and Springgay 2019). Further, any ethnographic tendency in my practice is always approached from the perspective of being an artist and curator, in the sense that such methods as field notes and interviews are never procedural, generalizable, or used as extractive data. For example, the field notes, annotated in Moleskine notebooks, have not been consulted while writing this book. They are, in fact, due to the pandemic, locked away in my university office. Even if they weren't, they served their purpose years ago. The graduate students and I met biweekly, sometimes with the artists and teachers and sometimes with only ourselves, and the notes served as *attention nodes* for our iterative conversations. They provided questions, responses, and tensions, and seeded new ideas and directions as the research-creation events unfolded. They were not intended to be data repositories but spaces that gathered and tuned in to the iterativity of research-creation events in that moment in time. They are not used to quote from, or as data mining. I use such notebooks on a daily basis—they literally litter my desk. There is one for this current book project where, even while on a Zoom call about unrelated matters, a word, an image, or a moment flutters in and I write it down in the pages between the dark, blood-red covers. There is another for WalkingLab.org, my other research-creation endeavor, and I've started one for the research-creation event of directing an art school. There are some that are miscellaneous that capture my everyday notations, lists, and fleeting thoughts. These notebooks once recorded notes from readings, but over the past few years I've transitioned to using my computer for such tasks. The act of writing by hand is part of a thinking-making-doing for me, and these notes are more diagrammatic, or scored, than they are a series of prose compositions like more typical field notes. George Maciunas, a Fluxus artist who will be explored in greater detail in chapters 3 and 4, created what he called *Learning Machines*, graphic notations on three-dimensional folded papers, much like flip books. They held an immense amount of information in visually scored diagrams, and the pages could be moved in such a way to suggest that the information was networked, entangled, and transversal (versus the linear page-turning of a conventional book). I consider the research notebooks to operate in a similar way.

When all of the residencies were complete, the teachers were invited to a day-long Teacher Institute with my research team, and together we examined the research-art ephemera that had been generated. This workshop with teachers resulted in the curation of a series of thematic galleries on the research website, called *Image Resources*, that highlight some of the curricular concepts that emerged in the various residencies. Importantly these concepts were cogenerated with the teachers and grew out of a desire to have more accessible resources available on socially engaged art and pedagogy. However, these online pages contain more-than-curricular resources; they act as catalysts for future action. They seed transversal lines of thought at the axis of art, pedagogy, and research-creation.

Too often art created in the context of schools, particularly art created with children, is undervalued. In a recent publication in conversation with the Cuban artist Tania Bruguera (2020), Claire Bishop challenges Bruguera's engagement with "demonstrable outcomes" in the project *Museum of Arte Util* (2013). Bishop asks, if art demonstrates beneficial outcomes, is it mirroring neoliberalism and the instrumentalization of art? While I can agree with Bishop that determining the value of a project on evidentiary outcomes is problematic, I appreciate Bruguera's insistence that the evaluation does not come from institutions (an outside) but is realized internal to the project and in relation to those who cocreated it or participated in it. Further, benefits are not quantifiable but reflect on a project's ethical and political responsibilities. Erin Manning (2020) similarly articulates value as the process of form-taking, its activation, and its potential to move an event into another. "Value," she writes, "is a capacity for intensification" (87). I return to the question of value and outcomes in chapter 5.

One of the ways I wanted to contextualize the residencies in the schools was to situate them within the larger art world and to provide robust critical reflection on what it means to do socially engaged art with students. To do so, Hannah Jickling and Reed Reed, the artists introduced in the opening scene of the introduction, engaged in a series of socially engaged discursive events with a number of artists and curators. The recorded conversations, like Bruguera's ethical and political benefits, pry open the complexities of working in horizontal structures with children and youth. The conversations were edited into online publications available on the research website, and form a *living archive* of socially engaged art as radical pedagogy. Formed through generative conversations, the *living archive* puts the residencies into relation with other artists and curators working with children, and with other socially engaged pedagogical projects. In much the same way that Bruguera insists on art's usefulness or its ability to mobilize civic change, the *living archive* engenders conversations regarding the outcomes, impact, and challenges of doing socially engaged art with children and in a community without evaluative metrics. In chapter 3, I discuss the ways in which I use ongoing conversations with contemporary artists as *living archives* of research-creation, not as extracted data but as moments of feminist accountability and responsibility. What is significant about the *living archive* is the work that it does. As living, the archives bring the past and the contemporary together pedagogically. They too, like the notebooks, are about *seeding* the research: attuning to it and moving it into something more-than.

I consider research-creation to be a generative practice. In the conventions of social science research, the method of data collection prevails. In research-creation, rather than thinking about existing data, to be mined and extracted from a research site, the generativity of thinking-making-doing germinates and seeds. Research-creation is not a thing but an event that emerges from the middle. To practice research-creation requires being inside a research event. This means that quite often an artist-researcher does not have a clear set of directions or procedures determined prior to beginning an inquiry. In *Knowings and Knots* (Loveless 2020) various authors remark that research-creation is a practice that starts in the middle. Randy Cutler (2020, 4) writes that the "process begins with permeable curiosity as an emergent mode of being and knowing," while Paul Couilliard (2020, 66) states that, rather than having an output at the beginning of a project, "it is the 'doing' that leads me to identify and clarify" concerns. Being inside a research event does not mean that one shows up in a research context with no plan. Rather, the porosity of the event is speculative, emergent, and always in movement. In the unfolding of an event of research the *what* (the questions we are asking) and the *how* emerge co-extensively of each other.

I have long argued that research-creation is composed by concepts rather than discrete definitions or procedures. For Deleuze and Guattari (1994) concepts are never simple. Every concept, they write, has multiple components. Concepts "link up with each other" (18) and require a "junction of problems where it combines with other coexisting concepts" (18). Concepts do not describe things; concepts *express* an event. Thus, research-creation is not definitive. Rather it is constituted through concepts that are constantly in the making, linking up and problematizing an event. Erin Manning (2020, 11) writes that a "concept is not a general category. It does not claim to encapsulate. It is not a metaphor. It cannot be debated. A concept is an intensive feature, an intercessor into thought." Concepts elicit touching encounters, where, in the speculative middle of a research event, concepts seed and germinate—or, as Manning (2020) contends, concepts create propositional paths to follow.

Research-creation, both in theory and practice, emerged during *The Pedagogical Impulse* events. The research in schools provided me with the spatiotemporal sites to experiment, innovate, and generate other ways of working with diverse publics. How I practice and theorize research-creation therefore emerged alongside my questions regarding radical pedagogy and socially engaged art. Research-creation as a methodology of thinking-making-doing materializes in the process of *doing* research; it is not known in advance and applied to a research problem. The first two chapters are organized around artist-residencies in k–12 classrooms and their socially engaged projects. There are other publications on the various residencies that can be accessed via the website.

For a second SSHRC grant I extended earlier questions regarding the Educational Turn with a specific focus on radical pedagogy in postsecondary institutions. I was interested in Fluxus pedagogy and its relation to contemporary art as pedagogy. Fluxus was an international group of artists from the 1960s and 1970s who emphasized participatory events over the autonomous art object. Many Fluxus artists taught in higher education and blurred the boundaries between Fluxus art and teaching. For this larger project, the research-creation examined archival material from Fluxus teaching alongside contemporary enactments of art-as-teaching. In addition to working in Fluxus archives, I involved postsecondary artist-teachers in the *living archive* project. These conversations examined the ordinary "stuff" of teaching—syllabi, course-based activities, and classroom atmospheres—that point toward the continued significance of scores and intermedia in contemporary teaching. This Fluxus-inspired work is detailed in chapter 3. The seeding of the Fluxus archival work produced a number of other research-creation projects in postsecondary classes that I explore in chapters 4 through 7. I weave material from historical archives throughout these chapters into conversation with contemporary teaching practices not to demonstrate a mimetic relationship but rather to generate a series of arguments about the nature of radical pedagogy today. My interest in the archives ruptures conventional art historical interest in Fluxus to focus on moments where art practices moved inside classroom spaces and were concerned with curricula and pedagogy.

Positioned in conversation with other texts on research-creation, *Feltness: Research-Creation, Socially Engaged Art, and Affective Pedagogies* enhances the theoretical debates put forward by Natalie Loveless (2019; 2020), Erin Manning (2013; 2016; 2020), and Manning with Brian Massumi (2014), as well as in previous work I have published with Sarah E. Truman on walking and research-creation (Springgay and Truman 2018; 2019a; 2019b; 2019c). Truman and I argue for a propositional approach to research-creation (Truman and Springgay 2015). Propositions keep the event of research-creation open, in flux, and oblique. I offer these propositions here:

Speculate: Research-creation is future event–oriented. As a speculative practice, it invents techniques of relation.

Propose enabling constraints: Enabling constraints are expansive and suggestive. They operate by delimiting process and possibility, although they always include more possibilities than any given event realizes.

Create problems: Research-creation is a practice that does not seek to describe, explain, or solve problems. Rather, it is an event that creates concepts that problematize. Concepts are not pregiven or known in advance. As an event of problems, research-creation brings something new into the world.

Think-in-movement: The aim of research-creation is not to reflect on something that has passed. Thinking-in-movement is to think in the act; it is a thinking saturated with rhythm and affect.

Note emergences, rework emergences: Concepts proliferate in research-creation, and with them, ethico-political concerns emerge. Once an ethico-political concern emerges, rework it to see what it can do.

More-than-represent: Rather than attempting to represent or report on research-creation, use it to propel further thought and create something new: new concepts, new ethico-political concerns, new problems.

Expanding these contributions to research-creation, the projects examined in this book are situated in school contexts and therefore not only offer complementary and extended theories about research-creation but contribute to questions and examinations of the intersections between socially engaged art and radical pedagogy.

Loveless (2019; 2020) and Manning and Massumi (2014) recognize the ways in which research-creation emerged in Canadian universities and granting systems alongside the institutionalization of artistic research that confined creative work to rigid criteria and impact metrics often determined by other disciplines and research methods. Manning and Massumi note that, at the time that the term was introduced into the Canadian landscape, there was inconsequential thought about how the concept would emerge through its conjunctive and would therefore amount to little more than an "institutional operator: a mechanism for existing practices to interface with the neoliberalization of art and academics" (2014, 88). Counter to this argument, one might claim that the lack of a distinct identity for research-creation may in fact have enabled its capaciousness, which in turn allowed those of us practicing and writing about research-creation to make sense of it as it unfolded in each unique instance.

As the language of research-creation gained momentum in the university, Loveless notes that anxieties emerged about the academicization of the arts and the pressure to become more "research"-oriented. This momentum, Loveless

(2019) and Lowry (2015) argue, was in part fueled by funding structures and financial bottom lines. However, despite these cogent critical reflections on the institutional and the problematic commodification of research-creation, most of the artist-scholars writing about research-creation are deeply committed to its conjunctive potential. As Loveless writes: "I continue to see research-creation as one of those cracks . . . that lets the light shine in, through its experimental and dissonant forms of practice, research, and pedagogy" (2019, 8). Her commitment to feminist, antiracist, and anticolonial art and scholarship creates openings for the potential of research-creation to disrupt the university as we know it and to create radically new ways of thinking-making-doing. Likewise, Manning and Massumi, through the SenseLab in Montreal, have been foundational in crafting research-creation through process philosophy, foregrounding the immanence of the research event and the emergence of research-creation as ecologies always in movement. Research-creation has enabled artist-researchers the opportunity to "re-story" our disciplinary practices within institutions and challenge questions about the legibility of art as research (Loveless 2015; Loveless 2019). Loveless writes, "In asking us to unhook ourselves from a primary alliance to disciplinary identity, the critical discourse of research-creation wedges open inherited forms of legibility and value that configure our daily activities as academic practitioners" (2015, 23). I read Loveless's text on research-creation intertextually with Dylan Robinson's (2017) writing about Indigenous public art and research-creation in order to notice ruptures in how we articulate research-creation practices. If research-creation is actively working to interrupt institutional norms regarding legibility and value in the university, we need to resist, as Robinson notes, settler modes of perception that are driven by settler legibility. Legibility is a continual process of centering whiteness and the violence of settler colonial genocide. To that extent, what becomes possible when research-creation operates through illegibility to institutional norms? Leah Decter's (2018) research-creation practice and scholarship pivots around the idea of *depremacy*, decentering the supremacy of white canons of theory and practice. Research-creation as more-than, as otherwise. However, the whiteness of research-creation, particularly the writing about research-creation, should not be ignored. By this I don't just mean the Euro-western theories that have often been relied on to craft research-creation stories but also the ways in which research-creation temporally negates Black, Indigenous, and People of Color's art-research practices that decenter and confront institutional violence and demands of legibility. Research-creation's claims of newness and intervention obscure the work that BIPOC artist-scholars have always been doing. Here I'm thinking of Audrey

Hudson's work on hip-hop that interrupts and intervenes into the prevailing whiteness of art, education, and the academy. Audrey Hudson, Awad Ibrahim, and Karyn Recollet (2019) and Syrus Ware (2020a) draw on speculative fiction and on Afro and Indigenous futurisms because such futurisms always already foreground cultural production while centering Black and Indigenous lives, ancestors, and arts practices. In prying open disciplinary logics and structures, research-creation must not create new silos or gatekeepers. Rather, in thinking otherwise, research-creation must expose the violence of settler colonialism and anti-Black racism in order to create more just and flourishing worlds.

My return to the university as a graduate student predated the term *research-creation* but came at a time that arts-based research was flourishing and rapidly changing the social sciences in Canada. As a practicing artist and curator, trained in fine arts and the humanities, I saw this as an exciting time to be in the academy. This moment was marked by significant changes in what constituted and was valued as a research methodology in the social sciences. In the field of education there is a long history of arts-based research, including potent rationales for doing arts-based work, theoretical frameworks, and various examples from the visual arts, fiction, poetry, performance, theatre, and music. Notwithstanding arts-based research's own challenges, tensions, and debates, which are not the topic of this introduction or this book, my position as a research-creation artist-scholar is predicated on the epistemological and ontological explications for doing artistic research that were already thriving in the field of education when I was in graduate school—and the University of British Columbia, where I studied, was a hotbed of activity in this regard.

However, I wish to mention a few specific challenges that are in conversation with Manning and Massumi's and Loveless's shared concerns. In the social sciences there were robust debates regarding the criteria of assessment for qualitative research, often mired in deliberations about the validity and generalizability of research. Such conversations dominated the field of arts-based research as I entered graduate school. This resulted in the creation of prescribed criteria for arts-based work that resembled existing language and criteria used to assess other qualitative methods. Research-creation entered into the Canadian lexicon in 2004 as I was finishing my doctoral work, and I held one of the first SSHRC research-creation grants. Although it would be many years before the early publications from SenseLab started to impact the field, for me research-creation's conjunctive opened up a theoretical moment to shift the question from "what criteria" to the "how" of a research event's doing and working. In other words, I was able to move away from the demands of how work should be assessed using external criteria to, *How does your work do what it is doing as it unfolds spatiotemporally?* This was significant for me because of my concerns regarding pedagogy as something open and emergent, and because of my interest in the creation of different publics as part of the research event. Research-creation enabled me to make sense of curating public performances and art projects outside of structural demands that it be evaluated by established rubrics in order to be understood as meaningful or valued as research. Instead, the research-creation events were accountable to the communities with whom the work was being made in collaboration, and mattered for the kinds of relations and solidarity for which it made space inside the research event; *this* was the doing and working of the artistic research. Natasha Myers shares similar concerns, noting that the arts offer her a means to disrupt "disciplined modes of inquiry." Research-creation engenders the asking of different research questions and forces researchers to "confront the limits of knowledge, what we can know and what we cannot know, and the accountabilities required to take stock of how we know" (Myers 2020, in Truman 2020, 227). Research-creation becomes a way of becoming responsible to the creation of different worlds, and to the telling of stories that matter (Haraway 2016; Loveless 2019).

Tangentially, another debate that seemed pressing in the early 2000s in the field of arts-based research, at least in education, was the relationship between process and product, inquiry versus output. Some arts-based scholars called for an emphasis on the artistic form of doing research while others saw merit in conducting research using traditional qualitative methods and then disseminating research through artistic outputs such as performed ethnography. Regardless of which side of these debates you landed on, the bifurcation of inquiry and dissemination cemented the boundaries between the act of doing research and the mobilization of that research. Research-creation facilitated a movement into the conjunctive to rupture such distinctions. In many instances the research-creation event is both the doing of research and simultaneously the mobilization of that research to specific publics—or the production of a public (see chapter 6).

This is the work of the conjunctive in research-creation; or the proposition *with* (Truman and Springgay 2016; Springgay and Truman 2018). Instead of perpetuating an idea of art as separate from thinking and writing, the hyphenation of research-creation engenders "concepts in-the-making," which, according to Manning and Massumi (2014, 88–89), is a process of "thinking-with and across techniques of creative practice." The conjunctive, Owen Chapman (2020, xvi) writes, "invites the juxtaposition of other terms, concepts, and categories." Manning and Massumi (2014, 88–89) consider the conjunctive as crucial to formulating an understanding and practice of research-creation. The conjunctive they write is "a mutual interpenetration of processes rather than a communication of products." Research-creation taken as a conjunctive whole becomes a "thinking-in-action" and a "practice in its own right" (89), as opposed to the combination of distinct disciplines where each discipline remains intact. For Manning and Massumi research-creation is experimental and catalyzes emergent events. Similarly, the proposition *with* is used to indicate associations and connections between entities. However, *with* is more than merely additive; it represents ethico-political (in)tensions brought to bear on research-creation. *With* is a milieu, an active set of relations that are composed of dimensions and vibrations that materialize a moment of space-time. If research-creation is composed in the conjunctive of response-able relations, as a practice of intimacy, then we can ask: *What grows and emerges within such a place?*

The conjunctive nature of research-creation shifts the language and emphasis on data collection and extraction, in one instance or register, and the output and circulation of findings in another. Rather, thinking-making-doing complicates linear proceduralism or methodocentrism, generating endless possibilities for doing research. For Loveless (2019) research-creation challenges the assumptions that monographs or peer-reviewed manuscripts are the only top-tier, valid forms of research outputs and skepticism regarding artistic practice as de facto research. She contends that research-creation as a hybrid, conjunctive practice has the potential, following Donna Haraway (2016), to tell other stories that matter. Research-creation practices, Loveless (2019, 24) writes, become "valid modes for rendering research public." For scholars trained in qualitative social science methods, research-creation offers a possibility to pry open established patterns of doing research. Research-creation, as Loveless so aptly describes it, becomes a crack, a movement of the not-yet-known where in its capaciousness it becomes a more-than.

In parallel to the debates waged against socially engaged art regarding its artistic merits, arts-based research became polarized by those who believed specialized training in an art form was needed in order to do arts-based research, and others who argued that the arts sanctioned varying degrees of experimentation and improvisation regardless of its artistic qualities. These debates about rigor are crucial but require attention that dismantles such dualisms. In a recent roundtable publication on research-creation, Erin Manning (2020, 238–39) noted that:

Rigour is an important concept; but not rigour as assessed and valued from the outside. . . . This kind of internal rigour is very close to Henri Bergson's notion of intuition as a practice that recognizes the difference between problems and false problems. False problems are problems that already carry their solutions. The institutions we work in are habituated in the deployment of false problems. [What is needed] is the sensitivity to the difference between a generative problem and a false problem. . . . This involves being moved by thought rather than seeing ourselves as its mover.

When Bishop (2012) argues that educational art lacks rigor because it is "unseen," she is applying assessment criteria that is already preformed, imposed from the outside. Research-creation demands instead that that rigor be internal to, and generated in and of, the event itself. As a highly transdisciplinary practice, research-creation, Loveless (2019, 33) contends, "fails to *fully* fulfill the criteria of any one disciplinary location. . . . It is an *in-coherent object*." I like to think of this failure in the way that Stefano Harney and Fred Moten (2013) refer to "fugitive knowers," modes of thinking not allied with governmentality, discipline, legibility, and order. Research-creation as a radical departure evades the capture of criteria already presupposed from the outside; it mobilizes other ways of mattering. The transversality of research-creation becomes a kind of radical illegibility. In the same roundtable, Natasha Myers (in Truman 2020, 232) argues: "Sometimes we need to forget and unlearn what we think matters. We need to rearrange our sensorium and sense making practices and disrupt disciplinary thought styles and ways of seeing so that other worlds within this world can come into view."

In the past decade in the social sciences, and to a greater extent in educational research, a new methodological shift has occurred called "postqualitative research," influenced by Deleuze and Guattari's rhizomatic and assemblage thinking, Barad's agential realism, Rosi Braidotti's and Haraway's feminist posthumanisms, along with various theories that fall under the umbrella of feminist materialisms and affect theory. Postqualitative research challenges the social sciences' methodocentrism, which presumes to know a priori what a research event might do and which privileges linear procedures of data extraction, analysis, and dissemination. Postqualitative research challenges the subject-object bifurcation that makes possible the extraction of knowable data and the humanist means by which research is carried out. Elsewhere I have written that postqualitative research and research-creation *are not* synonymous, and that postqualitative researchers problematically use art practices and forms to demonstrate that they are doing research differently (Springgay 2019). Cutting up transcripts, putting them in jars, or weaving them together with glitter and glue is not the work of research-creation. However, postqualitative research demonstrates the extent to which academics from different disciplines are working to dismantle the ways in which research is executed, valued, and circulated within institutions. If research-creation, as Loveless contends, offers a feminist, antiracist, and anticolonial mode of working to disrupt the institution as we know it, then much of the work produced under the framework of postqualitative research similarly (albeit quite differently) aims to deterritorialize the status quo of research methods. In this way research-creation works against a sense of deep alienation and an incapacity to act. Instead, research-creation as feltness expands the dimensions of knowledge and research methods both critically and politically and as radical pedagogy.

The concept of radical pedagogy has many different meanings. For some, radical pedagogy is connected to the avant-garde and involves innovation, experimentation, and unorthodox approaches to teaching and learning. For others radical pedagogy necessitates an analysis of the social and political aspects of educational institutions, policies, and practices. Radical pedagogy is also concerned with social justice, including antiracist, anti-ableist, and decolonial approaches (DiAngelo and Sensoy 2014). Here, radical pedagogy examines privilege, oppression, and ideology in order to challenge and dismantle educational inequality. Radical pedagogy centers a subject's positionality to examine how it informs and shapes their opinions, reactions, and knowledges. All of these meanings are enmeshed in the socially engaged art as research-creation projects discussed in this book, but so too does the work of these projects and the analyses in the book aim to expand and magnify radical pedagogy as feltness.

Interdependencies: Collaboration, Coauthorship, and Feminist Care

Staying alive—for every species—requires livable collaborations. Collaboration means working across difference, which leads to contamination. Without collaboration, we all die. (Tsing 2015, 28)

I open a discussion on collaboration with this passage by Anna Tsing, which shapes a particular understanding of multispecies interdependency and relations. For Tsing, human and nonhuman subjects are transformed through encounters, or, in her words, human and nonhuman subjects *become contaminated*. Through contamination, new directions and assemblages occur, and each participant in the collaborative encounter is made different from that relationship. I read Tsing's contamination along with Alexis Shotwell's (2016) scholarship on purity and compromise. There is no pure state, environmentally, bodily, or otherwise, but purity politics have conditioned heteronormative, racist, ableist, and settler colonial notions of what counts as human. Against possessive individualism and boundedness, contamination means being responsible and accountable to the kinds of encounters that take shape and to the results of those relations. Interdependency, then, Shotwell argues, requires that we displace habits of thinking with modes of attention and care: "To say that we are entangled is to say that we are responsible by virtue of our relationships to near and distant others" (107). To be contaminated is to be accountable to difference.

The socially engaged research-creation events that compose this book were created in collaboration with teachers, students, artists, and a team of graduate student research assistants. Part of practicing intimacy is being accountable to the various collaborators, coauthors, and co-composers with whom I have been in relation over the past two decades. I have been privileged to conceptualize the *how* of research-creation: to materialize a number of research-creation events and projects with diverse publics, and to coauthor with colleagues and graduate students. This book would not be possible without these interlocutors, and their words and insights are part of the felted fabric of this text. And while this book and the writing contained within it is the product of my labor, very little of the research-creation eventing would be possible without the collaboration and work of many others. Aubyn O'Grady, Andrea Vela Alarcón, Julie Smitka, Zofia Zaliwska, James Miles, Arden Hagedorn, Lee Cameron, and the many artists that will appear throughout the book have co-composed my thinking-making-doing.

In the book I oscillate between the singular pronoun *I* and a collective *we* to account for the students, teachers, artists, graduate students, chocolates, funeral flowers, fabric nets, boxed publications, and all the in-betweens of human and nonhuman circuits that generated this work. The universal *we* can be problematic, and I don't intend for it to flatten relations or issues of diversity and equity. But because the teachers, students, and schools must remain anonymous, while artists who choose to be identified in the research are named, the oscillation between *I* and *we* seeks to pause within these tensions, not to erase them. In writing *we*, I am accountable to the we of my research team, which co-composed itself in multiple and mutable ways over the past twenty years. *We*, similarly, articulates other compositions of artists and students in a grade-six classroom. *We* contaminates *I* like interlocking wool fibers in felt making; once fulled they are forever changed and altered into a new form, a co-composition. My use of *we* recognizes the interdependent and entangled web of relations that are necessary to do research-creation, socially engaged art, and radical pedagogy. In shifting collaboration from inclusive participation to radical relatedness and a feminist ethics of care we must ask: *Who and what are we accountable to in our research-creation relations? Who do we show up for and how are we present for their needs? How do we listen, attend to, and tune in to the differing relations of collaboration?* In caring-with others, we mobilize in direct action to create more just and flourishing worlds. Collaboration as feminist ethics places care front and center in research and teaching. Feminist care acknowledges that forms of care are entangled with gender, race, and disability that have pathologized dependency, and the labor of care work. Care must also be recognized as deeply embedded within historical and ongoing violence while also fostering strategies for living (Nash 2019). When collaboration means interdependent kinships and responsibilities that "proliferate outward," this requires "a more capacious understanding of care" (Care Collective 2020, 41). In the words of Donna Haraway (2016), collaboration must be accountable to noninnocent knottings.

A constant tension within socially engaged art is its participatory nature and the complexities of collaboration. When we conceive of collaboration in convivial terms, participation becomes a symbolic gesture that fails to dismantle racism, settler colonialism, and other forms of ongoing intersectional oppression (Springgay and Truman 2018). When we talk about socially engaged art as participatory and collaborative, as if those two concepts make the work inclusive and thereby transformative, then the events fail to engender a radical pedagogy of feltness. Rather, what is needed are questions about the *how* of collaboration as a feminist ethics of care: *How do we come together? How are we in relation? What contaminations are flourishing? What are not?* Astrida Neimanis (2012, 216) astutely notes, "To collaborate is a doing-in-common, more than a being-in-common." Collaboration must, Neimanis insists, recognize that not all comings together are benevolent but can be fraught with tense negotiations. Collaboration is not what the artist, or research-creation scholar, wishes a participant to do but the activity of the work's potential as opened up by the process of coming together itself. As Loveless (2019, 102) eloquently notes, research-creation "is attentive to how form makes worlds," where the worlding is micropolitical "from inside the belly of the beast: the classroom." For Loveless, pedagogy is how she cares: a pedagogy that is feminist, anti-oppressive, and imbued with curiosity, eros, and the uncanny.

If collaboration is predicated on interdependent care relations that contaminate, then part of what research-creation needs to do is to dismantle the structures, knowledges, and research conventions that have created careless institutions, states, classrooms, and communities. The ethics and politics of doing research-creation with diverse publics means that we must create conditions for other ways of living and learning. This means troubling our relationship with institutions and transforming the kinds of value we allow for particular forms of knowledge and research practices. Foregrounding intimacy and feltness requires that we turn from extraction-based practices to ones conditioned by transcorporeality, reciprocity, relationality, and care. And like Loveless (2019), who claims that not all research-creation is enacted in this way, I am also tenacious enough to insist that it *should be*. Research-creation as intimate and capacious has the potential to generate new kinds of research relations and to seed the flourishing of diverse publics and worlds co-composed by the research encounter.

I opened this introduction with the *Upside Down and Backwards* residency and the *Endless Paintings* on the banks of the Don River; I now turn to another rainbow composition, this one of institutional chairs inserted into the library at the Ontario Institute for Studies in Education (OISE), University of Toronto. Jickling and Reed, in addition to working with elementary students, were artists-in-residence in the teacher education program at OISE. The *Extra Curricular Curriculum Vitae* residency culminated in an installation of old, colorful furniture—arranged in rainbow sequencing and stacked precariously—and a series of performance lectures by teacher education candidates. Incorporating a set of odd instructional slides found in the OISE basement, the teacher candidates drew on the educational archive and "the course of their lives" to illustrate an incidental curriculum through performative lectures. The rainbow furniture was the stage for the performances, while simultaneously amplifying and queering curricular objects, such as school chairs, that condition the educational body in particular ways. Lecture topics included the importance of shoes, experiencing allergies to parents, bathroom anxiety, and learning through the nose. The performance lectures enact what educational scholars Madeleine Grumet and Bill Pinar ([1976] 2014) call *currere*, which shifts the curriculum from a set of static objectives and content to complicated conversations that entangle the self with social, political, and ethical frameworks. Examining one's own experiences as shaping a "living curriculum" (Aoki 1993) emphasizes a fluid, dynamic, and iterative process of learning, much like research-creation. Currere emphasizes the role that curriculum plays in a subject's becoming. As a recursive method entwining past, present, and future, currere interrogates our lived experiences and, in doing so, makes room for the possibility of becoming altered and undone (Miller 2005; Mishra Tarc 2015).

As a way of being in the world, socially engaged art as research-creation, like currere, is a practice that discovers things it wasn't looking for; as Tsing (2015, 278) writes, "Muddling through with others is always in the middle of things; it does not properly conclude." The socially engaged art as research-creation attended to in the pages of this book emerges from an accountability to education as living, as liveness, imbued with the intimacy of feltness.

How to Make a Classroom Function Like a Work of Art

Writing about socially engaged art as research-creation moves the felted, trans-corporeal, and affective forms of thinking-making-doing into a text-based plat-form that is incomplete. It is my hope that, in the enfolding chapters, readers engage with the complex, messy, and nonlinear instantiations of doing this kind of work in public elementary and secondary schools, as well as in the university.

Chapter 1 is situated in two different elementary schools and classrooms and thinks with two socially engaged art as research-creation events that con-verge around the idea of children as tastemakers. The projects rupture and intervene into normative and racialized conceptions of the child as incomplete and as one with uncultured taste. Repositioning the school as a candy factory and a flower boutique, where students engage in a range of experimental proj-ects that examine, disrupt, and cultivate different visceral taste sensations, the resulting collaborations question childhood, value, labor, and economy and position elementary school students as changemakers. The chapter engages with art criticism that often devalues artwork produced in collaboration with young children, arguing that this position is conditioned by normative and colonial understandings of taste. When positioned as tastemakers, children become socially engaged artists in their own right, disrupting the overdeter-mined value of art and education.

Chapter 2 continues to unsettle the ways that particular bodies, knowledges, and affects are regulated and governed in schools, where certain curricular mo-ments are undervalued. The chapter contextualizes artist residencies in nonart spaces through an examination of the Artist Placement Group (APG), who or-ganized a number of artist residencies in industry and government in the 1960s in the United Kingdom. The APG approached their practice through a method called the "open brief," which emphasized relationality, unknowability, and curiosity. Guided by the notions of placement, and of art in a social context, the APG is considered one catalyst for socially engaged art and artist residen-cies. The open brief method, I argue, creates conditions for an imponderable curriculum to flourish. Examining three artist residencies that were situated primarily in secondary schools, the chapter questions dominant narratives of what counts as educational, foregrounding moments of liveness, ridiculousness, and humor that enable youth to reimagine their situated worlds. Extending debates on socially engaged art and the Pedagogical Turn regarding the aesthetic value of the artwork—or its efficacy—the imponderable foregrounds the *extra-* of pedagogy as art—extrarational, extraordinary, extraeducational— and the unexpected and indeterminate ways that youth remix, remake, and reimagine future worldings. The chapter makes the case that the significance of socially engaged art practices as research-creation is an expression of speculation and futurity; a future that has not happened yet *but must*.

While the APG was influencing significant change in art in the UK, another group of artists working primarily in the United States in the 1960s and 1970s, though with international connections, was Fluxus, known for their method of scoring. Scores are open-ended propositions that catalyze an event and encourage an art practice that is indeterminate, performative, and situated within the ordinary. Understood as *feltness*, scores invite intimate participation either through collaborative inquiry or through embodied and sensory performance. Chapter 3 focuses on curricular materials that Fluxus created to impact educational reform. These curricular materials, such as course planning calendars and syllabi, were rendered as tarot cards, board games, and other score-influenced materials. These historical archives are examined alongside a living archive of artists teaching in postsecondary institutions. I consider the ways that the ordinariness of the score, its situatedness in everyday objects and actions, emerges in similar mundane aspects of teaching and learning such as syllabi, assignments, and classroom atmospheres. It is this ordinariness that conditions radical pedagogy as art, both historically and in current postsecondary classrooms.

In addition to the score, Fluxus artists often created Fluxkits, box-type publications that contained small objects—scores, booklets, photographs, containers, and objects—that were typically housed in an attaché-style case or box. Chapter 4 engages with counter-archiving and anarchiving research-creation practices that disrupt conventional narratives and histories and seek ways to engage with matter not typically found in official archives, as well as the affective experiences and lived histories of human and more-than-human bodies. While my interest in the Fluxus archive was initially prompted by a desire to examine the history of radical pedagogy, as the research-creation project unfolded the question needed to expand and transform. Accountable to the lack of Indigenous, racialized, queer, and trans contributions to the Fluxus archive, and responsive to the *living archive* of current artist-teachers, different questions emerged at this juncture: *How do we want an archive to function now? What can an archive seed?* This chapter explores anarchiving as research-creation and the *Instant Class Kit*, a mobile curriculum guide and pop-up exhibition of fourteen contemporary art projects dedicated to radical pedagogies and social justice. Produced as an edition of four, the *Kit* brings together contemporary curricular materials in the form of artist multiples such as zines, scores, posters, games, diagrams, newspapers, and other sensory objects. The lessons, syllabi, and classroom activities produced by this new generation of artists, many of whom are queer, trans, Black, and Indigenous, address topics and methodologies including queer subjectivities and Indigenous epistemologies, social movements and collective protest, immigration, technology, and ecology. Anarchiving as research-creation becomes a practice of responding to and countering the colonial logic of the archive while attending to its ephemeral and affective qualities. It is also fundamentally about practicing an ethics based on reciprocity, response-ability, and care that centers relationships to land, human, and more-than-human bodies. Thinking with the *Instant Class Kit*, this chapter lays out a theoretical framework for anarchiving as indeterminate, as felt, and as response-ability. Research-creation as anarchiving, exemplified by the *Instant Class Kit*, becomes a way to distribute and enact radical pedagogy.

Four multiples of the kit were assembled and three circulated to classrooms via mail to be activated by instructors and students. Chapter 5 engages with various activations of the *Instant Class Kit* in postsecondary classrooms and the various conditions of feltness that opening and unboxing the kit enabled. The conditions of feltness the kit seeds prioritize touching transcorporeal encounters and attune themselves to affective assemblages that undo or refuse humanist logics that dominate institutions for a practice of study that is committed to antiracist, anti-ableist, and anticolonial frameworks. Conditions create spatiotemporal openings to widen our attentions and to tune into the *how* of research-creation. Conditions ask questions about what art or research-creation *does* as a way of being in the world. Conditions affect how we come together in relations in response to something urgent, an impulse that requires situated and accountable responses. Conditions shift research-creation from content to anarchiving incipient form.

Chapter 6 engages with a series of publications produced within a semester-long course at OCAD University, Toronto, titled Pressing Issues and taught by the artist Shannon Gerard. The course is a seminar-studio hybrid course with a syllabus that consists of one score or proposition: *Make a Public*. The course blends readings and seminar discussions with field trips, explorations into the field of nanopublishing and artist multiples, and culminates in the students directing a publicly engaged community publication project. Playing with the concept of *public/ation*, I turn to public pedagogy scholarship to think with the public/ations—the publics and the printed matter—that emerged in the semester-long course. As more postsecondary institutions create socially engaged programs and courses, and more scholarship on the teaching of socially engaged art proliferates, it is crucial that different pedagogical theories be explored—including public pedagogy. In connecting publications, publics, and public pedagogy with socially engaged art, my arguments extend current scholarship on public pedagogy to consider more-than-human public/ations and their role in a radical pedagogy to come. Further, the chapter will consider the kinds of interdependent ethics of care needed in socially engaged pedagogies given the nature of moving inside and outside of classrooms while working with diverse publics.

The final chapter, chapter 7, returns to the *Upside Down and Backwards* residency and the *Endless Paintings* on the Don River that opened this introduction to consider the outcomes and impact of research-creation as vectors and impulses. The chapter illustrates a number of other research-creation projects concerned with questions around art and pedagogy to suggest that the pedagogical impulses discussed throughout the book are not only urgent but deeply connected to other research-creation events—and that, in and of itself, becomes a way to think about impact. The chapter also makes a case for the idea of research-creation as pliable.

Chapter One

Bitter Chocolate
Is for Adults!

Matters of Taste in
Elementary Students'
Socially Engaged Art

Ask Me Chocolates is a socially engaged art project coproduced by a group of grade-six students from Chocolate Elementary and the artists Reed Reed and Hannah Jickling.[1] *Ask Me Chocolates* is a series of limited-edition chocolate multiples with accompanying story fragments. Multiples are artworks that exist as handmade copies. While the copies appear identical, because they are made by hand each is unique. Mutiples are often traded or sold (Dyment and Elgstrand 2012). There are twenty-eight unique chocolate multiples, each produced as an edition of ten and packaged in a cellophane wrapper with metallic embossed printing. These chocolate multiples are the culminating project from a six-month socially engaged artist residency that investigated value, trade, labor, artists multiples, and counter-economies, poo humor in art, and the history and politics of the chocolate trade including child slavery.

The propositional concept that activated the residency was trade, a concept explored through a series of field trips, classroom-based research, lectures on a range of contemporary artistic practices, guest artist presentations, and a number of artistic research experiments.

Each student created their multiple out of Sculpey clay, which was then cast into a food-safe silicone mold. They also wrote their own accompanying text for the packaging. Students and the artists took over the school's staff room to melt and pour their chocolate multiples. Like chocolate bars, these multiples were designed for movement and distribution. These chocolate multiples were subsequently traded with other students in the school, and with parents and artists from the community, in exchange for songs, services, and objects such as books, a light saber, a can of tuna, an autographed baseball, a serenade, dancing, and a headstand.

On a field trip to the horizontally traded social enterprise ChocoSol, the artists noticed that most of the samples of chocolate provided to the students had not been eaten, and in some instances they had been thrown out after one bite (Jickling and Reed 2017). Weeks later, when determining the type of chocolate to be procured to make the chocolate multiples, the artists suggested using chocolate from ChocoSol. Students responded: "BITTER CHOCOLATE IS FOR ADULTS!" Dark chocolate would render the chocolate multiples worthless in a school economy where they were to be traded among peers and friends.

This chapter examines two socially engaged projects through *matters of taste*. While young children are often understood as lacking taste, or are assumed to have underdeveloped taste receptors, these projects instead position children as tastemakers—where taste becomes material, relational, and felt. If taste is conventionally assumed to be an adult quality, something young children cultivate to acquire, these projects rupture normative conceptualizations of taste in the context of school, young children, and art. Repositioning the school as a candy factory and a flower boutique, where students engage in a range of experimental projects that examine, disrupt, and cultivate different visceral taste sensations, the resulting collaborations question childhood, value, labor, and economics and position elementary school students as changemakers. Thinking with matters of taste as affective, visceral, and relational foregrounds bodily, affective, and felt encounters within socially engaged art and pedagogy. Additionally, the chapter asks questions about the radical potential of children as socially engaged artists engaged in research-creation, and problematizes current art criticism that devalues pedagogical art with children.

Children are often described as lacking taste or having underdeveloped taste palettes. This is most commonly used in reference to gustatory taste but is likewise implicated in aesthetic judgment and the discernment of behavior. The hierarchy of the senses in colonial contexts rendered taste as the lowest of the senses which, through moral cultivation, could be developed into refined sensibilities (Classen 1993; Springgay 2008). Linked to class and education, taste has been allied to notions of good or bad that are both subjective and universal. As Jim Drobnick (1999, 69) notes, both smell and taste were historically viewed as uncivilized senses, senses "of the primitive, infantile and animalistic." Considered the "chemical senses," he writes, smell and taste were "intimately linked in the evolution of species and in everyday acts of eating" (75). Colonialism was built on disciplinary regimes that sought to regulate the sensibilities of taste and comportment in colonial subjects, while denigrating the Indigenous and the enslaved as lacking bodily propriety. Educational institutions were a powerful site for the colonial apparatus to naturalize the cultivation of taste and moral behavior.

The myth that children lack taste corresponds with the figure of the child as incomplete (Farley 2018) or in a "suspended state of an adulthood-yet-to-come" (Sonu and Benson 2016, 231). As not yet fully formed adults, the incomplete child is trained and cultivated, by adults, toward gustatory and aesthetic wholeness. As Lisa Farley writes, "If children are incomplete, they are also malleable—and so can be made in the image of adult desire" (2018, 11). The making of the child into an adult has been described using universal models of development. The problem with such models, Mindy Blaise (2014) claims, is that they are predicated on mythical norms, built around the white, cis-male, middle-class, able-bodied child, that cannot account for bodies (or tastes) that diverge, and that continue to bifurcate nature and culture. From the vantage of development, a child's taste naturally and educatively matures over time regardless of race, gender, class, and so on. Yet childhood, Farley (2018) reminds us, has never been historically, culturally, or socially universal. Race, gender, religion, and class mediate the ways in which childhood is both conceptualized and lived.

Feminist postcolonial scholars such as Parama Roy (2010, 7) account for the ways that food and the sensorium intimately connected colonizer and colonized, "generating new experiences of desire, taste, disgust, and appetite and new technologies of the embodied self." The racialized subaltern was invariably reduced to a corporeality, the tastes of which had to be refashioned. She writes:

Colonial politics often spoke in an indisputably visceral tongue: its experiments, engagements, and traumas were experienced in the mouth, belly, olfactory organs, and nerve endings, so that the stomach served as a kind of somatic political unconscious in which the phantasmagoria of colonialism came to be embodied. (7)

The biopower of carnality continues to inflict violence on the bodies of the subjugated, including upon the racialized child. Kyla Tompkins (2012) similarly examines how eating and ingestion have been used to control racial and gendered positions. Attending to the sensory life of the colonized subject requires, according to Neetu Khanna, "a reorientation to dominant imaginaries of the body" (2020, 29). This in turn demands an affective and relational account of decolonization, one that includes a material and visceral understanding of taste. Khanna writes, "The revolutionary potentiality of the visceral is characterized by the volatility and unpredictability of its energetic activity, and how it unfolds in unruly and erratic ways" (18). The visceral enfolds mouth, gut, and anus in the politics of taste.

The politics of taste is further complicated in the figure of the child. Debbie Sonu and James Benson argue that the term *child* is used as a marker of inferiority. They write, "To act childishly is to act without thought, immaturely, without reason or rationale. The term *child* has been used to define and denigrate certain social groups perceived as inferior: colonized peoples, slaves, and women. *Child*, in this way, denotes dependency, powerlessness, and inferiority" (2016, 234). Children's preference for cheap candy, which is often distinguished from proper food, marks their taste buds as substandard. Children's taste, with their proclivity for candy and sugar, is viewed as unhealthy and harmful. The term *sugar ecologies* has been used to denote the racial capitalism of sugar and its toxic accumulation and effect on Black bodies (Hatch, Sternlieb, and Gordon 2019). Sugar ecologies include the colonial labor of harvesting and producing sugar, the manufacturing and consumption of processed goods, and the racial disparity of diseases like diabetes. Racialized and socioeconomically marginalized children are implicated in sugar ecologies and the environmental toxicity such ecologies produce.

Yet, Jickling and Reed (2017) assert that children's sustained interest in candy, at least in school contexts, is because it is regulated and forbidden. Gum, for instance, is banned in most Canadian public elementary schools; and public discourse shuns schools and families that make "poor" lunch choices while using the rhetoric of health and obesity without critical reflection on race and poverty as environmental factors. In education, children's taste is governed and controlled, where taste is fundamentally about power. Taste, while regulated because of its associations with "too much" viscerality, has simultaneously become disembodied and scrutinized.

Unsurprisingly, then, Jickling and Reed (2019) emphasize that what is most important to children about eating candy is "mouthfeel." This is "the feeling of something touching the sides of your cheeks, your tongue, your teeth. A little more than texture—does it make your mouth water? Does it pop? Is it slimy? . . . It's a slippery aesthetics, fuzzy authorship and tactile information that goes beyond our typical knowing." This resonates with Mann et al.'s (2017) tasting experiment, where they ask questions about what it means to taste through their fingers. In eating with the hands, taste, they contend, "viscously spreads" and includes such reactions as pleasure and embarrassment, erotic titillation, and discomfort. Clearly the senses are not autonomous, but rather cross over and interpenetrate. Some foods in fact can't be distinguished by taste alone but require the addition of smell; and, as mouthfeel suggests, tasting has a lot to do with touch. It is the affective, sensory, and felt dimensions of taste that guide my exploration of two socially engaged projects enacted with elementary school students. While "matters of taste," as an idiomatic expression, implies that taste is individual and personal, it also indicates that taste is an inherent quality of a thing, further bifurcating nature and culture. In bringing feltness to bear on these projects, I argue for an understanding of taste that is emergent and that accounts for the touching encounters, between human and nonhuman bodies, that are material, visceral, and affective. My arguments are situated alongside queer, feminist materialist, postcolonial, and decolonial scholars' articulations of affect as a nonindividual, unbounded force that is volatile, lively, productive, and self-organizing.

Tasting, whether through the mouth or the fingers, is affective and fundamentally about incorporation and encounters. Taste is profoundly a means of transcorporeal encounter, where all bodies—human and nonhuman—are enmeshed and coimbricated in each other's becomings. The materiality and corporeality of taste insists that taste is neither an inherent quality of a thing, nor a human attribute acquired through developmental processes. Rather, taste is a dynamic and emergent activity that requires intimacy; and this intimacy engenders *transmaterial* relations between diverse bodies. To taste is to make felt—and to make oneself felt. Taste as *feltness*: MOUTHFEEL! This feltness, as I wrote in the introduction, is about affective, material, touching encounters. In shifting taste from something cultivated to that which arises in the event of an encounter, taste foregrounds corporeal relations, and in doing so asks questions about how we are in relation. As Haraway (2008, 36) elaborates, "Touch ramifies and shapes accountability." Transmateriality renders taste as emerging from situated practices that are constantly in formation. This then foregrounds touching encounters—feltness—in matters of taste. Haraway writes, "Accountability, caring for, being affected, and entering into responsibility are not ethical abstractions. . . . Touch does not make one small; it peppers its partners with attachment sites for world making. Touch, regard, looking back, becoming with—all these make us responsible in unpredictable ways for which worlds take shape" (2008, 26). If taste is configured not only by the papillae on our tongues but as transmaterial feltness, then taste opens us to becoming responsible for matters of taste that are produced in a relational encounter. In the felt encounter we must become accountable to differences in taste, but also to how taste is valued and circulated, and how it shapes knowledge. *What (or perhaps who) do we taste when we taste a chocolate?*

Elspeth Probyn (2016) likewise argues that taste is about encounters that are entangled with intimacy, desire, and disgust. Writing about oysters, she claims that tonguing and tasting are things you do with your whole body. Thinking with Annemarie Mol's work on matter, Probyn argues that "matter is never matter by itself" (52). Chocolate is never just chocolate but "matter-related," conjuring indeterminate, felted, and knotted assemblages of relations.

In proclaiming "BITTER CHOCOLATE IS FOR ADULTS!," the students were advocating for their own childhood taste preferences and kid knowledge. However, the matters of taste they expressed were not based on poor or underdeveloped sensibilities but on opinions shaped transmaterially through months of research-creation and lived experiences into how value is determined, circulated, and multiplied. Their desire to use milk chocolate had everything to do with labor, trade, and school and community economies. The school was composed of more than 95 percent new immigrant families, families of color, who are socioeconomically marginalized and for whom English was not the language spoken at home. Most of the students in the grade-six class were not born in Canada. All of the students lived in a series of high-rise and subsidized apartment buildings that surrounded the school, in a very urban and densely populated community. Bitter chocolate wasn't for *all* adults; it symbolized a product that was expensive, exclusive, and not sold in their local neighborhood shops. Bitter chocolate was white. As tastemakers, those who decide or influence what is popular or fashionable (what is in good taste), the students asserted situated kid knowledge over the artisanal and, in doing so, articulated the politics and power of taste. The students' racialized and economic sensibilities affectively attuned them to the specific geohistories that produce bitter chocolate.

Writing about the politics of taste, Annemarie Mol (2008) narrates the story of eating Granny Smith apples in her youth. These apples were always associated with the taste of violence because they traveled to the Netherlands (her home) from their origin in Chile and were thus always connected to the violence of dictatorship. Thinking with Mol, Lindsay Kelley (2019) argues that taste "connects international politics, national identity, and sensory encounter, creating new knowledge through otherwise disparate connections." The bitterness of the ChocoSol chocolate became associated with the students' research into the cacao industry, including child slavery, their own relationship to chocolate and taste, and the National Bitter Melon Council, an arts collective introduced to the students in one of their many lessons. The collective is organized around the bitter melon, a vegetable not well known in the Western world. In their project *Bitter Barter*, participants were invited to trade a personal object—stuffed animal, water bottle—for a bitter melon. Their projects use the "foreignness of Bitter Melon, the concept of the flavor that is also an emotion, to instigate situations that, through bitterness, create an alternative basis for community."[2] In the residency, bitterness mobilized a series of pedagogical encounters that *exceeded* the flavor of bitter chocolate. This is what Probyn (2000, 9) means when she writes that "eating sends us off in unexpected directions and orders alternative connections." And, in doing so, she argues, "it roots actual bodies within these relations" (9). Student conversations about bitterness connected to different learning events from the residency but also to the bitterness of their personal and collective experiences of transnational movement, migration, learning English, and schooling. As Khanna (2020, 27) contends, the visceral regimes that reproduce taste are always "inextricable from colonial and postcolonial regimes of racialization." As one student wrote about their chocolate multiple, *Bitter Gourd*:

> I chose bitter gourd which was known by the group of artists called the Bitter Melon Council. I'll be more talking about the taste of bitter. Bitter is the most sensitive of all the tastes to me, or maybe it is. Well, common bitter foods and beverages include = coffee, coco, mate, marmalade, bitter gourd, beer, bitters, olives, and peel. I think the big idea of bitterness is sadness like sadness is life. The bitter melon council traded bitter gourd for monkey and other stuff. It was kind of interesting to me because I never thought you could trade a toy for an eating thing and it gave me a new idea of what I could trade with my classmates.

Tasting, Probyn maintains, "becomes a visceral reminder of how we variously inhabit the axes of economics, intimate relations, gender, sexuality, history, ethnicity, and class" (2000, 9). This is vitally at work in both socially engaged projects as matters of taste, where matter becomes accountable to transmaterial relations connecting mouth, gut, and anus with chocolates, migration, slavery, and capitalism.

Excremental Taste: The Affective Force of Poo Humor

Snowball sales, field trips turning the subway into an experimental studio, guest artist workshops, and research into child slavery and the global chocolate economy were just some of the many micro-research-creation events that made up the residency.[3] Jickling and Reed worked with the students and the teacher to think about trade beyond neoliberal, Euro-Western, and settler colonial narratives of conquest and progress, engaging the students in creating their own objects that had meaning and value on a personal and community level. These objects were circulated and traded among the students. As the research-creation events shifted to focus on the global chocolate economy, as a way to ask questions about local and global economies, students visited a Cadbury chocolate factory and the horizontally traded social enterprise ChocoSol. It was here that the students witnessed (and helped) the chocolate ooze out of a pedal-powered molino (chocolate grinder). This was followed by uncontrollable giggles and some bathroom humor, feelings of pleasure and delight coupled with disgust and shame. These affects coursed through the classroom over the remaining months of the project and stuck to different bodies differently (Ahmed 2010).

Jickling and Reed responded to the students' appetite for bathroom humor affirmatively and introduced them to a number of contemporary artists who work with chocolate, feces, or other unusual materials. Part of this pedagogical process was to expand the teacher's and the students' knowledge about contemporary art practices, particularly projects that incorporated chocolate and commented on the violence of trade and capitalism. For example, students were acquainted with Janine Antoni's *Gnaw* (1992) and *Lick and Lather* (1993–1994), works made from lard and chocolate; *Sweet Ass* (2002–2003), a chocolate toilet by Art Domantay; and Bill Burns's *Chocolate Hand Grenades* (1987), chocolate replicas of four mid-twentieth-century hand grenades. They were also familiarized with *Guarana Power* (2003) by the collective SUPERFLEX, a project that works with cooperative farmers in Brazil to challenge multinational corporations' monopoly on the guarana economy. Many artists' projects also challenged notions of aesthetic taste: for example, Dieter Roth's multiples *Bunny Dropping Bunny* (1968), a chocolate Easter bunny made out of rabbit shit; and Stephen Shanabrook's *Morgue Chocolates* (1994), chocolate molds made from wounds collected at morgues. Jickling and Reed (2017) note that shit art is often framed as abject because of its association with racialized otherness, filth, and disgust. In showing the students a range of scatological artworks, the artists argue that "this movement beyond the borders of social respectability satisfied our own desires to run with threads of discussions that challenged etiquette in productive and playful ways" (89). Excrement has been used to justify racialized and class-based hierarchies, where sanitation and cleanliness become part of the colonial civilizing project (Gerling 2019). The colonizer subject is distinguished by their "distance from excrement in comparison with that of their colonial subjects, whose sexuality and excremental habits alike were carefully scrutinized and used to support the narrative that darker skin meant excremental and sexual promiscuity" (629). Classroom management, particularly in colonial elementary schools, is a primary site of control in the production of nationhood and civilization. In bringing poo into the classroom and attending to the students' visceral responses, Jickling and Reed opened up the otherwise sanitized space of the classroom and ruptured colonial, normative, and adult understandings of taste.

The viscerality of poo amplifies the affective and felt dimension of the pedagogical encounter. The unruliness of student bodies and artistic works and the contagion of kid laughter expose how disruptive and nonnormative forms of knowing and being can propel anti-oppressive and social justice education because this is where the material and affective forces go askew. When introducing artists and artworks to the students, Jickling and Reed were mindful of who is typically represented in the art world (and in the art school curriculum) and who isn't.

Pushing against the forms of socialized behavior acceptable in schools, the students' chocolate multiples embodied a transmateriality of taste, where different bodies became porous and open to different compositions. Writing about their chocolate multiple *Ding Dong* one student states:

> I was inspired by the artist Hazel Meyer of her creation of a *Ding Dong*. I did the *Ding Dong* because I liked it. And also it was an activity we did in class. There were two different colors of *Ding Dongs*. The colors were only pink and green. I also did the *Ding Dong* because they were nice and squishy. I liked pouring milk chocolate into my mold.

Meyer was a guest artist in the class and her *Ding Dong* works are colorful, floppy, tensile constructions made of knit bikini fabric. Alongside the *Ding Dong* works were two squishy fabric sausages made from pink and green fabric.

What wasn't captured in the chocolate multiple but is hinted at in the student's narrative is the playful way the students engaged with these materials in the class—fashioning poo, a penis, and a breast. Uncontrollable laughter erupted, and, for a moment, matters of taste slid, stuck, and circulated, dislodging the norms of discipline and control so central to classroom life. Khanna (2020, 20) argues that it is "where visceral logics misbehave, where the volatility and 'mindedness' of the somatic unconscious is most vividly on display that the possibilities of decolonization are imagined." The kinds of values and economies afforded in the classroom offered different pathways for the students to navigate their own positionalities in relation to the formal curriculum on the chocolate trade. The affective requires the body of the other to respond. Deleuze and Guattari's (1987, 284) writing is helpful here: "We know nothing about a body until we know what it can do, in other words what its affects are, how they can or cannot enter into composition with other affects, with the affects of another body, either to destroy that body or be destroyed by it, either to exchange actions and passions with it in composing a more powerful body." It is in the intensive corporeal encounter and exchange that anti-oppressive and social justice pedagogy becomes possible. Poo humor, shit art, and the affective dimensions of an excremental pedagogy refuse to comply with the logics of taste. The titillation of ding dongs and chocolate merge touch and texture with mouth and anus, foregrounding feminist articulations of the biological and the material in accounts of embodiment and affect (Wilson 2015). Touch as a surface and skin contact sensation merges with the touching encounters of eating, digesting, and shitting.

Shit art and ding dongs take things normally considered private and render them public and social. Making public what is normatively considered disgusting can become a potent way to challenge power, class distinctions, and moral values. In her book *Against Purity*, Alexis Shotwell (2016) argues that to be against purity does not mean one is in favor of toxicity or harm. Rather, "it is to be against the rhetorical or conceptual attempt to delineate and delimit the world into something separable, disentangled, and homogenous" (15). I'm not arguing that all poo humor is always welcome in a classroom but that the affective dimensions of an excremental pedagogy have the potential to disrupt individual boundedness and racialized distinctions of taste. As Ahmed (2010, 33) notes, "To experience an object as being affective or sensational is to be directed not only toward an object, but to 'whatever' is around that object, which includes what is behind the object, the conditions of its arrival." This is important because it shifts affect or feelings from being located in an individual to emerging from relational touching encounters: from feltness. Affect is useful in thinking with matters of taste because it engenders a politics and bodies as "processes of circulation, engagement, and assemblage rather than as originating from the position of a sovereign subject" (Lara et al. 2017, 34). Scholars who articulate the relationship between affect and politics attend to the ways that power circulates and flows (Bertelsen and Murphie 2010; Clough 2008; Puar 2012) and categories of animacy that condition corporeal hierarchies such as the incomplete child (Chen 2012). Attending to affect disturbs normative fantasies of taste and disrupts the visceral logics that regulate and condition bodies. Affecting subjectivities, which brings affect theory into assemblages with intersectional theories, focus on the ways that disability, class, race, and other sites of oppression are affectively produced (Ahmed 2004; Blackman 2017; Nishida 2017). Affect theory helps us rethink the assumption that agency and politics begin with the human subject or that the human is the only animate agent. As Puar (2012, 154) argues, "Affect entails not only a dissolution of the subject but, more significantly, a dissolution of the stable contours of the organic body, as forces of energy are transmitted, shared, circulated." The stickiness of affect reminds us that the material and intensive feelings that accompany excrement and melted chocolate are not housed in an individual body, nor are they autonomous and disassociated from subjectivity and identity, but rather that they emerge as an assemblage of conscious and nonconscious matterings (Lara et al. 2017). The radical potential of affect, argues Lisa Blackman (2015), enables alternative worldings to emerge, other ways of living, being, knowing, and making, beyond conventional arrangements of progress and development. In fostering an excremental pedagogy, Jickling and Reed created space for the affective and the corporeal to *matter*. Against a rhetoric of moralizing taste, shit art, ding dongs, and oozing chocolate destabilized instrumentalized and normalized ideologies of childhood and contravened against the logics of taste as good or bad. Taste became viscous and unruly where flavors and feelings entangled in complex ways that connected mouth, gut, and anus.

Tasting, eating, and food as art challenges ocularcentrism and the sterility of the white cube of the gallery space. If vision is conceived of as objective and as the faculty of reason, then taste brings the aesthetic experience into intimate and proximate relations (Fisher 1999; Springgay 2012). Writing about the ways in which smell and taste operate in artworks, Drobnick (1999, 74) writes, "The compelled intimacy of taking nourishment and air into our bodies challenges the distance and detachment central to visually based aesthetic theories. Artworks that atmospherically envelop or undergo digestion break the illusion that viewers exist solely as scopic viewpoints, that is, without bodies, sensations or feelings." As tastes or foods are incorporated into the body, the artwork transcorporeally co-composes with the audience's bodies.

Reed and Jickling refer to the chocolate multiples as story fragments of the residency. The accompanying texts, written by the students, generate nonlinear relational associations to different ideas, questions, research, artworks, field trips, and other classroom-based activities. They might also be understood as pedagogical ingredient lists that detail the concepts, ideas, narratives, references, and curricula that went into each chocolate. This multiple ingredient list is apparent in this student's story fragment, where taste, biology, and economies of excess are entangled:

> I created an intestine chocolate. The intestine is a machine [Cloaca] created by Wim Delvoye. It makes poop and shows how our intestine is important because if you didn't have an intestine the digested thing wouldn't properly come out. So, if it didn't come out you would have pain by getting constipation and other painful sickness. The artist also packages the poop and sells it, it is important there is more than one poop.

Jack Halberstam (2011) writes that so often students are not asked to author their own lives, or to theorize them. The chocolates, although a collaborative and much-negotiated project between the artists and the children, foregrounded their affective assemblages and their refusals to perform "good taste." Here the unruliness of bodies ruptured the doctrines of classroom management and censored body parts. The affective created a kind of pedagogical intimacy that was fleeting and emergent. And while ding dongs and artwork made from rabbit shit might not be everyday curricular materials in an elementary classroom, I would argue that matters of taste are reminiscent of what Kathleen Stewart calls "ordinary affects." As ordinary, taste "passes through the body and lingers for a little while as an irritation, confusion, judgment, thrill or musing. However it strikes us, its significance jumps" (Stewart 2007, 39). It is this force that propels us to make sense of it, to incorporate it into our world making. Or in the words of one of the students:

> I wanted to make a Bolani chocolate because it reminds me of an art project called the Conflict Kitchen, which was created to serve food from countries that the United States is in conflict with. Even though Canada is a different country. I thought this was an interesting way to think about Canada and Its Trading Partners. And the larger idea of international relations. The Bolani made by the Conflict Kitchen was wrapped

in relay nice packaging with information from Afghans living in both the United States and Afghanistan. I love that the food wrapper is used to tell stories to hungry visitors and the Conflict Kitchen.

The cellophane packaging with the students' story fragments are what is left in the event that a chocolate is eaten. Wrappers mediate between the candy and the elements, preserving and protecting it. Wrappers "stall and stimulate appetite, instilling hopes of future pleasure. Like giftwrapping, they create anticipation and excitement" (Hecker 2019, 135). Wrappers themselves arouse an affective force enriching the edible contents contained inside.

Using the form of the artist multiple, the chocolates question the circulation of social justice narratives. The rhetoric of social justice education is too often fueled by well-meaning savior narratives that position the white, Western, liberal subject as enlightened and full of individual agency. Social justice knowledge and its accompanying actions are based on a logic of legibility and knowability. Injustices are identified and then curricula and pedagogy are mobilized to *overcome* these shortcomings. The global chocolate trade is bad. Horizontally manufactured and traded chocolate, which is typically bitter chocolate, is good. Ruben Gaztambide-Fernández (2013) contends that the arts are often used to justify such social justice aims. Many arts advocates, he argues, are trapped in what he calls the "rhetoric of effects" (215), which focuses on demonstrating how the arts can transform students or society. The arts, when reduced to advocacy statements, "typically evoke the arts as a substance with the power to influence any number of educational outcomes and individual experiences, or even to transform the consciousness of individuals. Instrumentalist approaches assert that injecting the arts can improve academic achievement; intrinsic arguments assert that the presence of the arts enhances individual experiences and perceptions of the world" (212).

Extending Gaztambide-Fernández's assertions, Sarah E. Truman and I, in our book *Walking Methodologies in a More-Than-Human World: WalkingLab* (2018), take up the logics of inclusion that participatory arts rely on. Participatory works are commonly framed as democratic and inclusive and invariably as against neoliberalism. Inclusion, we maintain, operates as a symbolic gesture that fails to undo the structural logics of racism, ableism, homophobia, and settler colonialism. Yet participatory works are often structured precisely via neoliberalism's focus on innovation and development. Participation does not guarantee an audience's ability to "alter the work's structure, only to assume [their] role within it" (Bishop 2012, 224). Max Haiven (2018) similarly argues that socially engaged projects too often adopt a rhetoric of participatory benevolence. He argues that "the imperative to 'participate' is germane to the logic of neoliberal financialization" (26). Artists thus need to recognize the ways in which their work might also reproduce such a logic. If participation as inclusion closes things in on itself, keeping things tidy, cohesive, and comfortable, then we need a way to think about participation that "keeps things unsettled, a push that ungrounds, unmoors, even as it propels" (Manning 2016, 202).

Jickling and Reed recognize these complex tensions in socially engaged art, particularly when working with children and in a school context where student attendance is regulated. However, working against instrumental logics of social justice, the artists rejected a falsely optimistic rhetoric about the global chocolate trade and resisted heteropatriarchal narratives of success that position the other as disenfranchised and deprived. The insistence of the racialized students on pushing the limits of affective comportment made possible a radical undoing of normative taste and liberal social justice and participatory narratives.

Matters of taste materialized in various ways throughout the project, including in some of the chocolates produced by the students—a dead bunny, a hand grenade, and a poo intestine. These (in)edible artworks expose the contradictory logic of neoliberalism, fair trade, global capitalism, and the value-neutral stories about the world that dominate school curricula. Each student got to eat one multiple in a frenetic chocolate orgy. However, the chocolates were more than edible treats consumed at recess time: as multiples, they eventually entered into a trade economy in the school and community.

Jickling and Reed never expected students to become more tasteful (chocolate) consumers. When the trade event commenced in the school for other classes to attend, students exchanged their multiple for light sabers, cans of tuna, social services such as carrying bags to and from school, and even a love ballad. A limited-edition birthday party hat (purchased on eBay for the event) was offered by a local artist as part of the community trade but was rejected for its seeming absence of kid value, while my headstand procured two chocolate packages.

While chocolates might infer habitual and recognizable practices, and are thus knowable, when we encounter them differently, when they refuse to conform to expectations, they become more than what we assume their functionality to be. In the words of Erin Manning (2013, 92), "they extend beyond their objectness to become ecologies for complex environments." Further, the chocolate multiples engender a "refusal of legibility and an art of unbecoming"

(Halberstam 2011, 88). Despite the tacit institutional desire for the students to craft tidy narratives empathizing with the child victims of the slave trade, the chocolates' affective force shakes our relationship to totalizing narratives and particular aesthetics of taste. This is not to suggest that the horrors of the chocolate industry be forgiven or ignored but that, in place of a curricular approach that assumes we can digest the pain of the other, the excremental pedagogy of the multiples "keep[s] us from taking the stance of the dispassionate observer, [keeps] us from falling into our selves . . . and so we become responsible before the event, in the face of it, in its incessant coming-to-act" (Manning 2013, 68). The toilet paper roll, the dead bunny, the intestine, the house, the snap hat, and others do not attempt to represent trade and its politics, as if the events of trade could be bounded and delimited; rather, through their refusal to confer and their affective force, they shape counterintuitive modes of knowing and being.

Commemorating Waste

Reed and Jickling also coproduced another socially engaged project with a different group of grade-six students at a different school.[4] *Your Lupines or Your Life* residency takes its name from a 1974 Monty Python sketch about Dennis Moore, an inept highway robber who, with his catchphrase "your lupines or your life," steals lupine flowers from the nobility to redistribute to the poor of his village. The sketch captured some of the ideas circulating in the artist residency regarding economic and material value. As a final project, the class acquired surplus floral arrangements from funeral homes and, with the help of a local florist, reconfigured these arrangements into wreaths and bouquets. Funeral flowers are regularly discarded after a service because of their grave appearance. The new floral arrangements became *Abject Awards* that were then bestowed to a public place or thing in recognition of its underappreciated qualities. Awards were granted to "The Loneliest Pigeon," "The Biggest Wad of Gum," and "The Most Eww-Worthy Lake."

In *Your Lupines or Your Life* the abject shifted from excrement to another form of waste: garbage. Through a variety of investigations incorporating field trips, exercises, discussions, and slideshows, the artists and students explored ideas surrounding supply and demand, relative value, and surplus. The school where *Your Lupines or Your Life* unfolded was located on the opposite side of the city from Chocolate Elementary. The students that comprise this school's population are socioeconomically marginalized new immigrant families and middle-class, predominantly white families whose children were typically enrolled in the gifted program and bused to school from adjacent neighborhoods. It was in a grade-six gifted class that this artist residency took place.

In one micro-investigation the artists had students create intricate packaging for garbage found in the schoolyard. In another, they created found posters for garbage. For example, students created found posters for a balloon knot, an ace of hearts playing card with a burn hole in the center, a rock, and numerous other items sourced from the neighborhood: items that conventionally had little to no value or that had been discarded as waste. These found posters were hung up in the school neighborhood, on telephone poles and the like, with my university office phone number listed. The absurdity of the posters challenged the ways that value is accumulated and circulated. I received a number of phone messages by members of the public playfully requesting their found garbage be returned to them.

Both the garbage packaging and the posters hint at a long tradition of contemporary art created from waste. While many contemporary artworks that incorporate waste capture the anxiety of increased ecological destruction, in the students' projects there is a kind of pleasure, sensuousness, and absurd humor in waste and what can be made of it. Waste has a complex role in the creation of value (Hawkins and Muecke 2003).

In addition to pointing at what waste tells us about value systems and beliefs, the accumulation of childhood commodities (balloon knot, playing card, chewing gum) lovingly restored and commemorated waste. Visualizing waste, making it present, honored, and celebrated, the students' projects interrogate their own patterns of waste but also global consumption. Memorializing and elevating the status of neighborhood trash, these projects present commodities that might seem benign or insignificant in larger conversations about waste as essential. "The aestheticization of waste," write Guy Hawkins and Stephen Muecke, "is an economic move, an attempt to invert value, to recuperate the negative" (2003, xi). The devalued, discarded objects are revalued as tastefully hand-packaged goods or belongings worthy of lost-and-found posters that "[demonstrate] the persistence of value even from the equalizing ground of garbage" (Boetzkes 2019, 28). The circulation of garbage through these projects, in the words of Amanda Boetzkes (2019, 28), becomes "a quasi-economy in its own right," expanding the arenas of value and exchange. The care given to the garbage by the students refuses any predetermined meanings about waste as offensive, dirty, or repulsive. The projects offer a taxonomy of the schoolyard and hint at the corporeality of the students who inhabit it: bodies conjured through teeth marks in chewed gum, candy wrappers, and hair clips. While a lot of waste art points at the global climate crisis, Jickling and Reed, as in the case of the chocolate multiples, steered clear of overarching moral narratives. Built upon the students' questions and interests, the projects focused on surplus, byproducts, and value and complicated the students' own preconceived understandings of aesthetic taste and art. To counter normalized understandings of waste as disgusting, which contribute to viewing public and community spaces as dirty and unworthy and, as such, bound up with racialized and class narratives, the projects amplified visualization and tactility to mobilize counter-values and counter-tastes.

In this residency, students were introduced to a variety of artists' projects, including Hannah Jickling's project in which she arranged chewed bubble gum into heart shapes on the streets of Glasgow, Ai Weiwei's *Dropping a Han Dynasty Urn* (1995), a series of black-and-white photographs showing the artist destroying an ancient vessel. They also learned about Diane Borsato's *Bouquet* (2006), a project in response to instructions by The Critical Art Ensemble to commit a crime with a humanitarian outcome, in which Borsato stole flowers from neighbors' gardens to create intricate flower arrangements. They were also familiarized with the design collective SPURSE and their *Eat Your Sidewalk* project about urban food foraging. The class watched the film *The Gleaners and I*, by Agnes Varda, which documents the history of gleaning intersected with contemporary urban practices such as dumpster diving and garbage picking.

Interested in rupturing matters of taste by repurposing worthless garbage, the artists and students conducted a playground excavation and neighborhood audit to find discarded items. They discovered an unexpected site of waste: a funeral home. Although flower arrangements are essential at many funeral services, they are quickly discarded because of their macabre appearance. Funeral flowers are an unacknowledged or invisible form of waste.

Discussions of flowers and value led the class to consider permanence and impermanence—cut flowers have a life of no more than five or six days. From the moment they are harvested, an intricate system springs into action to deliver this expiring cargo to its destination. Together the class researched where flowers are grown and how they are consumed. Through further investigation into the economy of flowers, the students learned about the Semper Augustus tulip bulb that, within Holland's seventeenth-century speculative marketplace, was worth the equivalent of one year's wages for a wealthy merchant.

As a final project, the class acquired floral arrangements from the local funeral home and, with the help of a local backyard florist, reconfigured these arrangements into wreaths and bouquets. These arrangements became *Abject Awards* that were then bestowed to a public place or thing in recognition of its underappreciated qualities. Awards were granted to Biggest Goober, The Biggest Wad of Gum, Rustiest Pop Can, Best Bag in Tree, and Moldiest Fruit. Repurposing surplus funeral flowers into *Abject Awards*, the students inserted new "taste sensations" into overlooked or insignificant spaces or things in their school neighborhood.

One student, who awarded the Loneliest Pigeon, wrote:

I did my abject award on "Loneliest Pigeon." I left the award near a tree in a grassy rocks place where all the pigeons are (near a high school tennis court on Jameson Avenue). I decided to recognize the value of this one lonely pigeon. Because since I was little, I always saw this white pigeon in a crowd of normal black/grey pigeons in an area near Parkdale Collegiate High school. And he/she always looked so lonely and sad and different. And I wanted people to recognize that pigeons have feelings to and that maybe he felt bad because he was white and not grey like everyone else. I wrote this all on a little note attached to the award.

Another student wrote:

My abject award was for the Best Sidewalk Crack. Well, the best one on my street, anyway. To be the BEST sidewalk crack, it had to be nice and straight with no breaks, clean, and nice and smooth. There is this beautiful sidewalk crack a few away from my house, so I put it there leaning against a telephone pole. On one side of the tag, I wrote "Congratulations for winning the cleanest, straightest, and smoothest sidewalk crack award! This goes to the best sidewalk crack on the street!" and on the other side, I wrote "Sidewalk cracks are one of the many things in life that we never recognize." By adding value to sidewalks, I'm pointing out something that has always been there, we use everyday, but isn't considered necessary for survival, or even cool. At first, when I came up with the idea, it just seemed like a wacky, funny award that I could put. Then I got thinking about it, and realized how I never think of sidewalks as some amazing invention, but it would be so weird without them.

Transforming the impermanence of funeral arrangements and flowers into a commemoratory award, the project disturbs the moral imperative of waste management and recycling. Boetzkes (2019) remarks that negotiating waste is a matter of contact, of touching and sorting. This shifts waste management from simply a moral obligation to a matter of taste that is affectively enfolded between bodies both human and nonhuman. Boetzkes writes: "A politics of becoming proceeds from those responses to waste that unsettle mastery, those intensities that signal not our differences from waste but our profound impli-cations with it" (42). In the various research-creation events in the residency and the culminating awards, waste takes on many forms: surplus, discarded, and recovered. Decaying flowers are lovingly restored to bouquets and wreaths and offered as awards to uncanny places or things. "Gleaning waste," writes Boetzkes, "is the aesthetic act par excellence because it severs the intentional relation between an object's designed utility and its economic destination" (51). Photographs that document the project depict the students in a formal photography studio setup with the flower arrangements in front of their faces; as if they are extensions of, or entangled with, the awards themselves. If the sweetness of chocolate became moments of poo humor that engendered an excremental pedagogy of refusal, then the awards inverted waste to become something precious, cared for, and commemorated. Both projects pervert nar-ratives of childhood innocence and incompleteness through strange and affec-tive matters of taste celebrating children's unedited pleasure as tastemakers.

Children as Socially Engaged Artists
Doing Research-Creation

Children are increasingly becoming present in and/or co-producers of socially engaged art. Consequently, critical conversations have emerged about their labor and role in specific projects. Leigh Claire La Berge (2019), in her book *Wages against Artwork*, devotes an entire chapter to the issue of children's labor in socially engaged art, considering the ways that children are put to work in often coercive and scripted ways. Similarly, Pablo Helguera (2010) has raised questions about the potential exploitation of children in socially engaged art, challenging institutions that commission or organize an artist to create a so-cially engaged project with children that is often driven more by corporate desires for opulent photo opportunities with marginalized communities than interest in quality educational initiatives. Children are being exploited, often in the name of diversity. As I have contextualized in the introduction, these conversations are in line with those being framed around the criticality of the Educational Turn. For instance, Janna Graham (2010) argues that when the autonomous artist is substituted as a model pedagogue, this only serves to re-inforce the hierarchical split between artist and educators. She contends that what is needed are methods and understandings whereby the artist becomes coresearcher or coinvestigator, a shift that would demand that the artist not only engage in cultural production for the sake of exhibition or careerism but actively employ creative participation in changing and sustaining the lives of the people they work with. In the context of the two projects discussed in this chapter, this horizontality was crucial. Further, the students were not mere materials and bodies used to create a work of art. Their labor and collaboration in the projects was generative, kid-oriented, and self-directed.

All of these varied conversations are crucial in realizing the radical potentiality of pedagogical art in school contexts. However, I want to pause briefly on a rather polemic text in which the art critic Claire Bishop (2012, 241) claims that "art is given to be seen by others, while education has no image." I introduced Bishop's arguments in the introduction but return to them here to further expand how we talk about value and socially engaged pedagogical projects. Her comments have raised a number of critical debates about the role of the art audience, which in her estimation is "ineliminable" (241). One of the tensions within pedagogical art, Bishop contends, is the gap between the primary audience of the students who coproduce the work and a secondary art audience, which for her is essential. Elsewhere I have written about the double ontology of socially engaged projects, where the forms and functions of art and education overlap in process but retain different criteria, expectations, and outcomes (Springgay 2014). As Bishop (2012) argues, we need to problematize the fact that artists disappear temporarily in practice and then appear as having been the primary authors all along in exhibitions, images, and documentation. The secondary audience is typically not present during the process of producing socially engaged art. "The secondary audience is ineliminable, but also essential," Bishop contends, "since it keeps open the possibility that everyone can learn something from these projects: it allows specific instances to become generaliseable, establishing a relationship between particular and universal that is far more generative" (272). Perhaps this double ontology is really a multiple ontology, with numerous and sometimes even unaccounted for audiences, where the work does different things for different publics. Take, for instance, *Ask Me Chocolates*. The students and teacher shaped an audience as they worked together over many months. But other publics inside of and outside of the school were also present, dipping into the project at different times. These audiences included my research team, the principal and vice-principal, parents, and other students and teachers in the school. The artists were in conversation about the projects with other artists, and the work was presented at conferences such as Open Engagement, thereby mobilizing the work within a web of arts discourse. As the chocolates circulated and were ingested, mouths, tongues, intestinal tracks, guts, and eventually bowels became part of the more-than-human entanglements of gustatory audiences. Writing about their own research-creation project on digestion, Randy Lee Cutler

(2020, 12) states that incorporation "tells us something about the movement of energies both inside and outside the body; it concerns transformations that operate at multiple scales and durations while pointing to the absorption of nutrients and experiences." The excremental connectivity of mouth, chocolate, flower, and waste upends Bishop's ineliminable audience: everyone and everything will eventually be excreted!

Excrement and waste challenge the idea of audiences as passive viewers of artwork by emphasizing bodily encounters: feltness. As the chocolates were traded and entered into wider circulation, and the awards were ceremoniously inserted into public space, the classroom-based socially engaged projects composed and recomposed themselves as ever-expanding multiples. Perhaps the question we need to ask is: *What does the work ask of us now?* This is what is generative about socially engaged art. In much the same way that the pedagogical process is emergent, as it circulates among different audiences in various contexts, the projects do not represent the work that was done in the classroom; they continuously reemerge as different pedagogical encounters. The question of whether an art audience is ineliminable magnifies the power and privilege contained within such a statement. This is an art audience that is already known, with prescribed values, tastes, and aesthetic sensibilities. The known audience continues to reinscribe normative and colonial configurations of taste, where only particular adults can be epicurean art consumers.

Research-creation scholars have similarly considered the transdisciplinary and hybrid modes of legibility. Natalie Loveless (2019) contends that the value of research-creation is that it does not feed into bounded individualism in the disciplines. Nor is it a mashing together of discrete parts that maintain their wholeness. Rather, she argues that "it fails to fulfill the criteria of any one disciplinary location" (33). It is, she claims, "incalculable" (33). This failure does not mean that research-creation, or socially engaged pedagogical art, does not fit into the discrete disciplines of art or education but that it *exceeds* them. In failing, it refuses to confer a bounded and normative logic of disciplinary legibility. Bishop (2012) raises similar concerns, citing Guattari's concept of transversality (detailed in the introductory chapter of this book). She contends that it is necessary to interrogate disciplinary logics, "to ponder the productive overlaps and incompatibilities that might arise from their experimental conjunction, with the consequence of perpetually reinventing both" (274). Much like the found posters of a balloon knot, and the conjunctive of research-creation, transversality expands the dimensions of classrooms.

However, while Bishop favors methodological transversality, to insist as she does that "education has no spectators" and that "the most effective education is a closed social process" (272) eschews decades of educational research and theory informed by queer, feminist, antiracist, and decolonial work and practice. When we assume that education lacks visibility, it becomes vulnerable to being rendered valueless. Bishop continues, "Institutional pedagogy never needs to take on board the question of its communicability to those beyond the classroom (and if it does, it only takes the form of wholly inadequate evaluative questionnaires). . . . The most successful instances of pedagogy-as-art today manage to communicate an educational experience to a secondary audience" (272). Education is in a continual state of communication beyond the classroom: to parents, to other educators, to researchers, to policy makers, to the media, and to the broader public. It could be argued that education is one of the most highly scrutinized public domains, often by audiences who have little to no knowledge of the intimacies of doing pedagogical work or educational research. Every aspect of classroom life is publicly dissected, from lesson plans to class sizes, methods of teaching math, the necessity of sex education, school dress codes, student lunches, academic readiness, and the list goes on. The surveillance of student and teacher bodies is always further impacted by race and class. One might concede that Bishop intended her comments to mean that the ephemera of schooling does not circulate or become visible to an art audience through forms—such as exhibitions, publications, and performances— that in her mind constitute the art of the art world. But curricular and pedagogical matter has been rendered visible and aesthetic for decades. Think of the secondary students taking to the streets to protest gun violence in schools, climate change, Black Lives Matter, and Indigenous land and water rights. Students are front and center in these creative and artistic movements. It is this messy blurring between pedagogy and art that I find so generative.

Yet, what is so telling about Bishop's comments are the ways that they reinforce taste as a matter of bounded individualism and discernment. In order for socially engaged pedagogical art to perform *as art* it requires colonial disciplinary regimes into the proper taste palette. It's not that education has no image. Rather, as Bishop describes, it is an image that needs the colonial master to develop it, mold it, and fashion it to reflect the tasteful subject (Singh 2018a). This is further compounded by the racialized child-artist: not a complete adult-artist, and also a subaltern subject in need of civilizing decorum. But as this chapter and the various socially engaged projects attest, children as tastemakers dynamically disrupt such colonial constructions. Children as socially engaged artists doing research-creation upsets restrictive ideas about legibility, knowability, and bodies. In a conversation on art, activism, and scholarly work centering abolition and disability justice, Black Lives Toronto cofounder and artist Syrus Ware claims that children and youth are central to activist spaces as valuable contributors. Part of the revolution is in imagining a future in which children have value beyond regimes of capitalism in which value is determined by one's ability to work and make money. He says: "Instead, we could say, oh, children are valuable just as they are, actually! Not as future workers but actually as they are. And our elders are valuable. Not as former workers, but as inherently just as they are" (Ware 2020a). This kind of valuation is fundamental to radical pedagogy. For me, the important questions aren't about art audiences and aesthetics, or even about whether the work is social or antagonistic or feel-good; they are about pedagogical encounters that create space for kid knowledge that is courageous, intimate, and a form of creative action. They're about their presence as children full of poo humor who see the value in commemorating a balloon knot. Instead of relying on the adage that children are still becoming adults and relegating their art practices to the invisibility of school, we need to recognize the agency and knowledge of kids and the ways that they can destabilize the status quo.

Education, schools, learning, and students are always already visible. We just need to shift our habits of attention and see them on their terms. Ware (2020a) argues that kids are already involved in the revolution. He says: "We just don't necessarily see them because it happens on the playground, or it happens when they're away from the grown-ups. They're already negotiating, figuring out ways to resolve conflict on the playground. They're figuring out all these [moments] that we as grown-ups are trying to figure out. That's what abolition is, figuring out new ways of resolving conflict, crisis, and harm. Kids are trying to do that." In no way am I stating that the students in these two projects were directly working to defund police, but they were creatively working toward more just futures for kids like them. On kid terms. Bitter chocolate is for (white) adults! This is the power of socially engaged art as radical pedagogy. Part of what we need to do as educators and artists is to retrain our habits, retune our attention. Making complex socially engaged work with children, we need to value their contributions to the projects, their ideas and opinions.

Intimate pedagogies require that we attend to, or "tune into," as Natasha Myers (2020) would say, the affectively charged compositions that assemble bodies, story fragments, mouths, guts, anuses, and waste into powerful configurations. Sensory methods of doing research, art, and pedagogy rupture the sterility and stasis of classroom life. Excrement seeds the revolution.

Classrooms are far from hermetic spaces. In much the same way that the Molino oozed chocolate poo, leading to all kinds of leaky epistemological and ontological matterings, the bodies and knowledges that stick to and flow between bodies in schools vector and seep, permeating classroom, home, and public worlds. As an intimate practice, pedagogy is not contained by the walls of a classroom; it is always more-than while remaining indeterminate and incomplete. I write the conclusion to this chapter as COVID-19 reaches pandemic proportions and schools respond to the new biopower that flows viscously between borders, institutions, and bodies, always already constructing some bodies as disgusting, infectious, and harmful. In an era of social distancing, how to practice an intimate pedagogy becomes crucial.

What if we take seriously the affective, visceral, carnal, intimate, and transcorporeal life of education? How might waste—excrement and garbage—challenge the ways we think, practice, and write about socially engaged art, research-creation, and radical pedagogy? How might matters of taste as affective, material, and felt alter our accountability and responsibility to anti-oppressive and social justice education? How are children authoring their own livable worlds and futures?

Ask Me Chocolates and *Abject Awards* are potent reminders of the excitable, intensive, and contagious processes of art and pedagogy and the possibilities that flourish when a classroom becomes a work of art. Celebrating students as tastemakers, Jickling and Reed complicated the separation of classroom and artist studio and the value of one over another. Jickling and Reed have often converted a canoe into a studio, which the students named the "Canoedio." Students were invited to turn their bedrooms, apartments, classrooms, and the public subway into places where the making and doing of art happened. At the end of the residency, as part of the tradition of the graduating grade-six class gifting or leaving a commemorative object in the school, the students developed a list of names for alternate classroom-studio configurations. These absurd and humorous names were screen-printed onto a poster, framed, and offered to the school as a departing gift. One hangs on my writing studio wall. As a practice of intimacy, Jickling and Reed did not reinscribe the colonial practice of embedding themselves in the lives of the other; rather, they reimagined a hybrid and situated space of transcorporeal relations, full of kid knowledge, poo humor, and the sickly sweet flavor of chocolate.

Chapter Two

Imponderable
Curricula

Living the
Future Now

The ways in which certain things are deemed to be "educational" and other things are not considered "educational" is interesting. Some of the Whoop Dee Doo encounters that you are describing, particularly the scenes of momentary confusion at the live shows, I feel like these kinds of things are the basis of education in some ways. The times when you become confused and disoriented and then you have to think or explore a little bit more.—REED REED, in conversation with the art collective Whoop Dee Doo

The gymnasium at Noteworthy Secondary School has been transformed into a performance installation.[1] Two forty-foot basketball nets, handcrafted by tenth- and eleventh-grade students with the artist Hazel Meyer using an assortment of braiding and knotting techniques, have been installed at either end of the gym floor. The nets extend the length of the gym and are tied together in the center, displacing the normative function of the net. Fifteen balls are being tossed around the gym, and students jump over the net, move through the knotted tendrils, and weave balls through its entwined core. A student on a drum kit beats out a rhythmic score, its tempo and the thud of balls vibrating the atmosphere. After weeks of braiding labor in the art room alongside other projects engaging with scale, language, play, games, and repetition, the project *Walls to the Ball* is being activated for the entire school population. It was an athletic feat to get the school administration to allow the project to be "exhibited" in the gym, a space that the art students say is designated for, or awarded to, athletes only. Typically, a small corner of the school library can be accessed for art shows, which are never performance-based and must be limited to a wall and a display case. The gym's spatial designation for sport-not-art was just one of many challenges we faced in activating the project in the gym; its gesture toward endurance, gender, transgression, amusement, and the absurd rendered the project neither sport nor art, but also "not educational." Not only was it out of place in the gym, it was inappropriate in the context of the school as a whole, where maintaining disciplinary boundaries ensured rigorous and standardized learning. While the project invited the student audience to move and sweat together, to become part of the work of art, the educational value was considered illogical, misplaced, and unreasonable. It was an imponderable curriculum.

While *imponderable* as a term describes the plausibility of something happening, or the inability to determine something with accuracy, it also points at the social, cultural, and political aspects of value and outcomes. For example, in the eighteenth century, magnetism was considered imponderable because it was incapable of being weighed or evaluated concretely. While the early meaning of *imponderable* denoted weightlessness, it has come to be interpreted as that which is unthinkable, with a double meaning: both unlikely (it's unlikely that *Walls to the Ball* is educational) and extraordinary (*Walls to the Ball* is a situated and speculative, future-oriented activation of learning). In the second meaning the imponderable suggests potentiality, where alter-worlds and futurities emerge. To that extent, this chapter works through the speculative possibilities within the imponderable, through its untimely proposition. It is in the unexpected and the absurd of the imponderable that the possibilities for radical pedagogy emerge.

This chapter picks up the thread from chapter 1 regarding the ways that particular bodies, knowledges, and affects are regulated and governed in schools, where certain curricular moments are never educational (enough). Through an attention to performance and time, pleasure and the absurd, and the intimacy of visiting and nearness—what I collectively refer to as imponderable curricula—I question dominant narratives of what counts as educational and foreground moments of liveness, ridiculousness, and humor that enable youth to reimagine their situated worlds. Extending debates on socially engaged art and the Pedagogical Turn on the aesthetic value of the artwork, or its efficacy, the imponderable foregrounds the *extra-* of pedagogy as art: the extra-rational, extraordinary, extraeducational, and the unexpected and indeterminate ways that youth remix, remake, and reimagine future worldings. This chapter makes the case that the significance of socially engaged art practices and research-creation is an expression of futurity; a future that has not happened yet *but must.*

Two of the residencies discussed in this chapter were in collaboration with secondary school students: *Walls to the Ball,* which queers our assumptions about gender, sport, and textiles; and *Friday,* a performance which parodies talk show aesthetics and teen talent shows. A third, *Museum without Entrance,* which decolonizes and decenters cultural institutions and practices of collecting, included a number of secondary schools and one elementary class. In thinking-with art, I also pick up a recurring thread in my work that art is theory (Springgay 2008; Springgay 2018). This is something I first learned intuitively but which I heard articulated by Irit Rogoff at a public lecture she gave when I was in graduate school (see Rogoff 2000). The idea that artistic practice is in and of itself theoretical is enmeshed in my understandings and enactments of socially engaged art, research-creation, and radical pedagogy. The chapter also considers the curation of artist residencies in school contexts and the method of the "open brief," which creates the conditions for an imponderable curriculum to flourish and grow.

Traditionally, artist residencies are understood as a home away from home, where artists and cultural practitioners can leave their daily obligations and routine activities behind so that they can gain time for reflection, research, and production. Today, however, artist residencies no longer occur only in specialized venues dedicated to artistic production but also take shape on farms and in campgrounds, airplanes, libraries, hospitals, and restaurants, even incorporating mobile platforms such as vans and bicycles. Residencies have operated as alternative schools making use of seminars, workshops, and discursive forms. It was with these new residency models in mind that I created the *Pedagogical Impulse* artist residencies in public schools. Rather than inviting an artist to enter a school to teach a particular art technique, or to guide students in making a predetermined object, I was interested in how the residencies could function as a site of spatiotemporal openness. This was a significant move because, while artists (and galleries and curators) were reimagining what an artist residency could be, public schools were rarely the site of such innovations, in part because of hierarchical distinctions depicting community-based or school-based art as unvalued or improper artistic sites of production.

I begin this chapter with a discussion of the Artist Placement Group (APG), a UK-based "artist consultancy and research organisation" from the 1960s that placed artists in nonart environments, such as industry and government, as a way for artists to relocate their art practices away from the studio (Hudek 2010). Guided by the notions of placement and of art in social contexts, the APG is considered one catalyst in the history of socially engaged art and artist residencies. My inclusion of the APG is driven by their method of the "open brief," a process that initiated each placement and which emphasized relationality, unknowability, and curiosity. In much the same way that the open score influenced the Fluxus group (to whom I turn in chapter 3) in the 1960s, the APG's emphasis on placement, propositionality, and spatiotemporal openness set the conditions for the school-based residencies. Examining each of the three residencies as imponderable, as portals of possibility, this chapter makes a case for radical education and a future that will have to happen.

The Open Brief Method

In the midst of the first year of the residencies, I traveled with Reed Reed and Hannah Jickling (the artists featured in chapter 1) to London to work in the APG archives at the Tate Gallery, attend an exhibition on the APG, meet the curator Antony Hudek, and interview the cofounder of the APG, Barbara Steveni. The APG was conceived of by Barbara Steveni in 1965 and founded a year later by Steveni, John Latham, Barry Flanagan, David Hall, Anna Ridley, and Jeffrey Shaw.[2] The APG placed artists in industry, and later in government departments, as a way for artists to relocate their practices away from the studio and gallery, and to redefine the role of artists in society. The APG believed that artists could offer different perspectives on social problems and the world of work, which over time would shape an alternative value system. At the same time, artists would develop new art practices because of their placement experiences. While films, performances, or sculptures were sometimes generated by the placements, for Steveni and Latham the intent was for artists and workers to be in relation while doing daily tasks. As Grant Kester (2004) notes, characteristic of the APG method was duration and dialogue. Latham believed that artists' long-term engagements in the workplace would intervene and shift decision-making processes, which he felt were often short sighted.

Critics have argued that the APG were unsuccessful in creating meaningful social change, that they were often overly concerned with management at a time when they might have been more productive thinking about labor from a Marxist lens, and that their placements were politically neutral (Bishop 2012; Kester 2004). However, the radical premise behind the placements was what the APG called the "open brief"; the placements were not directed by the host organization, there was no obligation or expectation of services rendered by the artists, outcomes were not determined in advance, and the artists were to be paid a wage by the host organization. Developing an art practice beyond the studio and exhibition space, the "artist assumes the role of facilitating creativity among 'everyday' people" (Bishop 2012, 163). The APG fostered the belief that artists have a "useful contribution to make to the world, and that artists can serve society—not by making works of art, but through their verbal interactions in the context of institutions and organisations" (164). The model developed by Steveni shifted the typical patronage or commercial ties between industry and artists, insisting that art was a valuable research and educational practice for these organizations.

Scholars have begun to draw parallel links between the work of the APG and artists working within socially engaged frameworks. A survey exhibition of the APG's practices, mounted at the Raven's Row Gallery in London in 2012 and curated by Barbara Steveni, Antony Hudek, and Alex Sainsbury, attests to the APG's ubiquitous influence on contemporary art. Claire Bishop (2012, 176) claims that their impact on contemporary art includes the development of a "post-studio framework for artistic production," the creation of "opportunities for long-term, in-depth interdisciplinary research," the reconfiguration of "the function of the exhibition," and the implementation of "an evaluative framework for both art and research that displaces any bureaucratic focus on immediate and tangible outcomes." Like their counterpart Fluxus, APG's antiart aesthetic and their interest in the aesthetics of daily life have had a lasting impact on contemporary art practices, including on socially engaged art as pedagogy.

The placements were negotiated with individual businesses such as British Steel, Scottish Television, Esso Corporation, and Ocean Fleets Limited and government offices such as the Department of Health and the Department of the Environment, and much later the Southwark Education Department. APG's emphasis on placement, context, and the artist as cultural worker sought to foster links between art and other disciplines whereby the "artist moves out of the closed art world into the domain of decision making and recognized areas of large-scale problem handling" (Southwark Educational Research Project memo, n.d., shared by Steveni, London).

In an undated memo, provided to me by Steveni, the APG describes the procedure for a placement to consist of a brief feasibility study followed by a longer fellowship period. The main feature of the placement was a structure in which the organization paid the artist without any commitment by the artist to produce a work of art with such funds. In the feasibility period the artist would spend time at the host organization to learn about the context of the placement, often using methods similar to ethnographic fieldwork, such as participation, observation, research design, defining objectives, and problem posing. Instead of asking industry to fund one-off projects by artists, or to provide resources and materials for artists to create art, the APG model emphasized that context is half the work. The APG's aim was to contribute to society by bringing creative practices to bear on problems or issues identified within the host organizations. The host organization did not predetermine a problem; instead, through the open brief, or a period of not-knowing, the artist moved through the day-to-day operations of the organization in order to focus on an area of interest. The artist—who would later be called the Incidental Person—was free to function as he or she wished and to discover relationships between previously unrelated areas. Grant Kester (2004) writes that the APG's durational process sought to engage with long-term problem-solving.

The open brief model is similar to the way I approached curating the residencies. I would first organize an ideation meeting with the artists, the teachers, and members of my research team. The ideation meeting allowed the artists to discuss with the teacher the classroom context and some general curricular concepts that could become a catalyst for the socially engaged projects. During the ideation period the artists did not fully plan a project or object but worked with the teachers to create entry points and propositions for the research-creation inquiry. Importantly, this process resisted the typical school-based art curricula that often incorporate art to represent or illustrate lesson topics. Instead, like the open brief, the ideation process foregrounded research, not-knowing, and exploration. The open brief is a speculative proposition that prioritizes the intangibility of expected results.

Latham's use of the label "Incidental Person," rather than artist, aims to remove the distinction between artist and nonartist. The Incidental Person is governed not by technical skills honed in art school but by "an awareness of her or his relative position on an infinite and infinitely variable temporal score" (Hudek 2010). Likewise, in the school-based residencies the students were valued as coresearchers and coartists. For an exhibition in New York, curated by Antony Hudek, which referenced the APG, Reed and Jickling created *Incidental Pancake*, a work using a 111-year-old sourdough culture from the Yukon Gold

Rush. For the exhibition, the sourdough culture was used in pancake batter at a New York restaurant and served with an informational placemat about the project. *Incidental Pancake* was introduced to students in the residencies, playfully disrupting ideas of who or what is an artist and of who makes art, and raising questions regarding the nature of collaboration.

In 1989 the APG changed its name to O+I (Organization and Imagination) in an effort to distinguish itself from neoliberal arts council–funded projects that situate artists in schools and which in the UK had also begun to use the term *placement*. The pervasive model of artist placements locates artists in schools on a short-term, project-oriented basis in order to supplement the regular teacher's art curriculum. Some of the challenges faced by such programs include a lack of collaboration between artist and classroom teachers and students, and an object-oriented focus that is not context-specific—in other words, what an artist produces in one school is similarly produced in another school without any regard for classroom or school context. Such an artist placement model is focused on the art object and on hands-on experiential learning that supplements existing curricula rather than thinking about how the classroom itself becomes a work of art. These kinds of artist placements are pervasive in Toronto. In curating artist residencies in schools, my aim was to counter such object-driven placements and to embrace the APG ethos of the open brief and of not-knowing.

In 1989 O+I established its first school-based placement, which was called the Southwark Educational Research Project (SERP) and was hosted by the Inner London Education Authority between 1989 and 1995. This placement took place in fifteen schools at a time when the responsibility for education was being passed to local authorities and a new National Curriculum was being established. O+I used film, interview protocols, and observational methods to examine educational change and to make a case for arts processes as educational research. In an era of outcomes-based research, the pressure to produce measurable results was not lost on Steveni. Instead she organized a community action at the local Town Hall where video documentation of the O+I placement was screened and various community members, teachers, students, parents, and artists used the artistic-practice-as-research methods to catapult conversations, actions, and new ways of thinking about educational reform. Unlike current models for artists working in schools, in which the artists' function and the projects' outcomes are predetermined, O+I's educational placement represented a radical departure for artists long before other school-based interventions had taken shape (Anthony Hudek, interview with author, London, 2012). Interestingly, the school-based placement is not well documented in art historical records, and I only learned of it through my interview with Steveni (it now has a website devoted to its revival). The absence of this placement in art historical texts and records about the APG (it was not even mentioned in the retrospective exhibition we visited in London) bore out my conjectures that art created with students and in educational contexts has been systematically devalued in larger art contexts and art history and yet it has made important contributions to the Educational Turn and to radical pedagogy. Discovering this historical precedent for the Educational Turn while in the midst of organizing the school-based residencies in Toronto reinforced the significance and impact of *The Pedagogical Impulse* research-creation event.

In 2018 the SERP project was reactivated by Barbara Steveni and Barbara Asante with Peckham Platform, a creative and educational charity in London, with exhibitions and programming at the Tate Gallery and at Flat Time House, a house where John Latham lived and worked and which is now a museum dedicated to his work and research. Part of reactivating the archive was to return to the original SERP schools and work with students, teachers, administrators, and policy makers on the school board to write the kind of curriculum they would like to see in the present and future. In the gallery spaces the transformation of the archive into pedagogical art becomes another way of mobilizing the open brief. The open brief, Steveni argues, is a process of not-knowing which becomes "the basis of action moving forward," and which in turn engenders a relational, felt, and touching encounter (Anthony Hudek, interview with author, London, 2012). Privileging and attuning myself to openness and relationality, I turn now to discuss three residencies in secondary schools and the ways that youth navigate and imagine future worlds. I return to the Southwark Educational Research Project in the final section in my discussion of the importance of speculative thought and futurity for socially engaged art as research-creation.

Imponderable Extraordinary Curricula

WALLS TO THE BALL: HIDDEN CURRICULUM

It's a crisp fall day and I have arrived at Noteworthy Secondary School, where the artist Hazel Meyer has been working for the past few weeks with groups of grade-ten and grade-eleven students in two separate classes. Julie Smitka, my research assistant, is already in the classroom. On my way into the school from the front doors, where I have been buzzed in through an intercom system, I pass the glassed-in front office where on CCTV monitors two police officers watch the entrances to the school, the hallways, stairwells, and parking lot. It is 2012 and there is still a heavy police force in racialized schools and communities in the Toronto District School Board (TDSB).[3] The walk down the hallway is sterile, and admittance through the locked door to the art room is afforded once I knock and show my school visitor ID. The atmosphere is heavy, carceral, and punitive. The school is located in the northwest quadrant of the city and is both a collegiate (academic) and vocational school. It is situated in a racially diverse and socioeconomically marginalized and underserved community. In education, writes Savannah Shange (2019, 15), "carcerality is most often viewed through the lens of the school-to-prison pipeline, whereby zero-tolerance-style disciplinary policies disproportionately impact students of color, resulting in their arrest, detention, and eventual imbrication in the prison system." Even in schools without a police presence, management styles, particularly at the secondary level, where a "zero tolerance" policy is enforced across the TDSB, are structured and conditioned to punish and dispose of Black and Indigenous students and students of color.[4] Shange names such policies and programs the "carceral-progressive paradox," meaning schools "can provide both culturally affirming and racially exclusionary experiences of a state space" (48). Noteworthy Secondary School was firmly entrenched in progressive educational practices that served marginalized students while also policing, dehumanizing, and monitoring their every move.

Inside the art room bodies buzz and swarm, moving around the room working on braiding recycled fabric into long strips of knotted textiles, punching out fabric buttons, or tossing a basketball into one of two red basketball hoops that have been temporarily mounted in the art room. Students work together in pairs, taking turns holding the end of long tendrils of fabric while the other knots and braids. Completed ropes are then tied to one of two red hoops which hang on either side of the classroom. These will eventually, months later, shape the *Walls to the Ball* performance installation introduced at the beginning of the chapter. Over four months, Meyer introduced the students to a number of contemporary artists and microprojects that explored various materials in relation to performance, gesture, textiles, athletics, pleasure, and the absurd. Juxtaposing seemingly disparate but overlapping ideas and issues, the project invited students to question sport, gender, race, craft, and school athletic culture and the illogical, ridiculous, or absurd associations resulting when different things are juxtaposed. Through an open brief method Meyer worked with the students to unlearn disciplinary and technically driven art practices and to consider everyday objects and actions as performance. For Meyer the open brief method foregrounded a research-creation practice in which students became part of the work. Rather than maintaining a practice that is concerned with meaning and interpretation, Meyer is intent on creating spatiotemporal events that facilitate provocations where new stories can emerge. The fantastical basketball net renders visible gendered, raced, and class assumptions about sport and textiles. In the final performance, the absurd net, fifteen balls, and a drum kit invite participants to engage with the work on their own terms; the rules of the game become ridiculous and simultaneously situated. Questioning who is included in and excluded from art and sport, both inside and outside of schools, the performance does not merely point at exclusionary boundaries but creates an artistic-athletic event where students invent new rules of participation and of being, moving, and performing in the gym. One student commented, "The installation in the gym was something that can't be described. It was messy and chaotic but incredibly fun and full of energy. I saw friends competing and strangers talking. I heard an incredible drum beat that made the games even more wild. I saw people falling but laughing and I saw confusion but smiling." Another student described the installation as "a big, yellow, awkward-looking thing sprawled across the middle of the gym, dividing it horizontally. It suspended slightly, bouncing to the rhythm of basketballs thumping on the group. As I went closer, it became clear was it was: a giant braid. Not just one, but also many? Many braids forming a tube from one net to another. I touched it." Additional comments converged around the inventive rules of the game: "It wasn't about who got a shot in the net, but what can you do with a net." And: "I always thought that the only way to play was to throw a ball into the net, but the installation changed how things work. We can always change the game up." Other artists, such as Germain Koh, also reinvent new ways to play a game. Her project *League*, which has been ongoing since 2012, invites participants to create games that evolve as players adapt to the environment, equipment, and shared participation. Writing about Koh's practice, Jim Drobnick (2016, 239) suggests that, rather than address the meaning of a work of art, we need to focus on the actions or "the dilemmas they create and how they expose systems of behavior." Describing Koh's practice as "incidental aesthetics" Drobnick reveals the "incidental exchanges" that involve "the body, senses, experience, and relationships" (239). In the unpredictability and imponderability of Koh's work, as in *Walls to the Ball*, "the profound masquerades as the inconsequential," which enables different and varying possibilities to emerge (239).

Yet, for the school administrative team, and for the music teacher from whom we had to borrow the drum set, disciplinary boundaries not only needed to be maintained; they existed so that learning was legible, credible, and visible. The police presence, locked classrooms, and hallway passes were used to manage dissent and teach that some bodies belong in some spaces more than others. Value was placed on educational structures and learning outcomes that kept bodies fixed, contained, and docile. Linear time was rewarded through adherence to schedules, hall passes, and confinement to chairs, desks, and locked classrooms.

Transdisciplinary, open brief, multitemporality, and hybrid research-creation practices inhabit uncomfortable spaces, and in this instance they rendered visible who gets silenced or denied in school spaces. The gym was for athletes, majority white students in the school. The drums were to be used only by students who "studied" music in the school, not by a self-taught musician and student of color with his own drum sticks (but no drum). The art room was marked as a space for students of color, many of whom were in the academic International Baccalaureate stream in the school or, alternatively, vocational students labeled as difficult, unsuccessful, and deficient. If we all stay in our respective spaces (locked classrooms) then school—learning—can go on as is: knowable, manageable, and measurable. Writing about postsecondary art schools, Justin Langlois (2021, 202) argues that institutions maintain the role of arbiter between the disciplines: "Courses are designed to assist with the replication of methods and methodologies that have produced the art world (and broader world)," a narrative, he claims, that forecloses "many other ways to cultivate, share, and sustain an art practice." Langlois contends that curricula, course syllabi, admissions processes, and the like render invisible hospitalities that welcome and unwelcome different students and that mirror a form of societal control. Langlois's articulations echo earlier work in educational scholarship on the nature of the hidden curriculum in schools, the norms and values that are tacitly taught (Apple 1979). The hidden curriculum's hegemony asserts its power through the regulation of what counts as knowledge, reproducing social and cultural inequalities. The artist Annette Krauss's project *Hidden Curriculum* (2007–2013) investigates such school erasure. In an interview conducted by Reed and Jickling as part of the *living archive*, Krauss (2013) says:

> *Hidden Curriculum* is an art project that focuses on the unidentified, unintended, and unrecognized forms of knowledge, values, and beliefs in the context of secondary school education. It could be explained as an investigation of everything that is learned alongside the official curriculum. On one hand these other forms of knowledge include various kinds of actions and tactics challenging enforced cultural values and attitudes

(e.g., punctuality, tidiness, etc.). On the other hand the project looks at practices that students develop in order to cope with the requirements in everyday life in school, investigating forms of subordination, hierarchies, and silent violence.

Working with students in various secondary schools in Utrecht and the UK, Krauss invites students to explore and analyze their proximate relations to hidden curricula and to develop performative interventions that respond to their direct environment.

As an imponderable curriculum, the *Walls to the Ball* residency and the culminating performance not only exposed the carceral, hidden, invisible, and neoliberal structure of schooling; in stretching the limits of art-sport and in taking over the gym for a lunch hour, the project became a kind of thinking machine with the entire school that, through endurance and transdisciplinarity, activated *extra-* modes of learning. In this instance the imponderable becomes more-than institutional critique and engenders speculative possibility and futurity. Guided by David Garneau's (Metis) convictions that artistic and aesthetic practices can be political gestures that create different future worlds beyond those imposed by settler colonial forms of dispossession, *Walls to the Ball* creates a space of extrapossibility where normative and colonial ideas can be perforated and torqued. He writes: "Art is the site of intolerable research, the laboratory of odd ideas, of sensual and intuitive study, and of production that exceeds the boundaries of conventional disciplines, protocols and imaginaries. . . . In the making and appreciation of art there is a space of difference, even resistance, where people can find refuge from the ideas that otherwise rule them" (Garneau 2013, 15–16). I'm curious about the ways that artists working with youth can make use of the absurd as extrarational, as that which pushes and cracks open extrapossibility.

Shange finds similar extraeducational moments in school hallways. She notes that the events that take place in school hallways (giggles, skirmishes, relief) do not end up on productivity reports from the school to the Department of Education: they are extra. Thus, hallways challenge productivity and what counts as or is represented as educational. The hallway, she contends, is a liminal space between "liberation and captivity—the peripatetic space of fugitivity" (Shange 2019, 90). She writes that "for those who 'do not have a place' to seize time, they have to reshape the content of both time and space in their own interests" (89). The hallways constitute a hidden curriculum: they teach students that hallway moments are uneducational and as such must be regulated and moved through efficiently; they instruct students that some bodies do not belong in particular spaces. But in the same way that Shange finds possibilities of fugitivity in hallways, the gym-art assemblage offers yet another hidden curriculum of extrapossibilities. In performing *Walls to the Ball* in the gym, the swarming gym-net-ball movement became a moment or event—within the otherwise coded school day—of extrarational, extraordinary, and extraeducational learning where students repurposed and remixed school on their own terms. Here the imponderable curriculum embodied a different spatiotemporal moment that was durational and expansive and that gestured toward a future otherwise. Hallways, writes Shange, or in this instance the gymnasium, "are the exception's exception, a space filled with the excess of those without access to place" (91). It is in excess or in the extra that possibility resides. As Halberstam (2011) argues, disciplinarity is a technique of power that is reliant on normalization, convention, and regulation that in turn produces institutional governance. To turn the gym into a performance space is to recognize that it already is one—a space where gender, sexuality, race, and ability are constructed, produced, and regulated. But the absurdity of an eighty-foot net and fifteen balls chaotically in play at once upended the legibility of art and sport, rendering them imponderable. Refusing legibility, according to Halberstam, "may lead to forms of speculation, modes of thinking that ally not with rigor and order but with inspiration and unpredictability" (2011, 10). Materializing humor and the absurd, *Walls to the Ball*, like *Ask Me Chocolates*, repurposes notions of appropriateness and bodily boundaries and impedes school habits, even if only momentarily.

A number of artists juxtapose art and sport to examine issues of race, gender, and sexuality. Meyer's ongoing multiparticipant performances of athleticism activate an arena of sweat, contact, and queer desire. *Walls to the Ball*, as well as her performance *Muscle Panic* (2015), employ the actions of drills, warm-ups, and locker room aesthetics to transform the associations of the sterile gallery or site of an exhibition or performance to a space of heavy breathing, sweat, and heat. Using touch and sweat to challenge gendered and heterosexual norms in sport, Meyer's projects take up space for bodies not typically privileged as sites of athleticism. Esmaa Mohamoud similarly transforms basketball jerseys and athletic equipment to examine and question sports' relationship to race, class, gender, and sexuality. In *Heavy Heavy Hoop Dreams* (2016), sixty solid concrete basketballs, some deflating and cracked, are installed on top of black plexiglass in six rows of ten balls each; their weight represents a conversation on the violence and erasure of Blackness in Canada. In *One of the Boys* (2017), Toronto Raptors jerseys are reworked into ball gowns (one purple, one red) and worn by Black men, their backs facing the viewer in the large-scale photographs, blurring gender and sexuality. While Mohamoud's works are very different projects from Meyer's, together they share a dialogue on gender fluidity, defiance, and legibility.

In addition to the gym-net-ball-bodies assemblage, threads that unraveled as the fabric was torn into strips was collected during the residency and amassed into a large ball, which was later mounted on the base of a golden trophy. The trophy was displayed during the event, and students wore handmade fabric buttons crafted from the same fabric as the net, humorously nodding to the only artifacts contained in the otherwise sterile school hallways: cases upon cases of dusty athletic trophies, ribbons, and other kinds of awards. The contamination of, or transmission of, bright yellow and orange thread perforated the musty pores of the gym. A student inserted their entire body into the knots of the net and got stuck. The TDSB art consultant, an invited guest to the performance, caught a ball to the head. Spectators gathered. Everyone laughed. Movement was infectious (Truman and Springgay 2015).

Back in the art classroom, during the preparation of the performance, the imponderable was embedded within the knotting labor. Students talked casually about the tediousness of the braiding labor that was simultaneously work and a kind of quiet boredom not often afforded in school spaces. The knotting and macramé required skills and practice that is labor-intensive, much like that which training athletes undergo (Cahill 2012). The making of the installation and the performance centers the body, endurance, and repetition. Students described the labor as monotonous. Yet, they also talked about the ways that such repetition afforded relations and collaborations between students: holding ends of the fabric, playing with the balls and the hoops together, talking about their daily lives as they worked. The physicality of making is rarely discussed in art education and art history, and in sport it is tethered to ableism and athleticism. In the art room the students were provided space through conversation and research-creation to navigate their own subject positions and experiences of art and sport. While early on in the residency the students were introduced to a number of different small projects and ideas, when the concept for *Walls to the Ball* emerged, the production of the nets took over the room. Students talked about how relaxing and comforting the labor became and the ways that its monotony created potential spaces for other intimate encounters to arise. As the students worked on different parts of the net, Meyer noted that the net and classroom "became this absurd and yet wonderful weird growth that we all created . . . where life just went on around it."

As is the case in many other schools in the city, Noteworthy's art program measured artistic success using criteria like accuracy of representation, favoring a particularly conservative and formalist attitude toward art based on the transmission of expert knowledge. The focus was on mastering techniques and a particular medium (most often drawing with charcoal or Conté) and emphasized a chronological approach to art historical periods. Students worked at separate desks, and most of the lessons focused on drawing still life objects selected by the teacher as "proper" art objects. Here the still life objects function as technologies of surveillance and regulation enmeshed with racializing assemblages (Weheliye 2014). The labor of drawing perfectly rendered still life objects becomes a lesson in aesthetics, taste, and behavior associated with white norms. Such drawings evoke colonial mastery that is materially and affectively reinforced in the daily curriculum. These racializing assemblages were not lost on the students, one of whom commented on the nauseating effects of having to draw Conté lemons for homework. By contrast, research-creation as art pedagogy embraces active practices of contemporary art with a transdisciplinary and hybrid focus that engages with social, political, and environmental issues. In particular, Meyer's project inserted students' active labor—producing the nets and activating the performance—as the research-creation event. As one student stated, "I really liked the idea of working on our own (making our own braids) but then combining them with everyone else's to form something larger. For once, art class didn't really feel like a place to create our own separate artworks, but a place to connect and have fun with others around us." I would not imply that the braiding labor altered racializing assemblages so inherent in schools; instead, it called attention to them, and in that instance destabilized them for a moment. The weird growth of imponderability, like Meyer's use of sweat and touch, created a space for the extraordinary and the possibilities that might open up. Importantly, *Walls to the Ball* is located not only in a school: the making of it and its performance take up questions of value and belonging central to education.

Museum without Entrance: Visiting

Rodrigo Hernandez-Gomez's *Museum without Entrance* (MWE), a work that he executed with five different classes (four secondary, one elementary) at a range of different schools in the city, reflects a similar openness to not-knowing and to unintended consequences as the open brief. Hernandez-Gomez is of Mexican Nahua decent, and his work explores Indigenous understandings of cultural value and time. MWE develops from the idea of decentering and decolonizing cultural institutions and the practice of collecting artifacts and cultural knowledge. The project brings together informal collectors, private collections, and students to create the MWE. For example, two secondary art classes visited the store ASP Locks in Toronto, where they had the opportunity to examine, close up, safes from the 1800s and hundreds of different locking mechanisms that highlighted the changing history and landscape of Toronto architecture, and experiment with locking themselves up using an antique set of handcuffs from the Don Jail. The MWE visits become an encounter with the collector's particular point of view, his or her motives and methods of collecting, as well as the particularities of the place where the artifacts are kept. The collection and the site together express a lot about local history and values, as well as the process by which one acquires a collection. This experience opens up a space that enables the students to draw connections between themselves, the artifacts in the collection, and the city. In a traditional museum, the relationship between the artifacts, the collector, and the visitor often maintain an impersonal quality and a complex symbolic distance. The intent with MWE is to provide students with an open experience instead of formal references or prescribed understandings about contemporary art. There were no lectures on Indigenous art content, but the structure of the work, of visiting, resisted the inclusion and integration that is so often about tokenism in education. Hernandez-Gomez centers Indigenous knowledges and practices not by describing them to the students, but by enacting them with the students. Similar to Meyer's enactment of sweat-sport-art, the field trips' experiential nature means that the project is doing the work of defamiliarization and decentering, not simply pointing at it. Too often curricula and pedagogy are framed around learning content: learning *about* Indigenous art. The MWE as a counter-gesture prioritizes relations as form and content. The project isn't about learning something about a topic, but, in gathering together, something imponderable will happen, and in that extraordinary moment learning takes place as emergent and indeterminate. MWE fosters an ethics of interdependence as radical relationality. Sharing space with others is intentional in the MWE; it is deliberately created and sustained. The intimacy between collector and inquisitive student becomes entangled with the act of decentering larger narratives around power and collecting. Similar inheritances can be found in the work of Sameer Farooq, whose practice exposes museum bias in collecting. Farooq employs a decolonial, queer, and critical race methodology to question how objects make their way into institutional spaces and how they are cared for and understood. Similarly, Hernandez-Gomez's MWE is a proposition for a different kind of institution that cocreates new cultural forms and new forms of relational knowledge.

Rather than validating the work from the outside, the project operates as a counter-curricular measure: placing students in an unfamiliar context, outside of the classroom and formal art structures, while intervening into private spaces and emphasizing being in situ. Like the APG, the MWE's placement shifts the conventional ways in which art and audience is understood, defamiliarizing and decentering art and aesthetic expectations. The collections provide a material record of the past-present and speak to the potential lives of the objects. During the visit, students, along with the artist and collector, considered the fraught and violent histories of museum collections and their colonial origins, structures, and practices. The imponderable in this example manifests in the informal collections and the kinds of value assigned to personal collections that are not narrated through capitalism and wealth. The field trips make visible unseen private collections while also working to destabilize colonial collecting narratives. Grand gestures of teaching students about Indigenous art were abandoned and replaced with intimate, quirky encounters. Instead of studying the other, in the way that conventional museums require of visitors, the field trips' imponderable curriculum engaged students in hands-on discussions of how collections materialize and how value and circulation are determined. Resisting the pressure for students to consume and extract knowledge, the MWE created new spatiotemporalities of wonder and disorientation.

Other collections visited included Jason Sanders's vinyl collection, folk art in the living room of Mr. Fujikawa, and the Contemporary Zoological Museum, a taxidermy collection in the apartment of Morgan Mavis. In each iteration of the project, students and the artist gathered outside of the home or storefront and enacted a ribbon cutting ceremony, parodying the significance instilled on the openings of official cultural institutions. In Mr. Fujikawa's living room students ate popcorn and drank hot chocolate while discussing and handling the folk art collection. In the Contemporary Zoological Museum, while passing stuffed snakes, rodents, and other smaller taxidermy pieces among themselves, the students snacked on homemade cookies and talked informally with the curator Morgan Mavis. These activities further ruptured the ways in which student bodies are expected to perform in cultural spaces and the dominant narratives about what knowledge is of most worth, and about who is the keeper of such knowledge. While the owner of ASP Locks put his collection on display, on the shelves and countertops of his functioning store, in the folk art "museum" students wandered through Mr. Fujikawa's house, examining the folk art pieces in bedrooms, bathrooms, living room, and kitchen. Most major museums function as authoritative spaces that are active in perpetuating settler colonial power and knowledge (Dewhurst and Hendrick 2017; Ng, Ware, and Greenberg 2017). Even when museums engage in the work of antiracism and decolonization, they remain implicated in regimes of colonial power. For many students of color, museums are unwelcome structures that exclude their personal experiences and knowledges. The intimacy of opening a family house, a short walking distance from their urban school, further pried open the disconnect that racialized urban students have with cultural institutions and their collecting practices. Here the open brief method of placement and nearness, of being in relation inside collectors' personal spaces, touching and handling collections, and experiencing indeterminacy regarding what they would encounter on the field trip, created moments of feltness. However, as the Mexican American artist and educator Jorge Lucero (2020) contends, nearness is more than just physical proximity; it is also how we attune to, or tend to, an experience or a thing. Nearness, then, is about fostering care, of becoming mindful of the kinds of *(in)tensions* we bring to a place, an event, or an object, where (in)tensions are ethical and political commitments and responsibilities (Springgay and Truman 2018). The MWE's nearness, its feltness, is germinated through touching encounters, handling objects, sharing cookies inside a stranger's home, and the decolonial ways in which different cultural knowledges are shared, examined, and explored—including the students' personal experiences and cultural practices. Questioning institutional validity, nearness ruptured the model of the expert, rendering the informal collector and the students cocreators of knowledge and cultural value. In contrast to the hard surfaces of a museum, metal cabinets, angular walls, and glass display cases, the MWE counters institutional absences and practices that sanitize complex histories.

Stó:lo artist and scholar Dylan Robinson (2020, 171) notes that many Indigenous artists doing socially engaged art incorporate gathering and visiting that "serve as a forum for intergenerational teaching and learning and move us away from normative settler cultures of display." He also contends that visiting can also be easily instituted or serve to extract knowledge and essentialize nearness. "Such instrumentalizations," he writes, "undermine the efficacy of visiting as a sovereign political practice" (173). Robinson cautions against the potential for the spectacularization of visiting when Indigenous practices are put on display. Visiting becomes political work when it is not simply about being in proximity but about a nearness that is attuned to responsibility and accountability to difference, where "gathering is not just a nice form of having tea and light conversation" (177). In the case of MWE, nearness engenders a political capacity through the open brief method of not predetermining experience or knowledge in advance of the encounter. In visiting the private collections, the students were not only decentering museum cultural expectations and hierarchies, but also examining who joins together and in what form, while creating space for racialized and urban students to center their situated knowledges, experiences, and processes of learning. Perhaps the MWE enacts what Cree artist and scholar Karyn Recollet (2018) calls "kinstillatory gatherings," spaces that stretch and create topologies for how we can be together to build and imagine a different future. Recollet's Indigenous futurisms counter persistent settler colonial fantasies of Indigenous erasure with spatiotemporal sites of transformation. She writes, "Something in me knows that when we gather, we are stronger" (51). Visiting and gathering have taken on complex meanings in 2020–2022, where gathering is under threat and regulated by social distancing, masks, and policed numbers. Yet, gathering is all too crucial in this moment in time, when people need to come together in solidarity, mutual aid, and care networks. The pandemic has forced us to pay attention to how we gather and how we are in proximity to one another. Our ways of gathering have transformed as we carefully consider whom we assemble with, and the how of our coming together, while also questioning what forms of futurity are made possible through intentional gathering.

Nearness, as Lucero and Hernandez-Gomez would offer, is about doing the work necessary to disrupt normative ways of being ameliorative and to consider alternative ways of coming together in action. The radical pedagogy of nearness, of gathering, is in attention, in attuning ourselves to why it is we have come together and what work needs to be done. Visiting and nearness are rarely understood in this way as sites of school-based learning. Both the MWE and *Walls to the Ball*, although in quite different ways, deploy absurd or incongruous juxtapositions to create spaces for other possibilities, where students repurpose, remix, and reimagine a future otherwise. Such a future, Langlois maintains, one that is based on decolonial, anti-oppressive, and equity-based politics, requires different versions of hospitality that are grounded in "care, curiosity, ethics, and complexity. It actively de-centres pedagogical practices that rely on the reproduction of existing relations of power" (Langlois 2020, 205). Dylan Robinson (2020) insists that our methodologies and practices must resist the already knowable that enables easy categorization and resist uncritical forms of being in relation. The notion of hospitality that Emily Johnson and Recollet (2020) offer is grounded in gathering, radical relatedness, or what they call *kin-dling*, a concept shifting between the notions of kin and kindling, small pieces of wood that catch fire and build the foundation for the fire. Kin-dling is a necessarily part of gathering; it is grounded in an ethics of care and mutual aid and supports and builds the foundation upon which we can convene to transform and create just worlds. Both *Walls to the Ball* and MWE inhabit learning otherwise, learning that is felt and intimate.

FRIDAY: THE DUBIOUS BUTTER DANCE

In this final example, *Friday*, the imponderable curriculum resulted in the shutting down of the school-based performance by the principal. *Friday*, a project that was undertaken by Sarah Febbraro and an art class of mixed grade-ten to grade-twelve students and that parodied high school talent shows, Kaprow-esque happenings, and flash mob performances, was so unthinkable in the school cafeteria that it was abruptly interrupted and censored. This residency took place over an eight-week period of time in a middle-class and predominantly Asian Canadian neighborhood. The school's art program was specialized and focused primarily on individual drawing and photography skills.

The performance-based project started with the question posed by Febbraro to the students: "What pop culture are you currently obsessed with?" The answers were broad and included K-pop (Korean pop music), *Harry Potter*, Taylor Swift, cake decorating, Kanye West, flash mobs, John Mayer, and paper airplanes with instructions. These obsessions became the basis for *Friday*, a combination of Febbraro's talk show aesthetic and the well-known tradition of high school talent shows. Central to *Friday* was the desire to parody talent shows and high school extracurriculars and to create a performance that would take place in an unexpected school space, while also prioritizing youth-led culture and interests. Originally the performance was to take place on the high school field, for which the students made an upcycled, kitsch-fabulous installation as a stage and undertook a practice installment a week before the final performance. Unfortunately, the last contributor to the project was a thunderstorm, and the final show had to be moved inside to the cafeteria opposite the stage, where the students cheered, judged, questioned, and participated in *Friday*. Performances included covers of John Mayer, Taylor Swift, and R. Kelly, as well as a flash mob dance to Michael Jackson's "Thriller." After "Kanye Wong" showed up to share his new love of dancing on butter, the show was cut short, and *Friday*'s audience rushed to decorate and eat cake—all part of the performance—before being ushered out of the cafeteria. Much like the performance *Walls to the Ball*, *Friday* pushed up against normative disciplinary boundaries and school decorum, but its quick censorship was not because the art happened in the cafeteria, which also served as the school auditorium with a stage: the cafeteria was the place where art, eating, and all kinds of school assemblies took place. In fact, this was a school that celebrated student performances regularly, including talent shows. Opposite the main entrance to the cafeteria-auditorium, a small foyer just outside the principal's office had been converted into a permanent wall gallery space for students in the specialized art program to showcase their work on a regular basis. These school spaces attest to what Shange (2019) refers to as progressive politics that have, on one hand, been instrumentalized to demonstrate reformist school policies and curricula, while simultaneously being controlled by school administrators. Neither cafeteria-auditorium nor foyer-gallery were spaces of youth agency and redistributed power; rather, they functioned to represent and to showcase normalized neoliberal progressive school politics.

There were concerns that the performance was not on the stage, but rather right in the midst of students moving around during lunch hour (we did not want it on the stage as it was intended to be enacted in situ, like a happening or a flash mob and not a formal performance). Apprehension was expressed that we had not reserved a "proper" space in the school for the performance (of course, we did not know in advance that it would rain), and fears were conveyed over lo-fi pop culture aesthetics, a departure from their "world-class art education," and inappropriate content for a secondary school. I'm convinced that, in addition to all of the above, the imponderable was the critique inherent in the parody and the power of laughter, with the butter dance being the final score. The students were in fact making fun of the very thing the school took seriously about itself: student exceptionalism and the showcasing of student talent. They were also sharing space together, on their own terms, exceeding those dictated by school rules and propriety.

As Halberstam (2011) so aptly points out, disciplinarity conditions the unlikeliness of the imponderable education: "Universities [and by implication high schools] squash rather than promote quirky and original thought. Disciplinarity, as defined by Foucault, is a technique of modern power: it depends upon and deploys normalization, routines, convention, tradition, and regularity, and it produces experts and administrative forms of governance" (7–8). Halberstam's writing here turns to the work of Fred Moten and Stefano Harney in *The Undercommons* (2013), where the work of "study" is to create thinkers—students—who refuse disciplinarity in favor of creating a new social order. Against legibility, Halberstam claims that we may want "different aesthetic standards for ordering space [and] more undisciplined knowledge, more questions and fewer answers" (2011, 10). Harney and Moten's *undercommons* refers to a counter-public inhabited by people of color and Black, Indigenous, and disabled and d/Deaf people who refuse to ask for recognition from a broken system but rather "take apart, dismantle, tear down the structure that, right now, limits our ability to find each other, to see beyond it and to access the places that we know lie outside its walls" (Halberstam 2013, 6). Deploying quotidian pop culture references and humor, the performance questioned dominant narratives of talent and mastery, fully embracing the pleasure of laughter.

Friday exists in conversation with other artist projects that use humor to make sense of complex events and to offer other possible ways of being. Humor exposes the structures of power and suggests creative means for dismantling oppression. *Friday* was very much about joy and pleasure; it was full of absurdities and nonsense. *Friday* invited viewers and participants to consider youth—a category often taken for granted—as an embodied and pleasurable experience. Febbraro's work with youth is embedded within research in youth studies that seeks to explore and reveal the visceral intensity and complexity of youth lives. The residency focused on youth bodies, expressions, and movements, as well as their tastes, interests, thoughts, culture, and leisure activities and exposed all the feelings that come with such an inquiry. In the context of this chapter, on the imponderable as extraordinary, in the final section I want to draw together *Walls to the Ball*, *Museum without Entrance*, and *Friday* as quotidian, unlikely, and expressive performances of youth futurity, while also making an argument for the importance of speculative thought and futurity for socially engaged art as research-creation.

Living the Future Now

If a few decades ago questions about socially engaged art and the Pedagogical Turn were concerned with aesthetics, efficacy, usefulness, antagonism, audiences, scale, whiteness, and the status of art and social work, what new directions might be proposed for the field today? More specifically, I'm curious about what speculative thought might mobilize for a future now. What might the imponderable as extra, as speculative, activate? In creating a space for speculative thought in socially engaged art as research-creation, I'm thinking of the generous work by Syrus Ware (2020a) on activism as speculative fiction and a radical reimagining of our world. Ware draws on the speculative fiction of Octavia Butler, among others, in which the world we live in is on the brink of collapse, where change is inevitable. This change, for Ware, citing Butler, means "that all that you touch changes, and all that you touch changes you; touch change" (2020a). He continues, "All activism is speculative fiction. We are always engaging in speculative fiction. When we try to envision a world without war, without violence, without prisons, without capitalism, we are engaging in speculative fiction." Tania Bruguera (2019) has also recently stated that we need to make art for the "not yet" and the "yet to come." We also see speculative criticism adopted by Claire Bishop and Nikki Columbus (2020) in their aphoristic review of the "new MoMA," a piece of writing that proposes institutional grappling with colonialism and that directly takes up the political. For artist-scholars like Karyn Recollet (2018) the speculative engenders radical relatedness, stewardship, and care. Alongside these interlocutors in my thinking about the importance of speculation in relation to socially engaged art as research-creation, I turn to the work of Tina Campt (2017) on futurity. Futurity, according to Campt, is a tense—the future real conditional. Futurity is "that which will have had to happen" and a "future that hasn't yet happened but must" (17). It is setting the (in)tensions for what you want to see in the future that is right now in the present. Futurity is about touching change and the inevitability of that change through touching encounters—touch change. Differentiated from utopian hope, futurity is noninnocent and unsettling; it is not necessarily heroic, loud, or determined. Rather, writes Campt, it is often humble, subtle, and quiet. Futurity, she contends, is in the quiet, quotidian, and unlikely places. For Campt quiet does not refer to the absence of sound but rather a sonic frequency, a hum, that affectively registers and vibrates and that requires one to listen attentively. In this way then, futurity is very much aligned with affect and the haptic: a feltness and touching encounter. Futurity is imponderable; it is extraordinary in a quiet and quotidian way. Its haptic frequencies move beyond stasis while touching and animating new worlds. In all three residencies, the socially engaged art as research-creation didn't point at an issue—art and sport, Indigenous knowledges, pleasure and youth culture—as Bruguera (2019) writes, "a posteriori reaction or comment." Rather, the residencies evented ideas, issues, and inquiry as practices while simultaneously engendering an imponderable futurity where a "future hasn't happened but must" (Campt 2017, 17). Take for example *Walls to the Ball* and its imponderable presence in the gym and in a school with a heavy police presence. To have made a work about abolition in such a school would have put students in direct danger, or into an oppositional position. Yet the imponderable futurity of an eighty-foot net and fifteen balls in motion was a performance for an abolition future that hasn't happened but that must: "abolition as the founding of a new society" (Moten and Harney 2004, 113).

One of the ways that these residencies grappled with "living the future now" (Campt 2017, 17) is through an attention to the importance of pedagogy as art with youth and in schools *as* contemporary art, not external to it or undervalued by it. The reactivation of the Southwark Educational Research Project

(SERP) by Barbara Steveni in 2018 is significant at a time when the arts and education are under threat from changes in policy and funding, when schools are pushing exams and standardized curricula and assessment models. The reactivation not only includes exhibitions of the overlooked archival materials, but recenters students and teachers in arts-led curriculum reform. The reactivation emphasizes that what Steveni catalyzed in 1989 is relevant and crucial in the current educational moment. It also underscores that, although the residencies discussed in these first two chapters were produced ten years ago, the impetus and need for socially engaged art as pedagogy is still paramount in the transformation of teaching and learning, a theme I will return to in the final chapter. The reactivation also speaks to a broader shift in contemporary art practices and the Pedagogical Turn, a shift in which art realized in collaboration with students and teachers inside of schools is no longer hidden, erased, and undervalued. Perhaps a significant outcome of decades of socially engaged work and the cogent contributions by queer, trans, and BIPOC artists is a redistribution of power from Euro-Western settler aesthetics and arts institutions to realizing that the politics of art resides in the ability to do the work where the work is needed. In other words, pedagogy as art inside of schools has the potential and extrapossibility of remaking teaching and learning.

At the time that these school-based residencies were happening (2012–2014), it was still a time within wider art discourses and critiques that vilified community-engaged art with young people. As I discussed in chapter 1, this was in part because of long-held beliefs about young people as improper tastemakers and developmental models viewing childhood as a state of incompleteness. It was also, as I argued, because schooling lacked conventional art audiences outside of the marketization and capitalism of the art world. Here I would add that pedagogy as art threatened art criticism because it was imponderable; it was extraordinary, and it offered young people an opportunity to author their own art worlds. Perhaps this fear was fueled by adults' fear of young people's resistance to adult monopolies on agency and power. In the time since, youth have been championing Black Lives Matter and leading the revolution against gun violence and climate change. And while I take up Bishop's (2012) insistence on schooling as a closed space in chapter 1, I also acknowledge her deep commitment to speculation and radical education as potential sites through which to remake art institutions. In her book *Radical Museology* (2014), Bishop examines three art institutions' efforts to curate and program alternatives to the blockbuster, colonial, and capitalist exhibition. Notably, she finds significance in alternative and radical educational initiatives for reshaping and reimagining the futurity of the art museum. Finding "new forms of mediation and solidarity," education has become the practice through which institutions can become an "archive of the commons," shifting educational programs and events from the periphery to the core of institutional activities and labor (Bishop 2014, 43).

In returning to Campt's insistence on affect and haptics within futurity, I am reminded of the quotidian, repetitive, and mundane labor of braiding yellow and orange fabric for months. In particular, Campt's sonic call to move beyond sight and the observer, and to listen to images, attunes me to the frequency of fabric being ripped into strips and the multiple spatiotemporalities of students holding ends of fabric for each other, and their conversations, and the rhythmic thud of basketballs. These sounds were audible variations of hums in the art room for months, almost imperceptible but extraordinary in generating a vibratory space of potential change. In listening to and tuning in to the haptic and affective, how might we live the future now?

Chapter Three

Fluxus and the
Event Score

The Ordinary
Potential of Radical
Pedagogy as Art

Make a salad. —ALISON KNOWLES, *Proposition #1* (1962)

The event score *Proposition #1 (Make a Salad)* is part musical composition, part performance, and part meal—given that, once the salad has been prepared, participants join the artist in eating the tossed greens. The score, which was first enacted in 1962 at the Institute for Contemporary Arts in London by the Fluxus artist Alison Knowles, invokes a recipe for action. Reenacted in 2012 on the High Line in New York City, the salad ingredients were mixed on a giant green tarpaulin while sounds of knives and forks clinking together augmented the musical performance. The performance emphasizes the processes of production (chopping, tearing, mixing) and the ordinariness of daily life as a musical event.

I love to reenact the score with my own students, chopping vegetables and tearing lettuce, allowing the sounds, smells, and textures to disrupt the otherwise sterile institutional space of a university seminar room. Sharing and eating the salad with students brings the immediacy and intimacy of bodies into the pedagogical encounter. Event scores are open-ended instructions or propositions that ignite the potential for future action. As invitations to activate and imagine different futures, scores are iterative but, while repeatable, are not concerned with predictable outcomes. Adopted by numerous Fluxus artists, event scores can be enacted by various individuals or collectives in multiple and mutating ways.

Fluxus was an international network of poets, artists, and musical composers who worked across different media and who sought to integrate art into everyday life. Primarily active from the late 1950s to the mid-1970s, Fluxus artists produced experimental concerts and performances as well as instructional works, ready-made objects, and printed editions. George Brecht is credited with the invention of the event score, which was taken up in many different ways by different Fluxus artists (Harren 2020; Higgins 2002). Some of the early Fluxus event scores were produced in John Cage's class at the New School for Social Research, in New York City, and at Black Mountain College, where I Ching and chance operations were introduced into the curriculum. Allan Kaprow, who was a student in Cage's class, later introduced scores as a method for teaching in 1953 at Rutgers University, which would eventually morph into what he called *happenings*: scored theatrical performance events.

While art historians have well documented the significance of the university classroom as a site for radical intervention, less analysis has been afforded to the teaching methods and the pedagogical materials—such as scores, posters, booklets, and games—that were produced as documents of radical pedagogy and curriculum reform (Harren 2020; Higgins 2002). For example, George Maciunas created a board game titled *Curriculum Plan*, as well as a number of *Learning Machines*—or diagrammatic scores—as new models for higher education. While not officially affiliated with Fluxus, Roy Ascott reorganized the entire second-year course calendar and curriculum at the Ontario College of Art in 1970, which he recorded on an LP titled *Aug.3* and then distributed to the rest of the faculty. He also generated a set of tarot cards for use as a new course calendar and promoted divination as a way to select courses and academic pathways.

In addition to material objects, Fluxus artist-teachers created research-based experiments with students that sought to challenge siloed, disciplinary education models. In 1969, Kaprow collaborated with the educator Herbert Kohl on an experimental school project called *Other Ways*, which invited artists, teachers, and public school students to experiment with performance and conceptual art by replacing curriculum plans with event scores. As a faculty member at the California Institute for the Arts (CalArts) and the University of California, San Diego, Kaprow often collaborated with his students in the production of his *Activity Booklets*, publications that were intended as instructions for art and collaboration. Similarly, Robert Watts, beginning at Rutgers and then continuing at the University of California, Santa Cruz, developed a laboratory-style approach to artistic research, which he called the *Experimental Arts Workshop* (1965; 1968–1970), that was in turn part of a larger research project eventually published under the title *Proposals for Art Education from a Year Long Study (1968–69)*.[1]

The Fluxus legacy, like that of the APG, is frequently mentioned within contemporary art—and in particular, in the genealogy of socially engaged practices—because of the emphasis on process, everyday actions, and open-ended collaborative and iterative performances and objects. And while the Fluxus label is often concomitant with radical pedagogy, what that radicality is, or how it might be enacted in today's classrooms, has rarely been explored. To reiterate my earlier claims, seldom have Fluxus's educational events or objects been examined in relation to socially engaged art and the Pedagogical Turn.

More recently, there has been some interest in Fluxus teaching. Emily Capper's (2016) dissertation *Allan Kaprow and the Dialectics of Instruction, 1947–1968* is a close examination of Kaprow's experimental teaching methods; however, the focus is on his time at Rutgers and other New York–area institutions. Capper's research does not extend to Kaprow's teaching in California and the *Other Ways* project. From an art historical perspective, the research is significant in that it focuses on the happenings that Kaprow produced with his students, arguing that many of the unorthodox aesthetic elements of the performance events were derived from campus life and that happenings can therefore be understood as "pedagogical scenes." As Capper remarks, examining the materiality of pedagogical history—syllabi, lecture notes, and course slides—offers a meaningful way to reconsider the Fluxus object, score, and performance event or happening in relation to, not external to, teaching.

Watts's *Experimental Arts Workshop*, and the subsequent publication from the year-long study, had limited circulation and impact at the time; however, renewed interest in Fluxus educational research includes recent work by

Natilee Harren (forthcoming), and such publications attest to the fact that there is much to learn from Fluxus about the radical pedagogy of the 1960s and 1970s and these artist-teachers' influence on art education curriculum and pedagogy. As with the APG retrospective that did not include the Southwark Educational Research Project, Fluxus art historical texts and exhibitions rarely tell the story of Fluxus from the perspective of education. This seemed a crucial inroad for my own research.

However, while I was curious about the Fluxus education archive, my interest in Fluxus pedagogy was entwined with questions I had about current pedagogy as art in postsecondary classrooms. In much the same way that the artist residencies in K–12 schools explored the possibilities of making a classroom a work of art, I was interested in the different ways that artist-instructors use the university classroom or curriculum as a site of creative practice. In other words, I was interested in the materiality of pedagogy as art in current postsecondary classrooms. As I argued in the introduction, much of the focus in the Educational Turn had to do with work being produced for museums, community-led initiatives, or large art fairs. Very little attention is directed at the Pedagogical Turn within classrooms, including postsecondary ones. This has led to a lack of documentation, archives, or complex understandings of pedagogy as art within current classroom contexts, and in particular how artists-teachers are redefining radical pedagogy alongside their students. Moreover, even within the focus on pedagogical social practice work in nonclassroom spaces, there is typically an emphasis on fully realized projects or events rather than on the materiality of education—such as syllabi, activities, or classroom atmospheres.

Expanding on what I had learned and germinated in the school-based residencies, I turned my attention to examining the different ways that artists entwine creative practice with pedagogy and supporting the documentation and archiving of coursework developed by postsecondary artist-instructors and their students. To do this I created a social practice research-creation project with seven postsecondary artist-teachers and their classes. This discursive work involved a series of recorded conversations with the artist-teachers about pedagogy, institutions, and art. Most of the classes also created blogs through which course materials could be shared, and in some instances the students joined in the conversation. This social practice work is related to previous conversation practices that were recorded between the artists Hannah Jickling and Reed Reed, and a number of international artists and curators as part of *The Pedagogical Impulse*. These conversations live on the research website as *living archives* about art and education. I use the term *living archive* after the artist Barbara Steveni's (the cofounder of the APG, discussed in chapter 2) project *I Am an*

Archive, a series of participatory walks taking place at the sites of original APG placements.[2] The walks include a conversation or exchange of ideas between Steveni and other artists while cooking food, hanging out, socializing, and making art, in order to explore the potential to reactivate the APG methodology. *I Am an Archive* does not function in the same way as the more historically focused APG archives, now located in the Tate Gallery, but is an active, live, performed reworking of APG material. The *living archive* as social practice incorporates the sociality and intimacy of conversation within the often sterile spaces of institutional classrooms. As living, the archive reanimates the Fluxus archive in ways that both accentuate its influence on current art education and also act as scores that privilege relations that are pliable, mutating, and ever transforming.

To situate the *living archive* research-creation project in conversation with Fluxus curricular and pedagogical experiments, my research team and I also spent time in Fluxus archives in postsecondary institutions such as the University of California, San Diego, CalArts, OCAD University in Toronto, and the University of British Columbia. However, this archival work was not driven by an exhaustive art historical focus, nor was it intended to establish a linear timeline of Fluxus work and practice. For a more art historical rendering of the significance of the score in the history of Fluxus, I recommend Natilee Harren's book *Fluxus Forms: Scores, Multiples, and the Eternal Network* (2020). Rather, through the lens of research-creation I approached the archives as an artist-educator interested in those moments in history when art and education collided in unexpected ways, and in the relations between the Fluxus archive and the *living archive* that made way for something new.

This chapter will begin with an exploration into Fluxus curricula and pedagogical materials. Key to the various Fluxus examples I analyze is the event score. Scores often foreground the body and the senses, providing a way to experience the world corporeally. They often appear simple, as in the case of *Proposition #1 (Make a Salad)*, but when activated they open up complex perceptions, generating numerous connections and meanings. Not all scores are written; many contain diagrams, drawings, and other visual imagery. The propositional nature of scores allows for different adaptations and for indeterminacy, where chance and improvisation are primary and where multiple renderings are made possible. Understood as feltness, scores invite intimate participation either through collaborative inquiry or through embodied and sensory performance. Following the discussion of Fluxus educational experiments, I turn to consider the ways that the ordinariness of the score, its situatedness in everyday objects and actions, emerges in similar mundane aspects of teaching and learning, such as syllabi, assignments, and classroom atmospheres. It is this ordinariness that conditions radical pedagogy as art, both historically and in current postsecondary classrooms.

Learning Machines, Board Games, and Tarot Cards: Scoring Curriculum

I delight in sharing with students and university administrators the learning machines, board games, and tarot cards that Fluxus artists created as course calendars and course management systems. It's exciting to consider how personal learning objectives, degree learning expectations, assessment strategies, and program structures could be communicated in such playful, graphic, and indeterminate forms. In this section, I trace the score through Fluxus curricular materials, examining their contributions to radical pedagogy. Focusing on the score in Fluxus curricular materials, I consider the following works: George Maciunas's *Curriculum Plan* and *Learning Machines*; Roy Ascott's tarot cards and his LP record; and the Fluxus Fluxkits. I also discuss Allan Kaprow's school-based project *Other Ways* and Robert Watts's *Experimental Arts Workshop*, both of which were directed at postsecondary art education or occurred within school contexts.

Fluxus remains a difficult movement or art practice to define, in part because, as Hannah Higgins (2002) writes, "Fluxus artists never seem to agree on anything" (xiii). In fact, even calling Fluxus a movement is misleading, as many individuals associated with Fluxus rarely understood themselves to be part of a common project or program. As Owen Smith (1993, 24) writes, it might be more helpful to consider Fluxus as an "alternative attitude toward artmaking, culture and life." The experimental and playful spirit of Fluxus is what should be remembered, as opposed to any of the art objects or performances that were produced. Fluxus artists were defiantly antiestablishment and anticapitalist. In particular, Fluxus resisted the commercialization of the art world. Central to Fluxus beliefs was the imperative to experience the everyday as art. Fluxus understood art as an in-between space made up of movement, space, silences, and holes (Sholtz 2018). Fluxus was, and is, a radical departure from traditional conceptions of art, with key members understanding their practice to be social and participatory rather than aesthetic. Owen Smith (2005) has argued that Fluxus explicitly rejected two dominant aspects of the traditional art world: first, that the artist is special (or a genius) and, second, that the art object is intrinsically valuable. Instead, Fluxus understood art to be grounded in social connections and interactions in which participation by many people was valued. Furthermore, the Fluxus attitude rejected the veneration and commodification of singular art objects, seeing such a belief as antithetical to the equation of art as life. To that end, scores enabled anyone, at any time or anywhere, to create art and to adapt and change the score to suit the needs of the group. As Natilee Harren (2020) writes, the score's iterability through multiple realizations meant that it would never exhaust further future possibilities and iterations; rather, a score is "an unforeclosable potential object" (26).

A key architect, organizer, and central figure was George Maciunas, who coined the term *Fluxus*, which he took from the Latin word *fluere*, meaning to flow or to be in a state of flux (Schmidt-Burkhardt 2003). Maciunas first planned for Fluxus to be used as a name for a publication, but it quickly came to represent a larger artistic vision and eventually an international network of avant-garde artists. These artists moved both into and out of their association and alignment with Fluxus, with the number of associated artists ranging from 30 to 350 over the years (Higgins 2002). For Maciunas, Fluxus was not to be seen as a new wave of artists or a new art theory or style, but rather as an international art stream that challenged the traditional art world and blurred the lines between art and life.

Though multiple dates have been suggested as the birth of Fluxus—such as 1961, with the publication of Maciunas's *Fluxus* magazine, or the public performance series held in Wiesbaden, Germany, in 1962—a key point of origin was a class in musical composition offered by the experimental composer John Cage at the New School for Social Research in New York (Higgins 2002). Among Cage's students in the years 1957–1959 were key members of what would become Fluxus, including George Brecht, Dick Higgins, Allan Kaprow, and Florence Tarlow.[3] Cage's approach to pedagogy, which would become so influential for Fluxus, was not to impart a body of knowledge; instead, Cage's students "conducted experiments using chance operations in a variety of formats including music, performance and poetry" (Higgins 2002, 2). Pedagogical innovations used in this class included understanding everyday actions as framed, minimalistic performances, an approach that would become an important aspect of Fluxus's practices. These experiments, alongside other chance events, scores, and happenings, would become the basis for much of the Fluxus approach to art and teaching.

One of the most explicitly articulated visions of the Fluxus philosophy can be found in the *Fluxus Manifesto*, written by Maciunas in 1962 (but never adopted by other Fluxus artists). The *Manifesto* defined three key terms that Maciunas believed were essential for promoting and clarifying the intentions of Fluxus: *purge, tide,* and *fuse* (Philpot 2011). The *Manifesto* was essentially a one-page collage of dictionary definitions of these three terms, with the addition of Maciunas's commentary beneath each. Maciunas's comments added that the intent of Fluxus was to "*purge* the world of bourgeois sickness, 'intellectual,' professional and commercialized culture. Purge the world of dead art, imitation, artificial art, abstract art" (Maciunas 1963). This was followed by Fluxus's desire to promote "a revolutionary flood and *tide* in art" that emphasized "living art, anti-art . . . to be grasped by all peoples, not only critics, dilettantes and professionals." Finally, *fuse* involved the fusion of cultural, political, and social revolutionaries into a united front. The revolutionary nature of the *Fluxus Manifesto* should not to be dismissed.

The objects, performances, and events associated with and produced by Fluxus members are often understood through the concept of *intermedia*. Dick Higgins in particular used the term *intermedia* to describe how Fluxus existed at the intersection of multiple forms of representation and could simultaneously include visual art, music, performance, dance, and literature (Schmidt-Burkhardt 2003). Intermedia was a significant concept for Fluxus as it blurred boundaries between disciplined art forms—which was essential for the larger Fluxus project of blurring boundaries between art and life. The Fluxus understanding of intermedia drew on a wide range of thinkers, including Marshall McLuhan and his book *Understanding Media* (1964), in which he argued that blurring the distinctions between art and life could disrupt or "break up habitualized forms of perception" (quoted in Schröter 2012, 17). In discussing Fluxus intermedia, Ken Friedman (1998, 247) asks us to imagine what an art form would be like if it "is comprised 10 percent of music, 25 percent of architecture, 12 percent of drawing, 18 percent of shoemaking, 30 percent of painting and 5 percent of smell." Harren (2020, 217) writes that intermedia was about "boundary conditions where one thing meets another, transcends a limit to become something else, or is exchanged with a proximate yet unlike thing." An intermedia approach meant that Fluxus works evoke a between-ness or liminal state that creates new zones of participation, interaction, and understanding. In the introduction, I discussed Natalie Loveless's assertion that research-creation is not simply the addition of two or more disciplines but rather a hybrid, something more-than that exceeds what the disciplines themselves can contain. Intermedia operated in a similar vein and sought not just to pull different media together into a form but to profoundly alter form altogether. Higgins's concept of intermedia defines the in-between state in which scores exist; where things are not merely mixed but in a state of flux.

Fluxus artists, and those associated with the group, began to develop ideas on how to reform or revolutionize art education, which they published in a number of texts, including Robert Filliou's (1970) *Teaching and Learning as Performance Art*, Allan Kaprow's (1972) *The Education of the Un-Artist*, Robert Watts's (1970) *Artist as Teacher*, and a collection of essays written by Maciunas and Robert Watts, among others, published under the title *Proposals for Art Education from a Year Long Study (1968–69)*. The common theme stretching across these publications was an embrace of an intermedia approach to education that encouraged play, experimentation, and choice and the rejection of what was seen as the rigid and stifling disciplinarity of existing institutional structures. "When art is only one of several possible functions a situation may have, it loses its privileged status," argued Kaprow ([1972] 1993, 105). In rejecting the rigidity of formal aesthetics, art becomes life.

In the essay *The Artist as Teacher* (1970) Robert Watts argues for a restructuring of art schools in terms of the way classes are convened and calls for an interdisciplinary approach to teaching. This publication describes the *Experimental Workshop* at Santa Cruz and the year-long project (later to become a publication) that had been implemented at the school. He writes, "Combining the artist with a biologist, a psychologist, a sociologist, a philosopher in an interdisciplinary arts committee could generate ideas" (59). Later in the paper he contends that students should not be trained in one method or approach but "encouraged to study by opening up the possibilities for creative exploration" through a research-oriented approach (60). I found a great deal of synergy between Watts's arguments in 1970 and the kinds of questions we are posing regarding postsecondary art education in 2021. He writes: "What does education in the arts mean for a student? Why should he [sic] want an art experience?" (59).

In addition to more formal or academic publications, many Fluxus artists created flux-objects to communicate their radical thoughts on curriculum change. Maciunas's *Curriculum Plan* (1970) was primarily concerned with the inefficiency of existing higher education models, which he argued led to premature specialization and a fragmentation of knowledge. The *Curriculum Plan* takes the form of a board game with multiple pathways and objectives for students to follow. The score of the game board allows students to break out of rigid requirements, prerequisites, and course sequences and permits students to move through the curriculum in a variety of ways. Durational workshops, some student-led, replace the structure of bounded courses in formal, discipline-specific areas. Framed as intermedia, the game board reflects the transdisciplinarity of Fluxus and their attitude toward education. Gesturing to his previous manifesto and its call to action to "purge," the game board spells out SOS, a plea that art schools needed to be reimagined. Mapping knowledge, the different letters on the board indicate the different levels of the new curriculum.

To counter what Maciunas considered to be slow, linear methods of information dissemination, like books, lectures, and films, he produced diagrammatic visual forms called *Learning Machines* (1969). In the place of so-called linear methods, Maciunas imagined and developed graphic representations of transdisciplinary information on paper that could be three dimensionally folded, providing different dimensions in which learners could move between areas of knowledge quickly, saving time and providing an unfragmented and integrated understanding of different topics. The diagrammatic form, Harren (2020, 65) contends, "maps out spatio-temporal arrangements of objects and actions, as if to enfold diagrammatic structure into language itself." Harren argues that the tendency to understand the score as only text-based neglects the many scores that were pictorial or that included other graphic notation that "privileges analogies, relations, and correspondences over arbitrariness of structural difference" (70). Reminiscent of children's picture flip books, where pages are divided into multiple sections that can be turned at random, generating different compositions each time, the *Learning Machines* argued for a networked or intermedia basis for curriculum reform:

> Maciunas used this chart-like taxonomy with its easily comprehensible structure to excoriate the slow, linear-narrative method of traditional sources of information such as books, lectures, television, and movies, as well as of newer computer technology. As one who did not really enjoy reading books, Maciunas replaced text-based knowledge transfer with a visual system of information that allowed a wealth of information to be grasped simultaneously. What he had in mind was a three-dimensional diagram whose main advantage would be its provision of a time-saving overview. (Schmidt-Burkhardt 2003, 65)

Similarly, in 1971 Roy Ascott, the new president of the Ontario College of Art (OCA) in Toronto (now OCAD U), gave a talk to all of the faculty and instructors teaching in the second level of the program. The talk, which was recorded on an LP record and given to all of the faculty teaching in the second-year program, argued that OCA's aim was not to further industry training but to create students who would create alternative worldviews: "alternative images, alternative forms, alternative structures, alternative systems . . . even alternative relationships between human beings" (cited in Wolfe 2001, 44). He later produced a set of tarot cards as the course calendar for the 1972–1973 academic year before eventually being removed from his position (Wolfe 2001). While there is little evidence that Ascott was part of Fluxus, his work in the Canadian context is an important connection and demonstrates how intermedia and scores were part of the Canadian landscape. Like Maciunas, Ascott saw the limitations of students moving through a discipline-focused and conventional art curriculum and was interested in collective, collaborative, and group activities. He wanted structured classes in skill development to be replaced by workshops, seminars, and score-type actions that were driven by student research and desire. Emphasizing what today would be called problem-based learning, Ascott wanted students to be presented with multiple problems in the first year of the program that would demand multiple solutions. From the second year on, students would need to pose their own problems. When he first arrived at the Ontario College of Art, he dismantled departmental boundaries, eliminating, for example, textiles and traditional sculpture, and he approached pedagogy from an intermedia and communications perspective. Part of the issue with the way Ascott implemented his curriculum reform had to do with pace (tarot cards notwithstanding): arriving in Toronto to take on the new leadership role in July 1971, he expected a fully new program to be ready by September, a timeline which understandably alienated many faculty and students (Wolfe 2001).

Acknowledging the toxic character of Ascott's approach to reform, one in which disagreement, transparency, and reciprocity were absent, I emphasize these historical moments not to valorize his actions; my aim is rather to examine the role of intermedia in postsecondary art education and the creation of curricula as art, the materiality of pedagogy as art. Rarely are the LPs, tarot cards, or board games produced by Fluxus artists and their counterparts examined for the ways in which they radically transformed art education. And while they were clearly "ahead of their time" in the 1970s, my contention is that they would still be understood as extremist in the context of education today.

It is crucial to note that, following World War II in the United States, many returning soldiers were able to go to university under the Servicemen's Readjustment Act of 1944 (known as the GI Bill). Subsequently, the 1950s saw enrollment numbers swell, which required new faculty recruits and also the construction of new college campuses. It was a time of mass higher education and the corporatization of the university, when many colleges were creating programs that focused on general education. It was at this time that many universities hired artists to teach not only courses in art and design but new interdisciplinary and general education courses.

As an artist-scholar who has just taken on a new role in the university, as a director of the School of the Arts at McMaster University, and as one who, with the collaboration of faculty and students, will be launching a new iArts program that captures the spirit of radical change of the 1960s and 1970s, I am eager to analyze the theory and moments behind these historical antecedents while also examining their limitations and failures. In imagining the future of iArts at McMaster University, with no discipline-specific boundedness (the school was previously composed of studio, art history, theater, and film and music) and an emphasis on intermedia, research-creation, and transdisciplinary practices, the history of intermedia in postsecondary art education is crucial.

If the politics of the avant-garde was in rejecting the institution of art, current methods of intermedia must put anti-oppression and social justice at the center. This requires that we center mutual care, disability justice, radical inclusivity, anticolonialism, and anti-oppressive work in our iArts curriculum and recognize the degree to which this requires collective responsibility, accountability, and time. I return to consider the implications of this new iArts program in the concluding chapter but briefly mention it here, as it tells the story of why I find the Fluxus moment in the history of postsecondary art education compelling, if not also problematic and complex. Writing about Ascott's time at OCA, Morris Wolfe (2001) cites a publication that Ascott published in *Art Magazine* in the spring of 1971. The article, titled "Art as an Alternative to Education, or, The Demise of the Jam Factory," claimed that the current state of art education was akin to a jam factory, where old methods and values were pickled and preserved. For Ascott, an art education of the future needed to be released from the past, not bottled or canned. The future of intermedia in postsecondary art education must not only make way for innovative and experimental practices, it must also decenter normative canons and actively embrace anti-oppressive frameworks.

I also want to imagine a future of the art school, embedded in a larger university institutional structure, that gives itself permission to create artistic forms and practices through which to develop and deliver curriculum and recruit future students (and faculty). It might not be a deck of tarot cards that we find most useful, but there is potential, I contend, in diagrammatically and graphically represented curriculum materials in the form of zines, chap books, and scores. For years my course syllabi and assignments were presented to students in the form of zines or artist books, and a larger project called the *Instant Class Kit*—a pop-up curriculum guide—will be discussed in detail in chapter 4. It is with a nod to the history of these Fluxus works that I reimagine radical pedagogy and the Educational Turn as sites of potential change in art educa-tion of the future. *How might the score become a thought exercise to reimagine the future university?*

Scores, whether in the form of text-based instructions, board games, or tarot cards, allow for the work to travel from place to place without the authority of the artist. Like the open brief, scores are highly improvised and open, with "many possible realizations of a given work" (Harren 2020, 7). Originally, scores were generally only used by the artist-performer, but as Fluxus publish-ing grew, scores were circulated for general use. Writing about her "Action a Day" project, which is derived from the Fluxus score, Natalie Loveless states:

> The daily practice instruction or event score insists on the value of *dai-lyness*, of the every day, of the quotidian. It does this in two important ways: (1) It carves into the flow of the everyday, insisting that the per-former *pay attention* to something else, and pay attention *differently*, de-familiarizing and re-routing and framing that moment as an aesthetic act or event; (2) It insists on the value of repetition. The things that we repeat, that we do on a daily basis, render the *shape* of our actions, of our attention, and our being-in-the-world. (Loveless n.d.)

Fluxus scores similarly insist on modes of attention that tune in to and shape lived experience. While the scores were a crucial part of reimagining what music, painting, or a work of art could become, what remains less often dis-cussed is the scores' central role in destabilizing educational structures.

Fluxus artists often referred to the score as an object, a kit, or a publication. An example is George Brecht's *Water Yam* (1963), containing a set of sixty-nine scores published in a box designed by Maciunas. These publications, along with a yearbook designed by Maciunas, eventually became what are known as Fluxkits. The first Fluxkit, *Fluxus 1* (1964), was conceived of by Maciunas and contained work by thirty-nine artists, not all of whom identified as Fluxus-affiliated. *Fluxus 1* transforms the act of reading into a haptic encounter, which is characteristic of Fluxus works in general. Fluxkits were boxed multiples that contained readymades, publications, games, written scores, and other multisensory stimuli such as balls, pom-poms, and found objects. The con-tents were intended to be touched and in many cases involved other senses such as smell. Rupturing ocularcentrism, Fluxkits were to be experienced, opened, experimented with, and remade in the process. Intended to be used by multiple participants, Fluxkits were highly social and experiential. "Fluxus encourages us to look at, listen to, and feel the environment, to learn from that experience and to remain open to new perceptions," writes Hannah Higgins

(2002, 206–7). Denouncing associations of high art, the content of Fluxkits were intended to be cheap and unprecious (Higgins 2002). The activations of the kits themselves is endless, as seemingly unlike objects were placed in relationship and could be activated in multiple ways (Harren 2016). Somatic, sensory, and haptic perceptions were important components to Fluxus work that challenged conventional ocularcentrism in art. Central to Fluxus work was the sense of touch—not just physical touching and the manipulation of objects and materials, but also a felt or affective experience. The incorporation of touch—of affect—as Sholtz (2018, 252) claims, "evidences the commitment of Fluxus to a contingent, unknowable future, and gives us hope that the future is possible, but only if we are able to find a way to resist or disrupt the present."

Many Fluxkits were used in postsecondary education, including in many happenings that took place in the Voorhees Chapel at Rutgers University (a space where many Fluxus events were programmed). The ethos of the kits was not about conveying particular didactic information but rather foregrounded the pedagogical encounter as corporeal, sensorial, and felt. For many Fluxus artists, teaching was not secondary to their artistic pursuits but rather a crucial aspect of their art. Joseph Beuys, who was loosely affiliated with Fluxus in Europe, said, "To be a teacher is my greatest work of art" (cited in Higgins 2002, 188). As Higgins notes, the idea of intermedia insisted that the artist-teacher was not present to transmit information but to create space for open-ended problem solving in a "teacher-as-facilitator role" (2002, 196).

At CalArts, the Fluxus artists Dick Higgins, Allan Kaprow, Alison Knowles, and Nam June Paik took up faculty positions and radically reimagined the school's course offerings, rejecting any set curriculum in their classes. Kaprow, as associate dean of the art school, had a particularly powerful influence. As Alison Knowles later explained, "Kaprow was the thinking behind the school as far as I'm concerned. . . . He had the vision of a school based on what artists wanted to do rather than what the school wanted them to do" (cited in Sarbanes 2012). While the modernist art school sought to emphasize the mastery of well-established art techniques, the Fluxus vision for art education included an intermedia approach that centered contemporary social and political issues and the everyday.

One such example is Allan Kaprow and the educator Herbert Kohl's project *Other Ways*, with classes from the Berkeley Unified School District. The project unfolded in a local storefront and was funded by the Carnegie Corporation. The project sought to bring an intermedia and art approach to the curriculum. Kaprow writes that, to this end, it brought together poets, artists, architects, happeners, and athletes with students, teachers, and administrators. In a sixth-grade class, the students were given cheap Polaroid cameras and encouraged to walk around their neighborhood and capture pictures of whatever caught their attention. The students, many of whom experienced inequality in schooling, were captivated by graffiti text, and Kaprow and Kohl capitalized on this everydayness to expand notions of literacy. The aim of the project was to create a model for learning based on playful, scored interactions outside of the conventional classroom and curriculum.

Kaprow tells the story of Kohl making use of discarded *Dick and Jane* readers, which the school board was throwing out because of their sexist and racist narratives. In addition to documenting graffiti, the students reworked the children's readers by adding their own drawings and text. He writes, "Our assumption was that the kids' sensitivity to these biases (the majority were black or Hispanic) would provide use the openings for frank discussion, and would make attractive the prospect of wholesale revision of the texts. We were right" (Kaprow 1994, 154). *Other Ways* also incorporated scores and happenings, some of which are documented in the performance poster *Six Ordinary Happenings* (1969). The scores that compose *Six Ordinary Happenings* emphasize Kaprow's use of play to incite inquiry into local phenomena and experiences. In 1969 Berkeley was the site of protests against the Vietnam War, and the National Guard had been brought in. While Kaprow's scores and happenings were not a direct comment on the protests, the students' films, photographs, and writings reflected the radical moment in the city. The six scores included *Fine*, *Charity*, *Pose*, *Shape*, *Giveaway*, and *Purpose*. In *Pose* students moved chairs around the city and were photographed sitting on them. *Giveaway* prompted the students to leave piles of dishes on sidewalks and to document the remains the next day, while in *Purpose* the students moved mountains of sand with shovels and recorded the sounds of the score. The scores used play, experimentation, and the students' bodies to invent a line of inquiry into their environment and their relationship with space.

In 1966 Kaprow wrote that happenings "deserve a place in contemporary public education—along with abstract painting, concrete poetry, and electronic music. As a uniquely social art, Happenings mark a growing trend in the arts, away from traditional intellectual alienation, and toward interpersonal relationships" (Kaprow 1966). He found a partner in Herbert Kohl, who believed that art could be the catalyst for reform in public education. The happenings, much like scores, overturned the conventions of art and introduced what would later become performance and body art. Writing about the project twenty-five years later for a book edited by the feminist artist Suzanne Lacy, Kaprow reflects on how at the time the work with the students was not valued as art because it did not adhere to the terms and conditions of what art should be at the time, and because it was decentralized in terms of the authority of the artist and was created in collaboration with public school students and teachers. The project was rarely discussed as educational, he contends, and, while the intent was to have a lasting effect on teacher education, training, and school curricula, he acknowledges that to be successful it would have needed to be sustained over a longer period of time. From my perspective, the devaluation of teaching is why this work is rarely discussed (except in footnotes) in art historical texts and why the Educational Turn instead reifies public, socially engaged work that gestures at education but which is formally accounted for as art. Practices of pedagogy as art, both historically and today, remain marginalized and under-analyzed. Most telling from Kaprow's critical reflection is the call for an ethics, an accountability to the intermedia, social, and community spaces in which the artist-teacher works. He contends that any evaluation of these kinds of pedagogical projects must shift from aesthetics to an ethics of encounters. The problem with valuing the work as art and education has everything to do with disciplinary boundaries, and with the notion of value as an external event. When value is conceived in normative terms as something applied to an object or event, it amplifies what is devalued. This type of value is also complicit with colonialism and slavery, where particular forms of life were rendered less valuable. In rendering ethics as a way to refuse capitalist forms of value, value takes shape in relations, (in)tensions, and in asking questions about the how of the event: what it is doing, what it is working. Extending Kaprow's arguments, I would argue that the value is in how the art as pedagogy shapes experience, how it co-composes and moves. What is valued is the scores' ability to shift habits of formation, to activate indeterminate formations from within. Erin Manning (2020, 23) writes that "value must also be activated each time anew. Art that truly engages with what has not yet found its form intuitively steers away from the mimicry of reproduction. . . . Art must never seek to define in advance its value." We cannot know in advance the feltness of the score.

Similar ideas about art and education could be found in the *Experimental Workshop* at Rutgers established by Robert Watts in 1965 and later in 1968–1969 at the University of California, Santa Cruz. Watts and three other instructors were invited to campus to pioneer an innovative intermedia arts program funded by the Carnegie Corporation. The three other instructors included the cultural anthropologist Edmund Carpenter, the art historian Sidney Simon, and the art critic Christopher Cornford (Harren forthcoming; Watts 1970). According to Watts, the structure of the new program included a large lecture course for art majors and non–art majors on contemporary social, economic, and political issues; smaller seminars on contemporary art; and Watts's *Experimental Workshop* in new media. While the courses were envisaged holistically, they were not convened to coordinate information among them. Students were expected to become responsible for their own inquiry and practice, which represented quite a different model from the traditional art school, which emphasized technical skills and disciplinary depth of knowledge. Experimentation, curiosity, and innovation formed the basis of the workshops. Visiting artists and scholars were also invited to give lectures and workshops and to meet with students (Harren forthcoming; Watts 1970). As Harren notes, "Representing diverse disciplines, the list of visitors reflected the research interests and personal networks of the pilot project's core team as well as the cross-disciplinary, exploratory spirit of the endeavor. The invitees were sought out because they represented a variety of institutions, but most importantly, because they were seen to be probing the limits of their respective fields."

Many of the workshops took place on Watts's property and involved happenings, performances, and multimedia projections. There was a pancake festival in the campus amphitheater and a number of other food-centric events (Harren forthcoming). All of the activities over the year were recorded, transcribed, and compiled for a published report of the year's activities, titled *Proposals for Art Education from a Year Long Study (1968–69)*. The publication questions the purpose of arts education and also speculatively reimagines its futurity. I return to an early mock-up of this publication in the next chapter in its role as a provocation for another research-creation project I curated called the *Instant Class Kit*. I turn now to consider how the score, intermedia, and arts education committed to social and political issues and the everyday manifests in current postsecondary classrooms.

The Ordinary Potential of Radical Pedagogy as Art

The Mexican American artist and pedagogue Jorge Lucero (2011, 15) posits that "teaching is the most sophisticated form of conceptual art practice." In his daily practice, writings, and educational commitments, Lucero approaches "teaching-as-an-art-practice" and suggests that teachers become artists in residence in their own classrooms. Part of what Lucero is advocating requires the dismantling of preconceived notions regarding expertise, production, and art. "Other than thinking," he claims, "there is no special art skill requirement for teachers to emerge as the premiere artists-in-residence in their classrooms" (23). Rather than seeing education as a skilled profession, Lucero asks teachers to think of themselves as artists everywhere and at all times. Influenced by Fluxus and conceptual artists, Lucero understands art as existing in the everyday gestures and actions that teachers and students do, including scheduling, recess, worksheets, and lesson plans. Lucero's words encourage K–12 teachers to give themselves permission to approach teaching as a creative endeavor. In doing so, he contends, emphasis is placed on everyday actions and knowledge as something a teacher has expertise in, thereby disrupting hierarchical expectations around art and knowledge. In proposing *Teacher as Conceptual Artist* (ongoing), Lucero invites teachers and artists to create a "hybrid practice that is simultaneously progressive pedagogy and conceptual art," whose "shared modes include—but are not limited to—negotiating relationality, testing the materiality of time, recognizing the body politic and the politics of bodies, theorizing the complexity and incompleteness of documentation, foregrounding the tense discourse between word and object, and pursuing a constant—almost utopian—aspiration for being wide-eyed in the world for the sake of the world" (Lucero 2011, 29).

I opened this chapter with Alison Knowles's score *Proposition #1 (Make a Salad)*, a minimalist set of instructions that are ordinary and yet open-ended enough that each iteration is different. Similarly, Knowles's score *The Identical Lunch* (1969) invites people to join her for her habitual daily meal: a tuna fish sandwich on wheat toast, with lettuce and butter, no mayo, and a cup of soup or a glass of buttermilk. Lucero, as a teacher-as-conceptual-artist, similarly opened his office during lunch hours for students, faculty, and staff to join him while he ate lunch. These scores invite reflection on mundane and quotidian activities. They foreground everyday gestures and rituals that are ordinary, yet full of aliveness. The etymological origins of *radical*, Lucero reminds us, are words for *root*, or *core*; that which is underneath a surface and which is fundamental to its being. He writes, "We can then understand *radical*—not as something that is more true, newer, or more impactful—rather as something that matures and becomes spectacular underground, out-of-sight, and over a mostly ignored duration" (2011, 34). The concept of teacher-as-artist, he continues, "is radical because it is ordinary, but when revealed, pulled out, harvested, and pointed out; it shows its colors, its size, its uniqueness, its interconnectedness, and its essential vitality" (34). This is a kind of intimate radicality, inherent in the everyday and the ordinary. The ordinary, writes Kathleen Stewart (2007, 3), activates "potential modes of knowing, relating, and attending to things [that] are already somehow present in them in a state of potentiality and resonance." What is radical is a palpable potentiality, a shift in registers that a score ignites. Fluxus scores disrupt ordinary perception and in doing so break open the latent potentialities of an event transforming our relation to the everyday. Fluxus scores were designed to be experienced materially by those who engaged with them. They were not meant to be precious or admired art objects. As Higgins (1998, 225) argued, "a masterpiece in this context was a work that made a strong statement rather than a work that would last throughout the ages in some treasure vault." The ordinariness of the score is countered by the unexpected and uncommon actions it ignites. It is the ordinariness of the everyday that enables artists to get close to things, to become immersed in an event and, in the attention to the overlooked, to make something visible, or tactile, or experienced differently. As Loveless remarks, daily practices and scores insist we pay attention and tune in to the everyday, to notice not just what we are doing but the how and why of our daily actions—our (in)tensions. (In)tensions are ethicopolitical concerns that emerge in practice; they are a way of thinking about problems as open-ended and in flux. Tuning in and attending to (in)tensions poses the questions: *What is being worked here? And why?* Meaning not only *what are we paying attention to that we might not typically experience* but *what responsibilities arise from such tending toward?*

Thinking alongside the Fluxus curricular and pedagogical archive, I was curious about the ordinariness of teaching in current postsecondary art education classrooms. The ordinariness, the everyday of teaching, is often quite remarkable for what it reveals and cracks open. The ordinary makes visible the labor, care, vulnerability, and responsibility of teaching and learning, while also decentering expertise and the individual. For Fluxus, the everyday as art challenged the privileged status of the art object, and the art genius, in favor of a more democratic art practice. Scores could be enacted by anyone and often encouraged collaboration and community. The everyday of the artist-teacher with a hybrid practice is ordinary. The ordinary is not the opposite of the extraordinary, the unusual, or the remarkable. Rather the ordinary enfolds the unexpected, the *extra-* as a double articulation. The artist-teacher's practice is ordinary in the sense that it is attuned to the everyday and often goes unnoticed. Yet, the ordinariness of the artist-teacher is quite unordinary, but its radicality lies not in grand disruptive gestures but in the attention to the everyday, the quotidian, and finds within the routines and rituals of schooling places of disruptive potentiality, or (in)tensions.

It is the ordinariness of teaching-as-art that is rarely documented or analyzed. Like the archives of Fluxus teaching, pedagogy as art in postsecondary art education has been obscured by more public pedagogical projects and events, most often attached to art institutions and curatorial platforms. Rarely are the classroom encounters of artist-teachers the stuff of analysis or worthy of being made visible or shared. An early question in the research process was *What are some of the particular ways that artist-teachers are blurring the boundaries or creating a hybrid practice?* But as the *living archive* conversations unfolded, the question itself morphed into *What is the ordinary potential of radical pedagogy as art?* While I was intrigued by the socially engaged projects that artist-teachers cocreated with their students, I became increasingly captivated by the everyday, ordinary materiality of teaching. And it is in the ordinariness—in things such as course syllabi, assignments, and classroom atmospheres—that minor gestures make way for anti-oppressive pedagogy and an "education to come." As Syrus Ware (2020a) says, "Activism is everyone and everywhere." As the *living archive* conversations will expose, radical pedagogy is in the force of things, no matter their size or volume. As feltness, radical pedagogy's potentiality is in paying attention to, of tuning in to, and in responding to things that matter. Stewart (2007, 12) writes that "the ordinary is a circuit that's always tuned into some little something somewhere," that "it amasses the resonance in things." As feltness, the ordinary becomes an impulse to be open to what we often overlook in our rush to value the oversized and the extreme. Lauren Berlant and Kathleen Stewart (2019, 42) remind us that we find the speculative in "rhythms interrupted"; and thus, the radical potentiality of the ordinary is felt as force, as affect, as an opening to something else.

In keeping with the ethos of the larger *Pedagogical Impulse* research-creation project, and in the spirit of socially engaged art, I invited seven North American artists to engage in a social practice *living archive* project that included creating class blogs to share and document course materials and content, as well as a series of recorded conversations between me (or someone from my research-creation team) and the artist-teachers on pedagogy, art, and institutions. With the emphasis on *living*, the conversations themselves were unremarkable and ordinary, as they focused on discussing the intricacies of individuals' teaching practices, which are always taxed with the excessive labor of the academy, capitalism, and the complexity of student engagement. Yet my curiosity and fascination in the routine, the insistence on the artist-teacher describing things as mundane as their syllabi, resonates with what Stewart (2007, 95) calls the capacity of "the ordinary [to be] a drifting immersion that watches and waits for something to pop up." Such unexpected moments can be violent, dangerous, banal, or replete with speculative potential, and we don't know what they will be until they happen. The ordinary of teaching-as-art moves something, it creates an opening for something unplanned, unscripted, and collaborative to happen.

As a social practice artwork, the *living archive* borrows from ethnographic methods of observation and interviews but foregrounds the ordinariness and open-endedness of the event score. Influenced by scores, my research-creation practice has always been informed by propositions, conceptual proposals that incite action or reflection with fluid or in-flux parameters and guidelines. As I discussed in the introduction, propositions start in the middle; they are not linear instructions or directions. Here the proposition *How is school?* became a starting place for our conversations. The conversations were happening at the same time that we were working in the Fluxus archives and so both could be said to inform the *living archive* project. Vacillating between the historical archives and the intimate exchanges, the vitality of the *living archive* makes palpable the ordinariness of education. In what follows I turn to the recorded conversations from the *living archive* to examine pedagogy as art in current classrooms and courses, teasing open the ordinary potential of radical pedagogy as art. I focus on the moments in our conversations where the artist-teachers shared thoughts on syllabi, assignments, and classroom atmospheres, school materials or events that are common to most postsecondary teaching and as such are rarely afforded much thought or concern. They are ordinary, but this ordinariness, I argue, holds within it great moments of flux and radical potentiality.

The Mundane of School

Shannon Gerard, an associate professor at OCAD University, Toronto, uses a score to create an open-ended syllabus. For example, for the class Pressing Issues the syllabus consisted of one statement *Make a Public*. To do this, over the duration of the semester, students engaged in numerous smaller projects, readings, field trips, and events, which then culminated in a publication. The entire semester-long class functioned as a social practice art project. In using the score, student collaboration and student-led inquiry drove the making of the syllabus and the direction of the course over the duration of the semester.

In another course, called Nano Publishing, Gerard made the syllabus for each student as a small zine "that folded out in three different ways and all the assignments were these little art multiples and students had to slide open a match box or untie a string; and it was all printed on acetate."[4] For another course Gerard made a Fluxkit in a cigar box as the syllabus, with the materials loosely contained in the box. In other classes she made a course reader with the students. Everyone printed the course readings in a zine-like format and then they sewed them together into little annotated folded zines. In our conversation, Gerard talked about the importance of multiples and publications in terms of their resilience, their ability to transform learning over time. Further, the multiples invited students to enter into each class through tactile, embodied, and multiple means. She states that "publications have a kind of inherent political reach to them." Here she references histories such as LGBTQ+ rights, where publication has had a strong role in the movement as a platform for marginalized voices. She continues, "It doesn't even necessarily matter what you're making a publication about; if you produce something in multiple, it implies a distribution system" that takes the work to other people. Multiples, she contends, have an urgent political momentum. This is often why she creates her syllabi as miniature publications. Intended for students registered in the course, they are also saved, shared, and exchanged with other students and artists; the politics of the syllabus is thus in its movement beyond and outside of the class. The Fluxus multiples, scores, Fluxkits, and other readymade objects all emphasized the collaborative approach to authorship. Conventional syllabi are functional documents produced by a teacher prior to the commencement of a course. Syllabi convey the curriculum as a static system that imparts disciplinary knowledge. In scoring and creating the syllabus within the course itself, and doing so collectively with students, the syllabus becomes relational, emergent, provisional, and excessive of their ordinary function. Unlike most syllabi, which today are digital or at the most printed out on letter-size paper, Gerard's syllabi are intended to be handled and touched, their object-pages-scores rearranged much like Maciunas's *Learning Machines*. Writing about Fluxkits, Harren (2020, 249) states that in opening up the box and activating the contents, "the functions and meanings of the objects contained within are drastically multiplied as they are thrust into relation with seemingly unlike objects and functions." What is ordinary—a syllabus—becomes more-than, or extraordinary, as the assemblages of information and knowledge multiply and mutate. The syllabus as a score does not predetermine the course or the learning; rather it acts as both an agitator or proposition and as a trace of the pedagogical encounter, the fleeting and ordinary moments of exchange. The value of Gerard's syllabi is not in suggesting that all teachers now need to create Fluxkits as a course outline; the emphasis lies in the repeatable, not as something to be done again, where the outcome is the same, but as a repetition of infinite and immeasurable possibilities. The tiniest, most intimate and ordinary gesture—a syllabus—ignites its radical pedagogy through unbounded relations, associations, and circuits. (Gerard's pedagogy as art practice will be discussed in more detail in chapter 6.)

Jorge Lucero, an associate professor at the University of Illinois Urbana-Champaign, went so far as to name his class blog Class Not a Class, writing:

This is not a class. It is an artwork. Even when it appears to have all the characteristics of a class (e.g. students, a teacher, a meeting time, a syllabus, assignments, a classroom space, grades, course credit, teaching and learning, etc.) it will never be a class. Much like René Magritte's famous *The Treachery of Images*—where the viewer's perception of a pipe is immediately rerouted to the obviousness of its being a mere picture of pipe—so will the participants of this class-not-a-class consistently oscillate between the appearance of a class and the pliable materiality of being in a class, at a specific time in history, in a location, focused on a specific topic, alongside a once-in-a-lifetime set of individuals. What this means is that this "class" is merely a set of materials and we—the participants—now need to decide what to do with that material.

In Class Not a Class Lucero sought to rupture normative expectations of what a class could be and open up the space for different kinds of experimentation. A starting place for Lucero is the syllabus, which he says needs to reflect generosity, openness, and emergence. Rather than a prescribed plan of action, the syllabus sets "up the triggers that make everything else go off." These parameters, or enabling constraints, Lucero notes, are not connected to expectations: what is set in motion has no anticipated result. Speaking to the indeterminacy of Class Not a Class, Lucero states: "I just kind of wanted to see where the raft would go. I wanted to see where it was being carried." Allan Kaprow ([1966] 2010, 57) noted that chance and indeterminacy break up "knots of 'knowables,' of groupings, relationships and larger structures which have become obsolete and habitual through over-use." In this sense, Lucero's syllabus becomes an invitation to imagine class otherwise but also a call to think politically about institutionalisms and accountability. The indeterminacy, for Lucero, is grounded in a particular ethos of care and generosity where, as in many Fluxus performances, he is both the artist directing the work and a participant who yields to the collective efforts of the group—what he calls "a horizontal exchange." In discussing some of the influences on his practice he states: "What I'm most interested about in John Cage's work is the way that he was able to set up the work so that it functioned in a way that he could also be a member of its audience."

Lucero's *Class Not a Class* was originally a permanent course (albeit with a different course name) that had been previously taught by a different instructor. The content, Lucero noted, "was troubling in that there were 27 readings assigned and 26 of them were written by men, and all 27 of them were written by white scholars." The homogeneity in the source material did not reflect the course's aims in art and cultural theory. Lucero introduced an online bibliography to the course, featuring over two hundred citations written by people of color, women, and queer scholars, and invited students to use this bibliography as a jumping-off point to cocreate the syllabus. He states, "It was a simple gesture, but a move I think we needed to make, to destabilize the sort of sedimentation that has occurred around this particular kind of study. And so, the syllabus was written like that, it was written in a kind of open way that invited the students to think about the curriculum as something you make along the way." Opening up the syllabus to student input, the syllabus shifts from being didactic to generative, where a different future is made possible. Schools conventionally invite and produce docile bodies; they become factories where rote learning is prioritized. Lucero's ordinary gesture of reworking the syllabus with his students enters into the gaps that are always present. When we refuse to call a classroom to order, as Stefano Harney and Fred Moten (2013, 27) suggest in what they refer to as the "beyond of teaching," a refusal emerges from within the ordinary. In the undercommons of Lucero's class, refusing the normative limits of a canon and restrictive ideas about what knowledge is of most worth, the ordinariness of a minor gesture, such as collaboratively and artfully creating a syllabus *as* the output of a course, and as an art practice, reimagines education otherwise.

Allyson Mitchell, an associate professor at York University, Toronto, similarly prioritizes the decentering of a canon with her syllabi. She spoke about the necessity of teaching through subcultural movements that are typically absent from the curriculum. She states, "There's lots of other pockets of stuff that has existed but that doesn't get canonized and made as the referential point." For example, the artist Will Munro introduced her to a group of queer performers from the UK, who influence the kinds of material she brings into a course: "They would live together in England in these collaborative households and they would do drag and costume-making. Their art practices encompassed their whole ideology, life, everything. I found that very influential because it was also definitely not funded, definitely not formally educated—it was queer, it was politicized, it was queer worldmaking." Mitchell centers feminist, queer, and disability art histories, or what she calls "feeling queer about feminist art." This requires not just rewriting a syllabus but thinking about how different people "access information." The syllabus centers crip-disability and critically questions the forms of institutionalization that render particular forms of knowing and bodies unequal. This, she states, is about being "queer- and/

or LGBTQI2SA-responsible." The syllabus, for Mitchell, becomes a means to foreground resilient webs of care that are accountable to differential distributions of care and which decenter dominant forms of care and kinship (Malatino 2020). While syllabi commonly function to provide sequential information to students about weekly class expectations and assignments, for Mitchell the syllabus is a place to begin the collective work of disability justice. Mitchell's words remind me of the ways that particular influences in the art world and art curricula get reinscribed. In researching Fluxus, I am conscious that I have left out the work of Judy Chicago, Suzanne Lacy, and Mierle Laderman Ukeles, among others, as feminist influences and postsecondary educators in the 1960s and 1970s. But Mitchell reminds us that this is only a partial story that leaves absent the queer, trans, BIPOC influences that shape our syllabi and our teaching. To that extent I want to acknowledge the following artists' contributions to socially engaged and community-based practices: Stephen Carpenter, Jorge Lucero, Peter Morin, Mary Tremonte, Hannah Jickling, Reed Reed, Dylan Miner, Anique Jordan, Camille Turner, Syrus Ware, Jess Dobkin, Lisa Myers, Alyson Mitchell, and Deirdre Logue.

Everyday assignments or tasks similarly shift the ordinariness of classroom routine. Jen Delos Reyes, the associate director of the School of Art and Art History at the University of Illinois Chicago starts every class with her *Phone Sculpture* activity. The activity asks students to do something specific with their phone at the start of class, which typically then leads to a group sculpture where the phones remain for the duration of class. In her conversation she reflects on the activity:

> I had this idea that we could put our phones together and make an artwork. . . . We ended up doing a Mondrian, so some people would be one of the white sections, and someone else would be a primary blue, yellow, or red, and then putting all the phones together and then documenting it—and once that was done, it would stay there. Then, it evolved [to] how can this be a way to introduce the work of an artist that I want to talk about that day; how can it be more related to the class plan? [For example] when I talk about Tom Marioni and hospitality, I introduce them to *Drinking Beer with Friends Is the Highest Form of Art* and show a video of this happening, and what I've learned about Tom's practice, and then everyone Google image searches a bottle of Pacífico and we make a "golden rectangle" together that you would see after one of those experiences with Tom. And then the phones would just stay there for the whole class. They are just out of our hands then, and we can move

on—which just felt like a much better way to handle the situation than just having the people put all their phones locked away. Sometimes it will be about sharing the work of an artist; other times it will be for a conversation starter. [For example, in a class where we were] thinking through issues of representation and appropriation in contemporary art and connecting it with postcolonial theory, [I asked students] to find an image that represents cultural appropriation in a way that upsets them, or they've experienced, or whatever, and then we all put our phones together and everyone gets that moment to talk about it; so it also becomes a conversation starter too.

Tuning into the ordinariness of syllabi and simple classroom activities with an (in)tension asks questions about what these routine educational activities do. *What is their force? Who are they accountable to?*

Bill Burns, at the Yukon School of Visual Arts in Dawson City, discussed the role of field trips in his teaching:

[We] go to the Cultural Center and visit with an Elder. This year we visited with Victor Henry, and he showed us a lot of tools that he made, and some of them his mother made, which are in the collection at the Cultural Center. [He showed us one tool that] is made out of pine, and he uses a green spruce stick to tap it, and it has notches all along the way, and you wrap the stick across the other stick and it makes a hollow piece of wood. The Tr'ondëk Hwëch'in used it as a kind of way to walk toward the caribou and it seems to have a hypnotic effect. Victor says you can walk right up to the caribou's nose using this thing. Victor explained that it's the same sound as the rattling of the horns when they are walking. In the classroom I do present a lot of things that are disparate. I leave the explicit explanation about why I'm doing this out. What works is when the connection comes from the student, when they say, "Hey, I get this connection," and usually it's something I didn't even think of, of course. That's the joy, that's the best part of teaching, when the students figure out something.

As in Watts's *Experimental Workshop* and Kaprow's *Other Ways*, students are required to make their own connections between disparate curricular moments; pedagogy therefore shifts from imparting facts to student-led inquiry. In much the same way that Fluxus kits present information through relations and assemblages, the field trip creates spaces for transconnections and new formations to be made.

Lisa Myers (Anishinaabe Ojibway, Beausoleil Nation), an associate professor at York University, Toronto, centers Indigenous knowledges and practices. For example, teaching a course on food, land, and culture, Myers used the Dish with One Spoon Treaty to discuss, from an Anishinaabe perspective, the importance of agreements between humans and nonhumans.[5] This framework, Myers states, lays the groundwork for how to examine food, land, and culture as interconnected. She notes that she is trying "to create a foundation around Indigenous art practice and its place and representation within institutions."

The everydayness of food and the ritual of eating is an important part of Myers's teaching. Myers often shares blueberries with students using small wooden spoons. People eat the berries with the spoons, which subsequently become stained. The spoons become a trace of absorption: stories, food, things we learn and witness. In one iteration of this work, Myers shared blueberries with participants who gathered at OCAD U for a four-hour reading of the Truth and Reconciliation Commission's (2015) Calls to Action. As people read aloud the Calls to Action, Myers invited people to share berries. She states: "We're hearing all of these things which could trigger people, bring up a lot of things for different people depending on who the audience is. . . . The berries were a way to help people in that moment." The berries brought people together. After sharing the berries, Myers collects the spoons and invites participants to sew them onto fabric along with beading. This, she says, becomes a different way to document the event. In her classes she also shares blueberries with her students. "I'll share berries with the students and tell them a story about why berries are significant to me. And then, so, in the act of sharing berries I would tell the story of my grandfather running away from residential school and following a train track to get back home while only living off of blueberries." The blueberries are about more than the act of eating together but about "teaching through storytelling. It's about sharing something that could change the way someone thinks, or change the ways that someone relates to the broader narrative of residential schools." This, she notes, is "an important gesture. It acknowledges feeding someone a thing, beyond yourself. It actually is a part of ceremony that is very important for Anishinaabe people. I'm not proposing that I am doing a ceremony when I am doing it, but it is a gesture that brings people together and I like that part."

Classroom atmospheres, whether centering disability, the politics of representation, or Indigenous knowledges and understandings of land, emphasize a transcorporeality where bodies, both human and nonhuman, become entangled in the pedagogical encounter. In all of the *living archive* conversations, relationality and responsibility were crucial to the ordinariness of teaching. Zoe

Kreye, a Vancouver-based artist who teaches at Emily Carr University of Art and Design in Vancouver, discusses how rather than teaching *about* social practice art (i.e., the history of this practice), her class becomes a social practice artwork. She states, "I was interested in doing social practice rather than talking about it." In the context of Kreye's class, issues relating to the new Emily Carr campus emerged, issues such as the corporatization of the university, gentrification, and the housing and real estate crisis in Vancouver. Many of the weekly exercises inside and outside of the classroom, as well as students' final course projects, intervened into the lived experiences of the campus structure and the physical environment.

For Kreye, having the class function as a work of art becomes an embodied experience. Using somatic exercises, Kreye allowed for student emotions to be present in the class. Like the Fluxus artists who sought to disrupt regulated institutional spaces, Kreye's somatic work "infiltrated the academic setting." The attention to the body and emotions Kreye attributes to the Brazilian artist Lygia Clarke (1920–1988), who created participatory work that enabled viewers to gain a heightened sensory perception, not only of the artwork but also of their relationship to the work and the surrounding environment. Kreye notes that not only does she value participation, relationality, and corporeality in her teaching, she understands art and pedagogy as a kind of healing process. Recognizing that healing is not conventionally addressed in institutions nor in contemporary art, Kreye's class as art facilitates an "unlearning practice": "lessons that one could do that might help unlearn the ingrained ways of being in school." Kreye notes that pedagogically she tries to keep the classroom open to varying situations and group dynamics, to how things evolve and shift as opposed to maintaining a preplanned curriculum and syllabus.

Other ways that classroom atmospheres are rendered malleable is by moving inside and outside of traditional classroom spaces. Lucero's class repurposed a storage room, while Kreye's class used movement exercises, shared meals, happenings, and group reading exercises to unhinge the typical function of a post-secondary classroom. Likewise, Mitchell challenges the boundaries between public and private space. In addition to holding an academic position, Mitchell previously curated and organized events out of the Feminist Art Gallery (FAG), a gallery and collective cofounded by Mitchell and Deirdre Logue that was run out of a garage on their private property in Toronto. Mitchell talks about the blurred or seamless demarcations between her teaching and the work that takes place on campus and in FAG. As a queer space, she notes, it breaks down boundaries between studio, gallery, classroom, private property, and home. In a move away from singular, artistic authorship and private, commodified gallery spaces, FAG insists on polyvocal contributions, where "something private can be lived in a public way."

I want to return to the scene of the score *Proposition #1 (Make a Salad)*. Twenty-five graduate students chopping vegetables, tearing lettuce in a dull, gray-brown classroom in a brutalist university building. The sharp burn of onion in the air. An assignment I have given students numerous times, one modeled after Knowles's score, invites them to teach, in ten to fifteen minutes, something to their classmates so that the teaching is participatory as opposed to didactic. The lessons must be aesthetic, in the sense that they should be bodily, affective, or sensory. They are not lessons on topics related to the course but convey an ordinary curiosity and openness, and perhaps correlate to students' own knowledge or expertise (though they don't have to). The assignment is called "Aesthetic Pedagogies." Students have given break dancing lessons, lessons on how to command a dog in Polish, how to do rhythmic gymnastics with a hoop, how to ferment cabbage, how to ride a unicycle, how to dry oregano, how to catch and identify spiders, and how to make small camping stoves out of paraffin wax. One year we even ventured to the university pool where, while learning synchronized swimming movements, we read laminated pages of the book *Swimming Studies* by Leanne Shapton. The actions are ordinary in their everyday environments, but in the context of a university seminar they become pedagogy in flux; we don't know where they will lead or the relations and assemblages that will be generated, but we do know that they affect intimate and felt encounters. Part Fluxus score, part DIY, the Aesthetic Pedagogies seed conjunctions. Less about imparting knowledge and more about creating a space or encounter of radical relatedness and emergence, the lessons produce new compositions and worldings.

In thinking about the ordinary as radical I want to return to felt. Like the Fluxus score, felt is produced through chance. Even though the process of felting is methodical, one can't predict how the interlocking fibers will fuse. The configuration of wool helices can't be determined in advance. Only through friction, chemical reaction, moisture, and heat do the fibers become entangled. "Felt is a material that takes its especial cohesion from its chaotic constitution, and perhaps more important it is a material enactment and embodiment of elements, tendencies, and forces that cohere most effectively because of, and not despite, the fact that not all strands have the capacity to connect with any or all others" (Thompson 2011, 30). The radical relatedness, the ordinary of felt, is its ability to cohere, or co-compose, without all helices touching each other. Between pressure points, one might say, exists the operational potential for different relations and intimacies to emerge. Felt creates relations that engender variations of encounters where relations don't happen between already knowable and static entities. As an activity, felting, like the score, comes into existence indeterminately. How a score alters a process, how it sets in motion an activation, a something doing, or a reorientation, is at the heart of the ordinary's radicalness. The work of the ordinary is to proliferate endless differing felted helices.

Chapter Four

Anarchiving as Research-Creation

Instant Class Kit

Kits, containers, and boxes have a long history in educational contexts, from early childhood education to museum and gallery programming. Kits provide teachers and students with hands-on resources to explore a particular theme, issue, or historical moment. They can contain lesson plans, toys, manipulatives, models, flip charts, flash cards, and more that aim to supplement the school-based curricula and stimulate experiential and hands-on learning. Referred to as teaching kits, curriculum sets, or school-in-a-box, kits are ubiquitous in most kindergarten to secondary school teaching. In the previous chapter, I introduced Fluxkits, boxed-type publications that contained small objects— scores, booklets, photographs, containers, objects, and other detritus—that were typically housed in an attaché-style case or box. While the majority of the kits were assembled by George Maciunas from a variety of works and materials, there are some, such as Alison Knowles's *Bean Rolls* (1963–1964), that were constructed by a singular artist. One of the box-type kits in the Fluxus archives contains a mock-up for the publication *Proposals for Art Education from a Year Long Study (1968–69)*. The publication documents a year-long experiment into art education curriculum reform at the University of California, Santa Cruz, supported by the Carnegie Corporation of New York. The box contains George Maciunas's original design for the publication, performance instructions, essays, posters, and an envelope labeled "instant class kit." The envelope contains headshots of students and instructors who took part in the year-long art education curriculum reform project. Unfortunately, because the box-style publication was too cumbersome for mass circulation, the publication was later converted into a book-length manuscript.

The kits, according to Hannah Higgins (2002), were to be opened, touched, and rearranged by whoever received them. Activated by an audience or participant, the kit conjured novelty, play, chance, and improvisation. "The boxes," writes Harren (2020, 160), "and the objects they contain give themselves over to the body—disappearing into it, being destroyed by it—at the same time that the body is forced to reckon with its all-consuming, possessive relationship to objects." Yet, the lived, unarticulated traces of bodies and lives are impossible to find in a conventional archive. Further, the Fluxkits are mediated by white gloves and no longer invite play and novelty. In the absence of bodies, affects, and the experiential nature that was at the core of Fluxus practices and pedagogy, the archive remains incomplete and insufficient. Moreover, archives are conditioned by values that center whiteness and erase queer, trans, Black, and Indigenous people and people of color (QTBIPOC). Feminist, queer, antiracist, and anticolonial contributions to archival thought and practice have provoked considerations of the authority given to the archive and what it does (or what it does not) contain.

More recently, the concepts of counter-archiving and anarchiving have been put to use to interrogate what constitutes an archive and the selective practices that continuously erase particular subjects (Thompson 2018; Ware 2017). Unlike static, stable, and linear colonial archives, counter-archives are grounded in accountability and reciprocity. They often emerge from community-based and collaborative processes. Counter-archives build on struggles from the past that continue to impact lives in the present. Further, counter-archives include what is traditionally understood as nonarchivable: affects, bodies, performances, and embodied events—that which is ephemeral and fleeting (Cvetkovich 2003; Springgay and Truman 2017). Counter-archiving and anarchiving practices are political, resistant, and collective. They disrupt conventional narratives and histories and seek ways to engage with matter not typically found in official archives, the affective experiences and lived histories of human and more-than-human bodies.

The question that prompted the historical research into the Fluxus archive—*What does the archive tell us about radical pedagogy of the 1960s and 1970s?*—needed to expand and transform as the research unfolded. By being accountable to the lack of racialized, queer, and trans contributions to the Fluxus archive and responsive to the *living archive* generated by current artist-teachers, different questions began to emerge: *How do we want the archive to function now? What can the archive seed?*

Playfully working with the instant class kit envelope found in the mock-up for *Proposals for Art Education*, and influenced by Fluxkits and other educational kits, my research team and I, along with Vesna Krstich, curated the *Instant Class Kit*. The *Instant Class Kit* is a mobile curriculum guide and pop-up exhibition of fourteen contemporary art projects dedicated to radical pedagogies and social justice. Produced as an edition of four, the kit brings together contemporary curriculum materials in the form of artist multiples such as zines, scores, posters, games, diagrams, newspapers, and other sensory objects. The artist multiples are housed in an archival black box that is 18.5 in. × 14.5 in. × 3 in., with a red vinyl typeface in the style of Maciunas's lettering. The contemporary artists who contributed to the kit desired to deliver a curriculum based on the values of critical democratic pedagogy, antiracist and anticolonial logics, and social justice and to continue the experimental and inventive collaboration that defined Fluxus. The lessons, syllabi, and classroom activities produced by this new generation of artists, many of whom are queer, trans, Black, and Indigenous, address topics and methodologies including queer subjectivities and Indigenous epistemologies, social movements and collective protest, immigration, technology, and ecology.

Curating the *Instant Class Kit* collaboratively, we approached research-creation as a practice of anarchiving committed to queer, feminist, antiracist, and anticolonial frameworks and ways of being and doing. Anarchiving as research-creation becomes a practice of responding to and countering the colonial logic of the archive, while attending to its ephemeral and affective qualities. It is also fundamentally about practicing an ethics based on reciprocity, response-ability, and care that centers relationships to land, human, and more-than-human bodies.

Thinking with the *Instant Class Kit*, this chapter lays out a theoretical framework for anarchiving as indeterminate, as felt, and as response-ability. The chapter commences with a brief discussion of the problems and limitations of conventional archives as repositories of power and ideology. From there, I turn to the practice and theory of counter-archives as a context for how the anarchive functions. Anarchiving is concerned with what it can do in the present-future: it germinates and grows. As such, the anarchive is less a thing than a process or an action. Research-creation as anarchiving—exemplified by the *Instant Class Kit*—becomes a way to distribute and enact radical pedagogy.

The Problem with the Colonial Archive

The collection and creation of an archive is closely linked to the social and political conditions at the time of its creation, as well as to the artifacts and information it contains (Derrida 1995). There are absences, distortions, and limits to a state archive that reflect larger state narratives about citizenship and agency. Imperial and colonial powers have traditionally controlled the archive and influenced the dispersal of history by wielding power through law, the state, order, and regulation (Sekula 1986). David Greetham (1999) argues that what gets included in an archive is reflective of dominant ideologies. For example, Canada's colonial archives have privileged white European settlers' stories and lives (Thompson 2018). Although archives may appear to be built on principles of neutrality and inclusion, they in fact reflect colonial violence. What is included in the archive is selected "to confirm the colonial invention of traditional practices or to underscore cultural claims" (Stoler 2002, 90). According to Greetham (1999, 9) "all conservational decisions are contingent, temporary, and culturally self-referential, even self-laudatory: we want to preserve the best of ourselves for those who follow." Due to this rigidity and the desire for classification and control, anyone lacking authoritative power or differing from the hegemonic group is put in a precarious position. They are either at risk of being written out entirely or of being further marginalized and labeled as deviant. As Cheryl Thompson (2018, 91) argues, "The invisibility of black subjects in Canadian archives has as much to do with past collection practices as it does with present ones. We continue to idealize certain aspects of our collective identity while demonizing others." Archives, Thompson contends, are more than repositories; they serve as technologies of power. They are ideological and political. She writes, "The choices that go into the creation of an archive, such as choosing certain images while excluding others, have implications on what is considered important" (92). Further, while some identities and voices are recorded and made visible in an archive, others are rendered invisible and absent. This is a not simply a matter of what gets collected and preserved but an issue with indexing. Thompson contends, "Where white bodies are named, described, and given agency in the archive . . . black bodies become disembodied, nameless, and/or appear inferentially in the archival record" (93). Syrus Ware (2017) similarly argues that conventional archives regulate what is allowed to be remembered. The archive, he claims, always begins with whiteness. Even queer and trans archives, Ware contends, are marked with erasures of Black and Indigenous lives. He states: "This erasure is part of a larger conceptualization of the black queer subject as a new entity, whose history is built upon an already existing white LGBTTI2QQ space and history" (172). For Thompson (2018), one of the ways to intervene into the logic of the colonial archive is to render the archive itself a subject of interrogation. She writes: "When we begin to think of the archive as subject, it means that we begin to interrogate its structure, its framing, and its contents as being part of the process of the archive, not merely taking archives as they are presented—as a 'source' where we go to 'find' what we are looking for when it comes to a research project" (82). As scholars and artists interrogate and disrupt the colonial archive, many turn to counter-archiving practices.

Counter-archiving and Future Worldings

Counter-archiving is more than a process of diversifying conventional archives. This means it is not simply about adding previously erased or hidden histories to an archive, but a method of interrogating the logic of archives. As Syrus Ware (2017) notes, counter-archiving is a practice of interrupting the whiteness of archives. For Ware, this means disrupting the narrative that Black subjects are new additions to existing archives and insisting that Black lives have always been present. This requires an unlearning and undoing of dominant narratives and cartographies. Cheryl Thompson (2018, 93) writes, "The act of locating black voices, then, requires that researchers become forensic investigators with clairvoyant tendencies. Stated otherwise, we have to not only read between the lines but also sense where black bodies might have been in relation to white bodies."

Counter-archives, according to Jin Haritaworn, Ghaida Moussa, and Syrus Ware (2019, 5), are about imagining "futures beyond displacement and dispossession." As Ware (2017) contends, this necessitates a move from damage-based research to what Eve Tuck (2009) calls a desire-based framework. Desire-based research examines "not only the painful elements of social realities but also the wisdom and hope. Such anaxiology is intent on depathologizing the experiences of dispossessed and disenfranchised communities so that people are seen as more than broken and conquered. This is to say that even when communities are broken and conquered, they are so much more than that—so much more that this incomplete story is an act of aggression" (Tuck 2009, 416).

In a similar way, counter-archives insist on a mode of visibility detached from state-produced documents and narratives. The goal is not "better representation" but to target and disrupt any claims of authority and value over the archive. Counter-archives become practices that are more relevant to lived experiences and histories. For Ware (2017), this means beginning from the position of Black, trans, and queer histories, to reorient how the past-present-future unfolds and to account for the change that is required in the future. Ware discusses the way that conventional white queer and trans archives privilege linear timelines. He contends that Black trans and queer lives operate through a different temporality and different entry points into timelines of resistance. Naming and calling forth QTBIPOC ancestors, Ware recounts the many spaces (academic, municipal, and community-based) where QTBIPOC archives reside and describes the kinds of materials that find their way into such archives: oral histories, banners, artworks, and other ephemera. Maandeeq Mohamed (2018) asserts that the absence of archival materials can leave space for "a recognition of the fact that what is/isn't archived is but one of many fictions (a dominant one to be sure, but still fiction nonetheless) that constitute blackness in public life." Likewise, a number of contemporary artists turn to speculative fiction and performance as counter-archiving practices. Syrus Ware's artistic and activist work is one such example, including his *Activist Love Letters* project (2012–ongoing), which will be discussed further in this chapter. Camille Turner's *Afronautic Research Lab* (ongoing) uses performance and counter-archiving practices to bring participants into an encounter with archival material that reveals the history of anti-Blackness in Canada. The research lab, a dark reading room filled with archival materials such as newspaper ads posted by Canadian slave owners, is attended by Afronauts, space travelers who have traveled back in time to reshape the past and present and point to a better future to come. Turner's performance, like many of her artistic projects, interrogates the logic of the colonial archive that insists that the past is terminated, when in fact the afterlife of slavery and settler colonialism persists. Turner's work allows for continuous activation of a counter-archiving retemporalization, insisting that the continuum between the ancestors, participants, and time-travelers is active, intersubjective, and embodied. The overlooked anti-Black history refuses to be seen as a resolved past but comes to assert an ongoing, lively existence of ancestral presence in opposition to archival erasure or accounting. This not only offers participants an embodied engagement with this particular narrative but invites them to consider employing counter-archiving practices more widely.

Counter-archiving is also about opening up the archive to affects, bodies, performances, and other ephemera not traditionally considered archivable. Alvis Choi (2017) argues that an archive should be understood as living bodies that "requires balancing between academic and community expectations, and forces us to engage in deep reflection, honest communication, and ethical practices of the kind that prefigure the kind of community we wish to be a part of." This means attending to the uncapturability of an event—its lived traces that are embodied in bodies and memories and that cannot be contained or recorded in a text. This requires that we consider the material, vital, and affective tonalities of archives and the ways in which nonhuman entities might constitute an archive of place (Springgay and Truman 2017). For example, Ann Cvetkovich's queer archive of feeling resists coherence in favor of fragmentation; it follows an archiving practice that is illogical, where documents represent far more than the literal value of the objects themselves and are "composed of material practices that challenge traditional conceptions of history and understand the quest for history as a psychic need rather than a science" (Cvetkovich 2003, 268). Although the materials and documents that constitute a traditional archive or a queer archive can be similar, a queer archive of feeling does not fulfill an institutional or official function. A queer archive of feeling is a form of counter–knowledge production, a dynamic that unlocks or liberates the archive. As an archive it is rooted not in a fixed notion of a past but rather in a futurity and urgency, shifting between fields of destruction, subversion, and regeneration. A queer archive of feeling seeks to share the affective tone of a process or event rather than relay strict chronologies or typologies of identification. The affective tone of an event outlives the event. Jess Dobkin's *Wetrospective* at the Art Gallery of York University (AGYU) reperforms the accumulated materials from past performances and performance documentations, rendering them live, affective, and in-the-making. The portable latrines staged as fleshy pink performance vitrines move the archive beyond preservation to reactivations that overflow with sensuality. This shifts the function of the archive. Rather than an archive that encapsulates what happened, the archive creates invitations to reactivate the event's core propositions.

Anarchiving as Research-Creation and Radical Pedagogy

In my research-creation practice I embrace counter-archiving entangled with the immanent techniques of anarchiving. Anarchiving is connected to previous writing on research-creation, which argues for an approach to doing research attuned to speculative middles, (in)tensions, and more-than-representational practices (Springgay and Truman 2017). Like counter-archiving, anarchiving is accountable to an ethics and a politics that is situated, relational, and response-able. Anarchiving means approaching matter from new perspectives in order to uncover unprecedented relationships between the works. Unlike an archive concerned with preservation and coding practices that aid in the retrieval of data, the anarchive aims at stimulating new nodes of production—what I refer to as germination or seeding. While an archive is concerned with an original artwork and its description, anarchives suggest new ways of using and produc-ing new work. Erin Manning (2020, 76) writes that the anarchive is about "generating techniques for sharing the work's potential" beyond documenta-tion and representation.

At the time of writing the grant proposal for *The Pedagogical Impulse* research-creation project, I imagined an exhibition of Fluxus educational interventions. As I noted in chapter 3, there is very limited scholarship on Fluxus curriculum and pedagogy, and most contemporary exhibitions (or reenactments) focus on scores, kits, and documentation of happenings. The confluences of art, research, and teaching that were central to Fluxus work are important precursors to socially engaged art and research-creation. It was crucial that the research have a public component to it that could be further enriched through programming and educational outreach.

However, due to the limitations of archives and the experiential activations necessary to fully grasp Fluxus educational experiments, a conventional exhibi-tion would fail to offer anything substantive. The Fluxus materials we encoun-tered in the archives were further mediated by white gloves and cataloging systems governed by the logic of the archive. Fluxkits and Fluxus editions have become precious, collectible artifacts. But Fluxus materials are meant to be performed and activated in order to fulfill their pedagogical function, not to be displayed as museum artifacts. While there were challenges to obtaining permissions for the loans of archival materials, an even greater disappoint-ment was the realization that the exhibition would be experienced behind glass frames and vitrines. Fluxus practices sought to challenge the mode of reception in which audiences are passive spectators. Rather, the event scores, happenings, and kits sought to infuse knowing through doing. Furthermore, particular sto-ries, histories, and bodies were absent from the Fluxus archives, and many of the overarching themes animated by Fluxus work did not fully resonate with contemporary issues. Taking my cue from contemporary art and curatorial practices of counter-archiving and anarchiving, our questions about radical pedagogy moved and expanded. I wondered: *What if my team and I curated a mobile exhibition that traveled via mail to postsecondary classrooms to be opened,*

P.1. From the residency *Upside Down and Backwards*. The image is of a student holding a round mirror in front of their face reflecting pond reeds (see introduction and chapter 7).

P.2. From the residency *Upside Down and Backwards*. The image is of two students walking with Elinor Whidden's *Rearview Walking Sticks* (see introduction and chapter 7).

P.3. From the residency *Upside Down and Backwards*. The image captures a group of students walking with Elinor Whidden's *Rearview Walking Sticks* along a path (see introduction and chapter 7).

P.4. From the residency *Upside Down and Backwards*. The image is of a student holding a round mirror reflecting the green landscape in front of their face (see introduction and chapter 7).

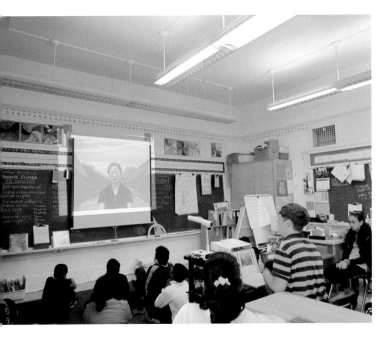

P.5. A slideshow presentation with students in their classroom. The on-screen image is from Jin-me Yoon's *Group of Sixty-Seven* (see introduction).

P.6. From the residency *Upside Down and Backwards*. The image shows students painting color bars (see introduction and chapter 7).

P.7. From the residency *Upside Down and Backwards*. The image depicts Hannah Jickling and Reed Reed with color bars in a red canoe on the Don River (see introduction and chapter 7).

P.8. Students arranging color bars on the beach from the residency *Upside Down and Backwards* (see introduction and chapter 7).

P.9. Color bars arranged on the beach from the residency *Upside Down and Backwards* (see introduction and chapter 7).

P.10. From the residency *Upside Down and Backwards*. The image shows color bars arranged on the edge of the river with reflection (see introduction and chapter 7).

P.11. Juice box color bars arranged on the beach from the residency *Upside Down and Backwards* (see introduction and chapter 7).

P.12. A student drinking from a juice box color bar, from the residency *Upside Down and Backwards* (see introduction and chapter 7).

P.13. Juice box color bars arranged on the beach, from the residency *Upside Down and Backwards* (see introduction and chapter 7).

P.14. A student's hand holding a mirror juice box, from the residency *Upside Down and Backwards* (see introduction and chapter 7).

P.15. Mirror juice boxes on a picnic table, from the residency *Upside Down and Backwards* (see introduction and chapter 7).

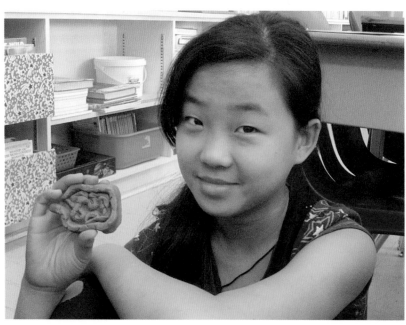

P.16. A student holding a chocolate multiple in packaging, from the project *Ask Me Chocolates* (see chapter 1).

P.17. A student holding two chocolate multiples in packaging, from the project *Ask Me Chocolates* (see chapter 1).

P.18. A student holding an intestine-shaped chocolate multiple, from the project *Ask Me Chocolates* (see chapter 1).

P.19. Chocolate multiples in packages laid out on a table, from the project *Ask Me Chocolates* (see chapter 1).

P.20. An artist offering to trade a retro birthday hat at the community trade fair, from the project *Ask Me Chocolates* (see chapter 1).

P.21. Two packages of garbage carefully displayed, from the *Your Lupines or Your Life* residency (see chapter 1).

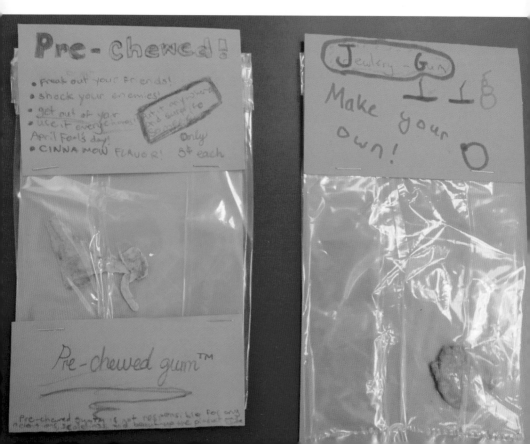

P.22. Found "card with hole" poster on a wooden street pole, from the *Your Lupines or Your Life* residency (see chapter 1).

P.23. Found "balloon knot" poster on a wooden street pole, from the *Your Lupines or Your Life* residency (see chapter 1).

P.24. A student holding their *Abject Award*, from the *Your Lupines or Your Life* residency (see chapter 1).

P.25. A student holding their *Abject Award*, from the *Your Lupines or Your Life* residency (see chapter 1).

P.26. Class photo of students holding their *Abject Awards*, from the *Your Lupines or Your Life* residency (see chapter 1).

P.27. The *Abject Awards*, from the *Your Lupines or Your Life* residency (see chapter 1).

P.28. Three students shooting basketballs in the school gym as part of the project *Walls to the Ball* (see chapter 2).

P.29. Thread Baby trophies and fabric buttons, part of the project *Walls to the Ball* (see chapter 2).

P.30. Two students jumping over the net in the school gym as part of the project *Walls to the Ball* (see chapter 2).

P.31. A student holding the center of the net as part of the project *Walls to the Ball* (see chapter 2).

P.32. Students placing a basketball in the center of the net as part of the project *Walls to the Ball* (see chapter 2).

P.33. Students holding various taxidermy specimens while sitting in a home living room as part of the project *Museum without Entrance* (see chapter 2).

P.34. Cutting the red ribbon as part of the project *Museum without Entrance* (see chapter 2).

P.35. Ribbon-cutting ceremony outside of the lock store, part of the project *Museum without Entrance* (see chapter 2).

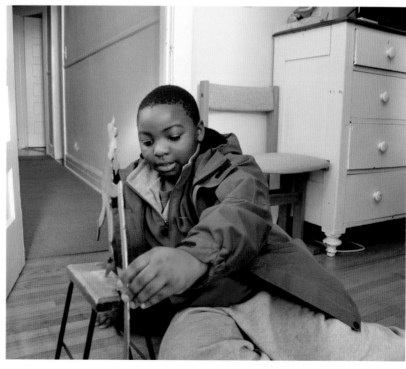

P.36. Three students examining a case of old locks as part of the project *Museum without Entrance* (see chapter 2).

P.37. A student engaging with folk art in a bedroom as part of the project *Museum without Entrance* (see chapter 2).

P.38. Two students singing as part of the *Friday* performance (see chapter 2).

P.39. A student doing a butter dance as part of the Friday performance (see chapter 2).

P.40. *Instant Class Kit* box lid (see chapters 4 and 5).

P.41. The contents of an *Instant Class Kit* (see chapters 4 and 5).

P.42. From the *Instant Class Kit:* Rodrigo Hernandez-Gomez, *Calling,* 2019. Seashell, textile, instructions. Dimensions variable (see chapters 4 and 5).

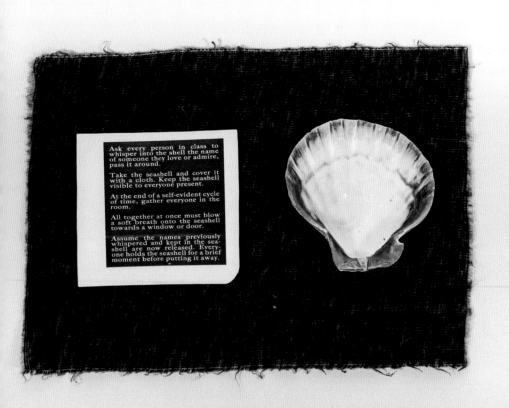

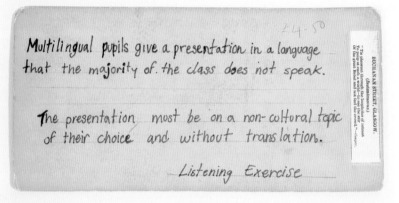

P.43. Rodrigo Hernandez-Gomez, *Listening Exercise*, 2019 (front), permanent marker on found postcard. Dimensions variable (see chapters 4 and 5).

P.44. Rodrigo Hernandez-Gomez, *Listening Exercise*, 2019 (back), permanent marker on found postcard. Dimensions variable (see chapters 4 and 5).

P.45. Jen Delos Reyes, *Phone Sculptures*, 2019, printed cards, acrylic cell phone case. 6 × 3 × .25 inches (see chapters 3 and 4).

P.46. Susan Jahoda and Caroline Woolard, *Making and Being Cards*, 2018, set of 171 cards printed and die cut on card stock with an instruction sheet. Booklet and excerpts from Making and Being Cards. 3.5 × 5.5 × 2 inches (see chapters 6).

P.47. Reed Reed and Hannah Jickling, *Tacky Forms*, 2019, vinyl envelope, prompts, chicle, mastic, and larch resin. 9.5 × 7.5 × 1 inches (see chapters 4 and 5).

P.48. Tania Willard, BUSH *Manifesto*, 2019, laser etched birchbark. Dimensions variable (see chapters 4 and 5).

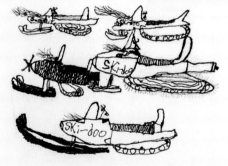

FUTURE SNOWMACHINES IN KINNGAIT

P.49. Anthea Black and Shamina Chherawala, eds., HANDBOOK: *Supporting Queer and Trans Students in Art and Design Education*, 2018, 6 × 9 inches, and Anthea Black, *Keep Queering the Syllabus*, 2019, 16-page zine with hand-stitched binding 7.5 × 4.5 inches (see chapters 4 and 5).

P.50. PA Systems, *Future Snowmachines in Kinngait* and *Resolution*, 2017–2019, self-published book and instructional insert. 11 × 7 inches (see chapters 4 and 5).

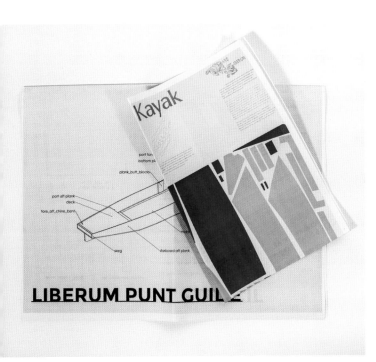

P.51. Elana Mann, *The People's Microphony Songbook*, 2013, newsprint. 9 × 11.5 inches (see chapters 4 and 5).

P.52. The People's Kitchen Collective, *Kitchen Remedies*, 2016, duplicate forms, ingredients, foil pouches, remedy cards. Dimensions variable (see chapters 4 and 5).

P.53. Mare Liberum, *Radical Seafaring Broadsheet*, 2015/2018, reprinted broadsheet with Punt stencils. 22.5 × 33 inches (see chapters 4 and 5).

P.54. *Celebrate People's History* posters, organized by Josh MacPhee, 1988–present, 14 posters, 2-color offset. 11 × 17 inches each (see chapters 4 and 5).

P.55. *Counter with Care* posters and envelopes created by Shannon Gerard and students during Pressing Issues, 2018, 4 posters and envelope, screen print. Posters 17 × 22 inches. Envelope 6 × 9 inches (see chapters 5 and 6).

P.56. *Counter with Care* poster (see chapters 5 and 6).

P.57. *Counter with Care* poster (see chapters 5 and 6).

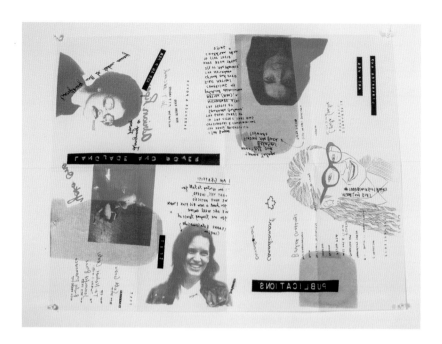

P.58. *Counter with Care* poster (see chapters 5 and 6).

P.59. *Counter with Care* poster (see chapters 5 and 6).

P.60. *Counter with Care* parade with a banner made at the Corita Kent anniversary event (see chapter 6).

P.61. *Counter with Care* parade on the beach with a banner made at the Corita Kent anniversary event (see chapter 6).

P.62. A student working on a banner at the Corita Kent anniversary event (see chapter 6).

P.63. Former students of Corita Kent with ocad u students working on a banner at a long table at the Corita Kent anniversary event (see chapter 6).

touched, smelled, tasted, and activated? How could an anarchive propose a radical pedagogy of the present-future? How might anarchiving seed? As I mentioned in the introductory paragraphs of this chapter it was crucial that the original question transform from, *What does the archive tell us about radical pedagogy of the 1960s and 1970s?*, to, *How do we want the archive to function now?* In the middle of writing this chapter, the question moves further, to, *How does the anarchive seed radical pedagogies and future worldings?*

In what follows, I explore research-creation as anarchiving: as indeterminate transformation, as felt, and as response-ability activated by the kit contents. In the next chapter I return to the kit once more as it circulated to classrooms to be activated by teachers and students. Research-creation as anarchiving is a practice that accumulates and propagates like hand felting. The layers of wool gather and amass, creating something new in the process. The stories that unfold in these chapters demonstrate the ways that research-creation assembles itself as the practice unfolds, in much the same way that Fluxkits and scores generate relations and assemblages that constantly shift the activation and meaning in the process. Research-creation is a practice of middles, of feedback loops and changes in direction. Anarchiving in this sense is about a "feed-forward mechanism for lines of creative process, under continuing variation" (Massumi 2016, 7). Anarchiving is excessive potential, or that which exceeds the knowable.

ANARCHIVING AS INDETERMINATE TRANSFORMATION

Kate Hennessy and Trudy Lynn Smith (2018) use the term *anarchival* as a framework for the transformations that occur over time to archival matter and to address the precarity and loss of the archive (including chemical reactions and insect infestations, to name just a few). The anarchive for them is the possibility of the archives' destruction not as a loss but as a generative force. While entropy is conventionally resisted in the archive, Hennessy and Smith attend to the potential of the anarchive as molecular transformation. Writing about traces of a pastel drawing that had seeped into a manila folder, Hennessy and Smith account for the drawing's lively activities and the new forms of association these material transformations conjure: "Anarchival materialities are these entropic forces of matter—the forces of things curling, catching fire, melting, or escaping. It is the processes of always being in-between—things in the state of transmuting into something else. However, it is also the emergence of the new and unexpected" (142–43). Research-creation as anarchiving "privileges contamination," they write (140). Brett Kashmere (2018, 21) addresses similar concerns about preservation, arguing that "preservation is an outcome of use," where that which is repurposed or created from an archive is most valuable. Counter-archiving, writes Kashmere, is a process of expansion through extrarational connections.

Anarchiving as indeterminate transformation occurs across multiple registers in the *Instant Class Kit*. Three of the four kits traveled by mail throughout North America for just over twelve months until their circulation was halted by the global pandemic. The kits were handled by students and teachers; paper edges were furled, torn, and folded. The piece of birch bark used for Tania Willard's BUSH *Manifesto* was living when it arrived in my university office as the kits were assembled. Moss and living microorganisms clung to the back of the bark. When the kits arrived back in my home office in March 2020, as the pandemic lockdown began, the bark had furled and dried around another object in the kit. The BUSH *Manifesto*, once slightly curved, is now a roll, its edges tightly bound within one another. The archival black boxes that constitute the *Instant Class Kit* are worn and no longer close properly, and the exterior shipping boxes are in tatters. Many of these exterior boxes have been added to, with stickers or notes from students and instructors who activated the kits in their classes. They act as traces, like postage stamps, of where the kits have been; a palimpsest of their circulation. When the kits can go back into circulation, the boxes and the contents will continue the process of anarchiving as indeterminate transformation.

This entropy reflects the ethos of Fluxus work: "There was also the sense," Dick Higgins (1998, 225) writes, "that if Fluxus were to incorporate some element of ongoing change—Flux—that the individual works should change. Many of the Fluxus objects were made of rather ephemeral materials, such as paper or light plastic, so that as time went by the work would either disappear or would physically alter itself. A masterpiece in this context was a work that made a strong statement rather than a work that would last throughout the ages in some treasure vault." Hennessy and Smith argue that these material transformations are significant because they speak to the dynamic and relational ways that humans interact with nonhuman objects. Entropy, they contend, "is the generative force of things breaking down on their way to becoming other things" (2018, 131). Over time, as the kits continue to circulate and are handled by hundreds of students and teachers, the contents—made from paper, fabric, birch bark, spices, a sea shell, and other fragile materials—will continue to show signs of use, where use points at the kinds of germination that occurred. The bodily traces of use, Sara Ahmed (2019) offers, show lives lived and the knowledges they hold. She writes, "A used object preserves a life even after it appears a life has been terminated" (38). The use of the kits brings the bodies of the students and teachers into proximity, mingling with the objects in the kit and with future distributions. When Hennessy and Smith (2018) talk of entropy, they are working with touch, felting encounters. For Ahmed (2019), use is a contact zone that infers maintenance: "to keep something usable requires taking care" (41). The kits remaining useful becomes a form of intimate and public care.

In excess of the physical change that the kits undergo, anarchiving as indeterminate transformation reveals how the kit is activated in the different classrooms. Each of the contributions in the kit invite participation. But the instructions for activation are scores: open-ended, indeterminate, and operative through an aesthetics of chance. When the kits arrive in a classroom they are out of my control. How they are used is indeterminate and iterative. Chance refers to operations where any number of outcomes can happen, that cannot be predicted in advance. Artists use chance mechanisms to establish an initial set of procedures the outcome of which cannot be predicted. As opposed to the idea that chance involves complete spontaneity and chaos, chance aesthetics typically include a degree of structure, similar to research-creation propositions and to the event score. Chance becomes "a way of introducing an element of uncertainty and contingency into the work, but it is not a matter of unbridled spontaneity or sheer chaos" (Iversen 2010, 19). Many of the works in the kit involve event scores. For example, Rodrigo Hernandez-Gomez's *Listening Exercise* instructs as follows: "Multilingual pupils give a presentation in a language that the majority of the class does not speak. The presentation must be on a non-cultural topic of their choice and without translation." Another example is Anthea Black's *Keep Queering the Syllabus*, a sixteen-page zine with hand-stitched binding that contains biographies and information on queer and trans artists. The zine contains information to be activated in class, but how this happens is left open to its activators. What kinds of new activities, projects, and events emerge out of classroom engagements, and how will they contribute to further transformations of the kit contents? Anarchiving practices invite embodied interaction, turning them, as Charles Mereweather (2006, 146) suggests, from "excavation sites into construction sites."

Jen Delos Reyes's *Phone Sculptures* consist of twelve scores printed on paper in the shape of a cellphone and housed in a clear plastic cellphone case. The scores invite students to collectively produce a phone sculpture with their phones at the beginning of class that will remain intact for the duration of the class session. Delos Reyes discusses this scored intervention as a pedagogy that produces multiple connections and entry points into class materials (see chapter 3). The project also functions to remove phones from students' hands and bags in a nonpunitive manner. Indeterminacy was central to Fluxus's scores and enacted a "form of resistance . . . resistance to a prevailing arts culture based on commodification, resistance to prevailing art forms, resistance to social normalisation, resistance to perceptual habitualisation, in essence, resistance to its present" (Sholtz 2018, 251).

Anarchiving is expansive: it seeds and germinates new ideas and new events, and they in turn encourage a practice that expands and becomes more than what is contained in a box. The works *Future Snowmachines in Kinngait* and *Resolution* by PA Systems (Alexa Hatanaka and Patrick Thompson) include a score for participants that is intricately connected to a larger project they have been exploring with youth in Cape Dorset Nunavut. *Resolution* is a score that invokes visualization strategies. It invites the participant to make tangible (through a small sculpture or a drawing) an intangible desire. This score is paired with the booklet documenting an ongoing project with Kinngait youth. Working through a similar score, the youth created small snowmobiles out of Play-Doh which were then 3D printed and enlarged into aluminum sculptures. The sales of these sculptures fund a youth leadership program which has purchased real snowmobiles for the community. The score alchemically turns desires into functional and needed machines. The indeterminacy of the score in the kit enables ordinary relations and assemblages to emerge that are deeply committed to a radical relatedness that is accountable and responsible to anti-oppression. Indeterminacy is about a contingent and unknowable future but one that is possible if we find ways to resist or disrupt the present (Sholtz 2018).

The opening of the kits is an important part of their indeterminacy: lifting the lid, unpacking the contents, making connections between objects and concepts, smelling, tasting, choosing what to tune in to, what to touch and hold, finding what repels you. Indeterminacy does imply a positive or comfortable relationship to chance. Often the contents unnerve students, forcing them to confront what they have previously understood as art, pedagogy, and knowledge. How the contents are assembled or put in relation each time unfolds uniquely. There is a liveness to the kit and its content; the objects move and breathe, they germinate and grow, ever expanding their modes of operation and activation. Disregarding the rules of archiving, the kits invite touch, they exude a kind of physical open access, they are free (my grant paid for their circulation), and they remix and improvise the Fluxus archive. As a practice of anarchiving, the kits rely on their circulation; otherwise they become hermetically sealed and die. As the pandemic raged across the globe, resulting in the suspension of in-person teaching, my collaborator Andrea Vela Alarcón took the lead in developing a series of ten online, self-guided, scored activations.

Available on the research website with accompanying readings, actions, and discussion points, the kits continue to be opened virtually. Although this removes the tactile nature of the kit, the provocations through the online scores become yet another indeterminate part of their transformation.

ANARCHIVING AS FELT

Many works in the *Instant Class Kit* activate nonvisual senses, including sound, touch, and smell. *Kitchen Remedies*, a work by The People's Kitchen Collective (Sita Kuratomi Bhaumik, Jocelyn Jackson, and Saqib Keval), invites participants to bring the stories, traditions, and wisdom of our elders and ancestors into the kitchen. Small pouches with food ingredients ask activators to smell and to put their noses and memories to work. For example, one pouch contains "sugar tit," a familial name for a baby pacifier made by placing a spoonful of honey in a small piece of cloth and then gathering the cloth around the honey and twisting it to form a bulb. The collective seeks remedies for everything from upset stomachs to the patriarchy (because we know that these are, in fact, connected). Ingredients hold stories of our resilience. In the face of oppressive systems such as white supremacy, capitalism, patriarchy, the prison industrial complex, and police violence, healing ourselves is an act of self-determination. Through the act of healing we feel the strength of those who have come before us. *Kitchen Remedies* includes four cards corresponding to four remedies from The People's Kitchen Collective. Open a container and pass it around. Read the matching remedy card. What does it smell like? Are the remedies familiar or unfamiliar? Is there a sensation or feeling evoked with each remedy?

Writing about queer archives of trauma, Cvetkovich (2003, 7) maintains that an archive of feeling is "an exploration of cultural texts as repositories of feelings and emotions, which are encoded not only in the content of the texts themselves but in the practices that surround their production and reception." *Kitchen Remedies* operates via this turn to affect and sensation, albeit not those exclusive to queer cultures, with food as the medium for memory and knowledge. Julietta Singh, in writing about the creative capacities of archives, ponders her own body as "a messy, embodied, illegitimate archive" (2018a, 27). I read Singh's introspections in line with anarchiving practices that become "a way of thinking-feeling the body's unbounded relation to other bodies" (29). Moreover, as she contends, these anarchiving affects are always partial and incomplete, never becoming representative of "her core." Anarchiving as affective recognizes the instability and the limits of knowability, its porosity. Singh reminds us that normative digestion is informed by colonial legacies; anarchiving as embodied therefore becomes a way to conceive of antiracist and anticolonial ways of affecting and being affected. Singh (2018b) insists that archives are more than brick-and-mortar repositories of matter: a body of literature is an archive, a literature review, a comprehensive field of study, a stack of books, a syllabus, a digital hard drive of data. A body—porous, entangled, the flesh of the world. Singh's words are significant because they remind us that everything is an archive—that whether or not you do research in an actual archive or with archival materials, you are in effect archiving (or hopefully counter-archiving or anarchiving).

The body as an anarchive is palpable in Reed Reed and Hannah Jickling's *Tacky Forms*, a series of chewing gum scores that invite participants to explore the sensory qualities of raw gum materials. They are encouraged to transform gum into an art material and create sculptural forms using tongue, cheeks, and teeth, using *mouth feel*. Luring participants to smell and taste raw ingredients, these ingredient-based projects encourage participants to consider the nose and the mouth as important organs of knowledge-making. The sense of viscerality is constructed through the juxtaposition of desire and repulsion—the raw gum has an unexpected and, for many chewers, an unpleasant taste. Chewing gum and then creating sculptural objects from it, mixing saliva and raw material—particularly in the context of a classroom—conjures up the disgust of fingers finding the chewed pieces of gum commonly stuck to the underside of desks or the regulation that prohibits gum in schools. Collectively—as multiple participants gather and create these gum-objects—there is a mingling of bodily fluids, further accentuating the visceral and the corporeal. This is part of the intimacy of these projects, their ability to put bodies in proximity in ways that might suggest desire but perhaps also the repulsion of playing with food-saliva-body. Instead of being presented with a direct body—the body of the artist, the body of the other—participants enter into contact with bodies via ingredients. Exposed to multisensory experiences—biting, chewing, and inhaling—the anarchive shapes a felt encounter with the materiality of what goes into our bodies, bodily archives of memories and the environments that raw ingredients come from. Eating and smelling, writes Elspeth Probyn (2000, 17), conjoins us in a network of the edible and inedible, the human and non-human, the animate and the inanimate. As The People's Kitchen Collective makes clear, and as is discussed in greater detail in chapter 1, eating is as much about sustenance as it is about power.

Reed and Jickling's work with elementary school students using chocolates and candy was explored in chapter 1 as a matter of taste, where children determine the materiality of tastemakers. I work with particular artists over many years and on many different projects and events; anarchiving practices are forged through long-term relationships and a sense of collectivity that is nurtured by the various research-creation events, but also the ways that such multiply mutating projects activate pedagogy in flux and as an impulse.

The People's Microphony Songbook by Elana Mann and an additional twenty-two contributors marks another sensory contribution to the anarchive. While the songbook is a paper-based broadsheet printed on newsprint, it enacts an auditory score that centers political listening. The resistance songs in the songbook are inspired by the People's Microphone, a human technology that enables public speakers at large activist assemblies to be heard without the use of electric amplification. The songs explore the human voice as material, political, and sensorial through various scores that amplify human and more-than-human sounds. Questions the songbook engages include *What does it mean to listen and to speak in times of polarization? What are the implications of repeating someone else's utterances out loud? How does the act of repetition through different and multiple bodies affect meaning? What happens when vocal sounds outside of language are introduced?* In the introduction to the songbook Mann writes that the many global uprisings of the past two decades function as both "protest and active listening sessions." The movements amplify voices that are silenced, occluded, and not heard. The People's Microphone, she writes: "expresses the inter-related desires of collective and individual voices to speak and be heard, to hear one's words spoken back through different mouths, and to digest someone else's word through one's own body." Once again, the mouth is positioned as an integral part of art, activism, and learning. But the significance of the microphone is about more than mere amplification through the mouth; it is also about critical and attentive listening through the ear. The songbook embodies not only amplification but active listening.

Both the songbook and Hernandez-Gomez's *Listening Exercise* animate listening. Both of these works trouble what Dylan Robinson (2020) would call settler modes of perceptual legibility. Settler listening, he writes, is part of normative, neutral positioning that structures the civilizing mission of the nation-state. He argues that resisting forms of hungry listening involve listening to sound but also to the situated and historical context, while accounting for our own listening privilege and aesthetic habits. Listening differently recognizes how listening has become fixed and often goes unnoticed. Undoing settler modes of listening and legibility requires that we collectively become "aware of normative listening orientations across a range of gendered and racial formations" (60). This, Robinson contends, "holds potential for listening otherwise" (60). One way of doing this otherwise is to intervene into the norms of the concert hall and include spaces of intimate listening, listening in relation to the land, where listening becomes actively engaged in critical forms of engagement. "In re-orienting our listening practices from normative settler and multicultural forms to the agonistic and irreducibly sovereign forms of listening, we must also reconsider what we think we are listening to" (45–46). *Listening Exercise* reorganizes our listening privileges and habits and emphasizes the responsibility of listening to difference. This is what Robinson calls "oscillating between layers of listening positionality" (61). Robinson's work is also important in the context of feltness, in that he underscores the problematic nature of a shared affective response to artistic work. He notes that affect can be used to suggest a "connective tissue" between performers and audience (205). While affect can be a powerful means by which art effects positive change, it is not enough simply to foster empathy or raise consciousness in non-Indigenous audiences. Such empathic practices are consumptive and crude and result in foreclosed resolution. Rather, what is needed are affects with political efficacy. This, he claims, means "moving beyond the position of intergenerational bystanders," making room for conflict and the recalcitrant (232). This requires moving beyond forms of inclusion to a more critical act of listening and witnessing, where the spectator and participant are not calcified by empathy but called to work through the complex field of affect.

ANARCHIVING AS RESPONSE-ABILITY

I begin this final section of the chapter with Rodrigo Hernandez-Gomez's score *Calling*. It is a palm-sized seashell wrapped in a thick piece of brown fabric, with an accompanying score printed on a piece of a record album. The first line of the score reads, "Ask every person in class to whisper into the shell the name of someone they love or admire, pass it around."

Imagine you are holding the shell, or perhaps you have an object that holds a particular personal story near you that you can hold. Whisper a name. Hold that name (in)tension for the remainder of the chapter.

Caring for the kits as they move from ideation to assemblage to circulation requires ethical and political response-abilities and obligations. It requires, like a name whispered, that we hold (in)tension the ways we are in relation to each other, to consider that not all relations are equal or neutral, and to actively work to create more just relations. *Calling* normalizes the practice of bringing ancestors and loved ones into the space. It requires that participants consider kinship ties and inheritances. Whispering a name, positioning ourselves in relation to our ancestors and to the places where we are from, is an exercise in intergenerational response of who we are in relation to land. Donna Haraway (2016) reminds us that stories do more than tell particular narratives.

Stories matter, and what stories are told matters, and being accountable to stories compels us to think otherwise about our relation to those stories and to what new stories can be told differently. Loveless (2019) similarly asserts that the kinds of research stories we tell create alternative worlds. The crafting of research—questions, theories, practices, experiments, art—is the crafting of stories, which in turn is "the crafting of an ethics" (Loveless 2019, 25). To tend to, become attentive to, be tender with, listen to, bend into, share through, and be accountable to collaboration and exchange—these are just some of the ways anarchiving is response-able. Practically and quite literally, tending and reciprocity entail legal contracts, payment for artist work and services, and proper citations. This ethics means being accountable to teachers' labor and to the burden of time. It also demands, when artists and artistic practices are brought into classroom spaces, particularly in spaces absent of critical conversations about the art market and representation, that these conversations happen, that students and teachers understand how their engagements with works of art become artworks that circulate publicly, and that they are given the opportunity to determine how and through what means that happens. The ethics of anarchiving requires material relations beyond institutional ethics requirements, which necessitate different practices in different contexts as opposed to a one-size-fits-all consent form. Sometimes, in the context of my own work, I share with students ongoing research-creation activities from *The Pedagogical Impulse*. This action situates what they are being asked to do within the context of a larger project on radical pedagogy and art. In other circumstances, students and teachers negotiate how and where their contributions to the project might appear and in what form. While their signatures on institutional ethics forms are necessary, they are simply not enough if we prioritize caring. As Martin, Myers, and Viseu (2015, 635) write, "If we were to hover in the moments before a researcher secures an object to care about, we would encounter an open field of potentialities—indeterminate subjects and objects, and expansive possibilities for forms and temporalities of response. To stay in this space is not to refuse to care, but to slow care down, to expose and to question the self-evidences that would otherwise prescribe its proper objects, as well as its seemingly necessary directions, temporalities, intensities, and forms of action." Assembling the kit was a collective labor: Amy Meleca coordinated communication with the invited artists, Vesna Krstich was in dialogue with the artists about the parameters of their submissions, Shannon Gerard designed and applied the red vinyl text on the kit box lid and designed and printed the accompanying newsprint publication, Andrea Vela Alarcón photodocumented the contents, and Anise Truman managed the circulation and lending of the kit. James Miles developed teacher resources on Fluxus, and the entire team workshopped the kit with Toronto high school teachers and the general public at numerous events. These graduate students, along with Sara McLean, Aubyn O'Grady, Christine Jackson, and Emmanuel Rutayisire, wrote and prepared four papers for a conference panel on radical pedagogy, three of which saw their way to publication. This matters. The debt I owe to the contours of collaboration, and to the students whose ideas, theoretical guidance, and nurturance are felted throughout these pages, exemplifies academic care networks par excellence.

Destabilizing whiteness and ableism are also necessary parts of care work. As a white settler scholar, it is important that I not only approach the research-creation events and projects by centering anti-oppression; I must also consider how I enter a classroom or school, what work I need to do to be invited in, and how to be there. How can I be a good guest? This entrance typically means time spent getting to know artists, teachers, or classroom spaces long before the research-creation begins. I also ask, What can I do to reciprocate or what can I offer in return? The reciprocity must be something desired, not something I have predetermined as valued. I have been asked to guest-teach, to compile some of the documentary photographs to gift to participants, to share a meal, to provide training and support to teachers, to show up for events beyond my research at schools, and to provide materials that are often much-needed in public schools. I have reviewed and helped assemble portfolios to apply for art school. I have assisted in filling out grant applications and school applications. I have invited participants from the projects to present with me at international conferences, funding their travel, so that I don't speak on their behalf. I have organized social events and chaperoned youth events. These networks of care, as Leah Lakshmi Piepzna-Samarasinha (2018, 46) states, entail a rewriting of what care means beyond a "one-size-fits-all" approach. In other words, care must be responsive.

The concept of care surfaces in Hernandez-Gomez's contributions to the kit (he contributed four interconnected objects). *Museum without Entrance* and *Class Feedback* instruct participants to teach art history from an Indigenous perspective or to visit the homes of informal collectors. *Class Feedback* is presented on amate, a Mexican-Indigenous type of paper that is typically painted with birds and other natural elements. In this instance the amate is painted in gold with text that states:

THIS YEAR OUR ART HISTORY SHALL BE COMMITTED TO:

1 ART BY NON ELITE WOMEN

2 INDIGENOUS ARTISTS

The paper scroll is interconnected with his ongoing project *Museum without Entrance*, discussed in chapter 2, where students take field trips to experience a personal collection. This project works to decenter and decolonize cultural knowledge and museums while also prioritizing visiting and relations of care. Aryn Martin, Natasha Myers, and Ana Viseu (2015, 630) remind us that "an attention to matters of care remains open-ended and responsive: one does not know in advance where this attention will lead." Tending and reciprocity simultaneously demand that we consider the noninnocent histories in which care circulates. To engage with care as innocent, or as an ameliorative good, only reinforces the ways that care already operates via capitalism, settler colonialisms, and other hegemonic structures (Murphy 2015). Situating how and why we care means "paying attention not only to acts of care but also to the very conditions of possibility for care" (Martin, Myers, and Viseu 2015, 635). As an anarchiving practice the kits set in motion this attention to care: *What kinds of care webs are germinated and accounted for?*

Syrus Ware's *Activist Love Letters* is similarly committed to such an ethics of care. A project that Ware created, and which has been performed in a number of galleries and spaces internationally, asks participants "to think about their role in sustaining a movement and supporting their communities." Inspired by the powerful and often hidden letters that activists and organizers have sent to each other—words of support and encouragement, words of rage and fear, cautions and inspirations alike—this project asks you to consider your own activism and that of the people you hold dear. The project asks, "If you could reach out to one person who moves you by what they do, who would it be? What would you say?" Included with a set of love letter scores are ten letters that have previously been shared between activists, short biographies of forty QTBIPOC activists, and a playlist of activist music. As a counter-archiving or anarchiving project, the letters, writes Ware (2020b, 284), "tell of a deep, intersectional knowing that can inform our understandings of our own lives today, direct our future activism, and help us build stronger communities rooted in care and justice."

In an interview with Ware (2019), Monica Forrester, and Chanelle Gallant, the three activists use the framework of an interview conversation as a counter-archival or anarchival practice. In addition to supplementing existing archival materials on queer and trans sex worker activism in Toronto, the interview, like *Activist Love Letters*, is grounded in lived experiences and personal narratives. The activism of the 1960s and 1970s is brought into the present-future through what Forrester calls a collective "mapping of lives" (Ware 2019, 42), or what I would refer to as a *living archive*. Similarly, the love letter project is about connecting through real and speculative writing to different people and about sharing in the response-ability of what that connection means. Ware asks people to mail the letters to the intended activists and to consider the kinds of actions of solidarity and care the writer will take in their own life. Gallant insists that this reciprocity and response-ability is paramount for white cis people: "You must really, actually, in concrete ways, support the leadership of poor and working-class trans women of colour around the work that they're doing, whether they're innovating the work or resourcing the work. . . . And then the other piece I see is really having those conversations and building up the capacity of other white cis folks to do that work as well, so that it is not left for trans people of colour to do" (Ware 2019, 44). The letter writing project proposes thinking beyond appreciation and thanks for activist labor and taking up the work and the response-ability it entails. In writing to activists, participants are asked to think about their own role in their community and in anti-oppression. The letters engender what the Care Collective (2020, 33) calls "promiscuous care," which can "multiply the numbers of people we can care for, about, and with, thus permitting us to experiment with the ways we care." When care shifts from an individual act to one that privileges interdependence and alternative kinship structures, "promiscuous care is an ethics that proliferates outwards to redefine caring relations . . . that remain experimental and extensive by current standards" (41).

Care, in the context of anarchiving and the kit, includes tending to the objects contained in the box, the contributors, and the participants and activators, while also expanding webs of care to the questions, issues, and lives that the objects and the kit summon. Part of the nature of the score is that it does not provide complete didactic information on a topic. Take, for instance, *Class Feedback*. The provocation is mobilized by the score, but curriculum content and pedagogical encounters become the work—the activism—performed by the class. The object asks: *What kinds of infrastructures are needed to care? What would need to be transformed in a school to do what this score asks?* Perhaps a way to think about this is through the form and practice of the anarchive. It's in the anarchive that the ethical and political work emerges, not just in the content. The point is not that it is a box full of QTBIPOC artist objects but that the anarchive challenges participants to do something with that, to do better, to care.

Of course, part of the indeterminacy of the kit is that such criticality might not happen. It can't be predicted or known in advance. It does, however, open up the possibilities for something more than what teaching and schooling has become. The kit creates cracks, tears, and slippages where touching and felting relations can flourish. This is what Irit Rogoff (2010a) calls *criticality*, the recognition of the limits of one's thought, the risk of not knowing or being able to articulate what that means. Part of criticality is giving up known methods, or the certainty by which one tackles a problem.

While many of the objects in the kit question institutional spaces, Tania Willard's (Secwepemc) BUSH *Manifesto*, which in the kit is etched into a piece of living birch bark, asks how gallery systems, institutional spaces, and art practices might be transformed by Indigenous knowledges, aesthetics, and land use. Willard (2019, 189) notes that land art, as an art form, is typically attributed to white male artists and often described as pioneering or avant-garde. Settler art histories replace Indigenous art practices. Indigenous peoples, she writes, "have been making 'Land Art' since time immemorial." She writes, "Art is one of these great forces, imagining impossible futures for disappeared bodies, languages, and generations. In my own practice of Land Art, land *is* art: an interconnected power to create, imagine, and make real connections to the world, as well as to those who fly and those who swim, in an ever-expanding stitch that coils us all together" (190). Land, writes Sandra Styres (Mohawk), is more than simply a geographical place for Indigenous peoples: it is "spiritual, emotional, and relational; Land *is* experiential, (re)membered, and storied; Land *is* consciousness—Land *is* sentient" (2019, 27). These ideas comprise what Styres calls "Land as pedagogy." This pedagogy, Styres insists, is deeply entwined with understanding and acknowledging whose ancestral lands we are on, our relationship to that place, and the work we are doing to understand the stories and knowledges contained within those lands. Styres emphasizes the importance of stories for Indigenous peoples but also for non-Indigenous students and teachers in grappling with their own place on the land and their part in ongoing colonial violence. This intimate process of coming to know one's own story in relation to land is an important part of what Styres calls "literacies of land," which represent one thread within the praxis of decolonial education. Willard's contribution to the kit enacts what Leanne Betasamosake Simpson (Michi Saagiig Nishnaabeg) calls "acts of resurgence." Simpson (2014) identifies practices that reinvest Indigenous ways of being and regenerate knowledge traditions as important parts of decolonization. The BUSH *Manifesto* is attuned to the land as it cares for past and future ancestors. As a nonhuman material, the birch bark brings the living, breathing land into the classroom. Peeling bark, Willard (2019, 196) writes, "is an act of intimacy, stripping back rough bark, revealing smooth, wet inner bark the color of stored sunshine, which it records in its rings, a memory of life on the land." The faint trace of a mossy scent still caresses me when I open a kit.

Anarchiving Seeds

Anarchiving is a practice that orients the curatorial goals of the research-creation project, its theoretical framework, and it informs the circulation and use of the kit in educational contexts: anarchiving as research-creation and as radical pedagogy. The circulation of the kits is crucial; without it the kit loses its anarchiving potential and becomes a static object. In circulating the kit via mail (made possible through my research funding), the mobile exhibition and curriculum performs a form of open access. Distribution as lending foregrounds movement and circulation, and it removes research from behind academic paywalls. Research-creation as a generative research practice often folds research activities into knowledge mobilization, which then becomes a different research event. The normative, linear method of doing research is blurred in favor of a felted and fused approach, where research activity and dissemination are imbricated with one another. Another way that the kit performs its openness is by being available for anyone to use, regardless of prior knowledge of or expertise with the contents, the history of Fluxus, or discourses of contemporary art. Writing about the Interference Archive, a community archive in Brooklyn, New York, dedicated to cultural production and social movements, Gordon et al. (2016) insist that what makes their archive radical is its open access. Rather than being defined by radical content, the archive is radical because of how it functions, who has access to the collection, and its public-facing programming. Being able to open boxes and search through the collection with hands rather than through a computer renders circulation intimate and relational.

Where these kits find a permanent home once their circulation has ended will also require an aspect of openness. University libraries have expressed interest in the kits, but institutional lending models would prohibit the kits from being handled or circulated to classrooms. In the meantime, when the pandemic shuttered the world, the kits were made accessible via the research website.

Anarchiving is about keeping the archive open. Anarchiving as a research-creation practice and as radical pedagogy is concerned with the event of research, an affective and indeterminate process under continuous variation and intensity. Each anarchiving moment triggers a new event and new chance encounters. The kit, unlike its name, did not happen in an instant: after years of labor in the archives and seeding the *living archive* conversations, the kits took a year to curate and assemble and then spent more than twelve months circulating and anarchiving new modes of existence, relations, and encounters. *Instant* is most commonly used to denote an infinitesimal unit of space and time, something immediate or direct; it also infers a nearness, something pressing, an urgency. The instant is the nearness, the feltness of the anti-oppressive work and radical pedagogy that is urgently needed in educational spaces.

Shout the name of your ancestor or loved one. Call their name and inheritance into the room. Find your own way in connection to the land.

Chapter Five

Conditions of
Feltness

Education has a love affair with quantitative capture, assessment, and met-rics. This capture is predicted and can be calculated in advance. Credibility rests on proof and impact. This infatuation requires teachers and researchers to procedurally plan and predict outcomes in advance of inquiry. Bodies of knowledge, literature reviews, and disciplinary frameworks must be identified, rationalized, and consumed. This obsession has been named *methodocentrism* (Snaza and Weaver 2015), *cognitive capitalism* (Rogoff 2010b), or *proceduralism* (Manning 2016) and is predicated on knowability and legibility (Lather and St. Pierre 2013; Maclure 2013) and on the continued emplacement of settler futurity (Tuck and McKenzie 2015). Against the logic of mastery, knowability, and predictability are incipient research practices that are propositional and in constant movement. Previously I have argued that we need to event research through speculative middles that insist on immanent and emergent modes of thinking-making-doing (Springgay and Truman 2018). Speculative middles can't be known in advance and shape a way of inhabiting the world. Additionally, (in)tensions arise in the speculative middle and attune to the *how* of the event. (In)tensions are the ethical-political responsibilities and concerns that become vectors and catalysts for new speculative middles to emerge. Propositions, movement, speculative middles, and (in)tensions counter extractive research methods and insist on conditions that are indeterminate, propositional, and nascent. Natalie Loveless (2019) hints at something adjacent when she asks, *What does the work solicit?* The kind of research-creation practices she finds most compelling, particularly in this moment of global crisis, are those that make knowledge emerge at the level of form (method or process), not content. Irit Rogoff (2010b) takes a different stance, albeit with similar intentions, when she states that artistic research should be less concerned with format and instead turn toward the knowledge formations that the work elicits. In relation to the Educational Turn, Rogoff (2010b) argues that the focus should not be on artistic and visual renditions of school-like formats but rather on the circulation of knowledges that vector and agitate. The discursive coming-together, she contends, should not be the focus of the work; it should be the knowledges that emerge in the midst of that taking-form. Both Loveless and Rogoff acknowledge the significance of worlding, of creating more just and liveable worlds, as a condition of research-creation.

This chapter engages with various activations of the *Instant Class Kit* in postsecondary classrooms and the various conditions of feltness that opening and unboxing the kit enables. Three of the kits circulated by mail to more than a dozen postsecondary classrooms, five Toronto secondary schools, and a number of art institutions, academic conferences, and workshops.[1] Instructors activated the kits in their classrooms in various ways and for different periods of time. Some classes used the kit minimally, while others built an entire course around the kit. After instructors had worked with the kit, we recorded a conversation together, and in some instances student work (writing and images) was shared with me digitally. It became apparent that the kits created particular *conditions of feltness* for radical pedagogy to emerge. Because conditions intervene into disciplines and capture, they vector and seep, much like anarchiving discussed in the previous chapter. Rogoff (2010b) argues that we need to think of education, the circulation of knowledge, as a vector "made up of both direction and magnitude." In this way the opening and unboxing of the kit contents continues the anarchiving practice of germination, spilling out as vectors of new anarchives and new knowledges. But this germination is not about form or content but conditions. Here again I think with Tina Campt (2017, 5) and her use of the sonic as a method that "opens up radical interpretive possibilities." Conditions are material, live, affective, vibrational, and propositional and they felt pedagogy, research-creation, and knowledge-in-the-making. Conditions create spatiotemporal openings to widen our attentions and to tune into the *how* of research-creation. Conditions interrogate what art or research-creation *does* as a way of being in the world. Conditions affect how we come together in relations in response to something urgent; an impulse that requires situated and accountable responses. Conditions shift research-creation from content to anarchiving incipient form.

Rather than use conventional subheadings, chapter sections are introduced by a score from the *Instant Class Kit*. Scores emphasize chance and improvisation, but they also engender the specific condition of feltness discussed in each subsection. Scores anchor the investigation differently. They are not direct procedural instructions but offer different entry points and urgencies. Scores activate conditions and perform material intimacy between the many multiples, artists, students, ecologies, and knowledges.

Tacky Forms
JICKLING AND REED

In elementary schools, quick hits of sensation are smuggled into classrooms while the brain gets trained. Fuzzy pens, all kinds of slime, DIY balls made with balloons and sand, flip-sequin EVERYTHING. In other words, anything to keep texture moving and improving through the hands of kids in an otherwise cerebral environment. Chewing gum is a sensory anchor that is restricted, if not banned. It's messy, it's sticky, it's loud—a prohibited substance circulated in seductive packaging, a non-nutritive conduit for outrageous flavours. We have included three plant-based gums for you to experience. Try one, mix and match.

The kit as a physical object to be opened, touched, and shared presented students and teachers with multiples, concepts, and sensory experiences not typically part of postsecondary seminar classrooms. While arts classes do involve touching materials by hand, the orientation is toward the manipulation of materials into a form and is less about what or how touch propagates. Contrasting against the backdrop of an increasingly digitized teaching space, the ability to touch and in some cases smell and taste the contents of the kit provoked an intimate and sensory way of coming to know different artists and issues. The condition of touch, one instructor noted, was significantly different from opening websites or working on a Google Doc. The tactility and immediacy of the kit created a space of generosity as students opened the box, took out individual items, examined them, and passed them around.

Touch infers tactility and contact. It is often set in opposition to the intellect and the mind as a bodily or intuitive form of knowing (Springgay 2008). Such binary thinking means that what or how touch matters has rarely been attended to in education, where the docile and regulated body is rewarded. But touch is complex. As a form of proximal mediation it is socially, culturally, and intersectionally experienced. Touch invokes intimacy and care but also violence and harm. In touching, one is simultaneously touched; there is a multiplicity in touching encounters with vibratory sensations that seep and flow. Touch instantiates transcorporeality, rendering material and affective entanglements in a felted, fleshy mesh. Touch is a conceivable and concrete expression, but it can also be imperceptible and imply proximity that can be felt but not measured. Touch generates and intensifies affects opening a body to another. Touch forms our immediate, everyday experiences and yet has been afforded little attention in relation to socially engaged art and research-creation. In thinking about touch in the context of the kit and art as pedagogy, I want to examine how touch matters, what conditions it seeds.

The texture of the birch bark (in Tania Willard's BUSH Manifesto), an instructor remarked, was an unexpected presence in the kit; its liveness and peaty smell was startling and curious. Natalie Loveless (2019) insists that curiosity is central to research-creation and can't be planned for or known in advance. Curiosity is a condition of being displaced (ignorance) and of coming to know something simultaneously, "the condition of knowledge making at its best" (47). Curiosity is bodily: one moves affectively toward a multiple in the kit, seeking out its contours and provocations. Touch is about being open to a curious encounter, to the coming to know something transcorporeally as feltness.

The textures of the kit mingle with the textures of our fingers and hands, creating a kind of skin knowledge (Howes 2004). And while we touch all kinds of things in our daily lives, and certainly in school, rarely do we tune into these skinscapes, or what Taina Kinnunen and Marjo Kolehmainen (2019) refer to as "touch biographies." Touch, they write, "constitutes bodies and their affective interconnectedness" (34). Touch biographies are affective accounts of diverse experiences of being touched. Touch biographies, Kinnunen and Kolehmainen contend, "highlight the intercorporeal and trans-subjective aspects of (human) life, and decenter the idea of autonomous individual subjects" (50). Using the method of touch biographies to explore Black women's material and affective experiences with black hair, Sweta Rajan-Rankin (2021) writes that theories of touch and intimacy often privilege a form of closeness predicated on Western values of heteronormativity and belonging. In contrast, she argues, we need theories of touch and intimacy that are situated, culturally coded, and accountable to diverse subjectivities. Touch, she states, can be "intimate, nurturing or laced with hostility" (162). Tuning into the materiality of touch demands that we consider the context, temporality, and memories of such affective registers. These kinds of situated touch biographies surfaced in the encounter with *Tacky Forms*, the multiple created by Hannah Jickling and Reed Reed.

This object pushed the affective and sensory dimensions of the kit to a limit. The natural and raw gum materials in the multiple—chicle, mastic, and larch resin—both enticed students and repelled them. Inviting students to sculpt with tongues, teeth, jaw, and cheeks, *Tacky Forms* invites a bodily and touching pedagogy that is distinctly unfamiliar in taste and in execution. For some students, the tastes evoked bodily memories of chewing mastic with their grandfather or associations with comfort food like a plum. Others wanted to spit out the gum, warning their classmates not to try it because of its strange and pungent taste. These taste experiences created conditions for discussion on the politics of taste (see chapter 1) that extended to packaging, consumer culture, and capitalism. Interestingly there was also resistance to *Tacky Forms*, as students questioned how this multiple was considered art, or how it related to pedagogy; it became imponderable. Classrooms are rarely places where we learn through our mouths and our bodies, and *Tacky Forms* is unsettling therefore because it invites you to use a bodily organ to seek information. *Tacky Forms* poses the question: *What happens when someone doesn't like the feel?* One instructor found these kinds of resistances generative because they opened up questions about what is educational and about what it means to learn through taste and the mouth. In contrast to the sterile PowerPoint lecture, the condition of feltness brought students into proximity with the multiples—and in the case of *Tacky Forms* they were invited to bring the work *into* their body, body and artwork becoming entangled and relational. Curiosity, in this instance, is both allure and threat, opening bodies to the unpredictable and unexpected.

The condition of feltness and of touching encounters attuned students to the webs of interdependence of food: precarity, consumption, supply, agriculture, and eating practices. *Kitchen Remedies* invited students to examine the kitchen as a site of knowledge production and to examine interspecies and intergenerational memories of touching, smelling, and tasting ingredients. Merging sensory exploration with social justice, the recipes translate the touch of cooking and eating into words. Circulating recipes in any language, students share geographical and cultural history. *Kitchen Remedies* asks questions about how people, ingredients, and places are interconnected but also how food can be weaponized and colonized (Kelley 2019).

While contemporary art is often introduced into the curriculum, increasingly teachers rely on digital forms. Rarely are students invited to touch and handle an original work of art. This of course invoked tensions, as students not used to touching original works of art were hesitant to hold and activate the multiples. The opposite also holds true: the multiples, unrecognizable as art, were approached less formally or, as one teacher exclaimed, leaned on, sat on, and tossed aside. Touching and activating the multiples created conditions of care for the objects but also enabled critical conversations regarding originality, preciousness, pricelessness, and value. This is part of the indeterminacy of anarchiving. The kits' ongoing molecular transformation, which I wrote about in the previous chapter, became increasingly evident as the kits circulated. The external boxes are tattered and adorned with drawings and stickers from previous classes, and multiples in the kits are torn, the spines of zines and books becoming worn, and the birch bark drying out, edges curling.

Alongside the tactility of touch, the kits conditioned proximal liveness. Instructors spoke about how the contents made it feel as if the artists were present in the classroom as invited guests and interlocutors. Students were generally unfamiliar with these artists and through curiosity came to know them and their work. Being proximate was alluring. *What is this object? Who made it? How can it function?* Speculatively inviting the contributing artists into the classroom space opened up moments of reciprocity and attentiveness to collective learning.

Rodrigo Hernandez-Gomez's *Calling*, a shell with a score instructing participants to whisper the names of ancestors into the room, likewise invited imagined guests into the classroom space. Such invocations of intimacy, of touching encounters, extend beyond family and kin to consider other ways of being together. Proximal liveness was similarly invoked through Syrus Ware's *Activist Love Letters*, which invites activists near and far into the classroom space. When hung on a clothesline or passed around like trading cards, the activist bios and writings permeated the atmosphere. Love, writes Carolina De Robertis (2017, 6), "is the blending agent that fuses the political and the intimate, providing urgency to the one and context to the other." Love letters are about connecting with the recipient, and creating a space to ward off isolation. Love works toward justice, care, and radical hope.

The collective nature of the multiples, scores, and propositions further complicated the idea that art making is a solitary activity that happens alone in a studio. The multiples, one instructor noted, asked students to consider how to engage with different publics and how the form is part of that responsiveness. The immediate liveness of the kit shifted engagement with contemporary art from looking at it (digitally or in a gallery) to participating in the work's activation directly. Instead of simply interpreting and discussing a work, the kit invited students and peers to set the work into motion together and pedagogically. In other words, student engagement shifted from looking at and analyzing a work of art to doing.

In her book *Autotheory as Feminist Practice in Art, Writing, and Criticism*, Lauren Fournier (2021, 135) examines various ways that artists make references to other works highly visible, by "working with citation as artist's material." Rather than understanding citation as a practice of quoting sources of influence, Fournier sees such artistic practices as methods of "intertextual intimacy and identification" and as a "practice of community formation" (135). Intertextual intimacy requires "queer feminist modes of being in relation with others in consensual, ethical, critical and life-affirming ways" (155). Referencing as a core element in art becomes a means of connecting community, "making visible the lineages and legacies of inspiration and support that make up a feminist art community" (192). Multiples like Anthea Black's *Keep Queering the Syllabus*, Syrus Ware's *Activist Love Letters*, and the *People's History Posters* by Justseeds artists similarly "destabilized hierarchies of influence as a movement toward a relational politics" (154). On the opening page of *Keep Queering the Syllabus*, Black's score speaks to this idea of citation as community formation. She writes, "The artists here are not historical figures we can only touch at a distance. They are colleagues, mentors, friends, and friends-of-friends." The multiples are more than lists of QTBIPOC artists and activists, and they affirm the value and capacity for community building.

Thinking with Cauleen Smith's *Human_3.0 Reading List* (2015), a series of drawings of books by BIPOC writers as a visual reading list, Fournier argues for the possibilities of intimate citation in creating more just and livable futures where queer, feminist, and BIPOC writers become allies. The multiples in the kit also invited students to add to, extend, and create their own intimate citational practices of relation. In making citation visible, in decentering Euro-Western canons, the multiples create capacities for other worlds to emerge. Katherine McKittrick (2021, 17) writes that references and citations need not succumb to mastery of knowledge but can express "how we know." McKittrick's arguments are specific to how referencing functions in Black studies and, further, how citations can become "suggestions for living differently" (19). Like Cauleen Smith's hand-drawn book covers, McKittrick makes a case for citations as a practice of unlearning and refusal while also sharing Black ways of knowing and being. She writes: "This does not mean names do not matter; it means, instead, that naming is enveloped in the practice of sharing how we live this world and live this world differently" (30). In her book *Dear Science and Other Stories*, McKittrick describes her practice of using a scrolling slide deck of images when giving a public talk. Like Cauleen Smith's book covers, this practice bears witness to the ideas that have shaped McKittrick's thinking and places music, art, poetry in equal relation to academic texts. She writes, "The images are not intended to carry clear meaning. They are looped, and the loop represents what I and what we cannot say or hear or see or remember just as it establishes a repetitive, circuitous, and circular but also inaccurate representation of coming to know" (15). This form of relational sharing and naming is taken up in Black's and Ware's contributions to the kit. Here citation is not a politics of representation; it creates conditions through which relationality, resistance, and care are fostered as artistic theory-making. Writing about the linearity of white queer and trans archives, Ware (2020b) begins his essay "Power to All People" by calling names as an act of remembering the legacy of Black queer and trans folks. Calling names, he writes, brings "the spirit of these activisms into the room with us, to remember that it is ongoing and enlivened by a consideration of the past, present, and (Afro) future" (280). Calling names of trans women of color and Indigenous trans and two-spirited peoples who are often excluded from the archives, Ware begins the process of collective memory work with trans people of color. This naming is what McKittrick (2021, 23) refers to as understanding how we know, where "radical theory-making takes place outside existing systems of knowledge." Citation as intertextual intimacy and relation conditioned through feltness orients radical pedagogy to know differently, to unlearn normative and racist citational ways of being measured and counted.

In addition to understanding citations as relational sharing, Fournier (2021) argues that they counter the entrenched violence of the theory-practice divide and the ways that particular kinds of theory (French and white and written) are authoritative and abstract while QTBIPOC theory and art are devalued and contested. Fournier refutes this distinction through intersectional and decolonial feminist politics centering locatedness and subjectivity in theory-making. Rather than understand theory as elite, inaccessible, and cerebral, the practice of theory-making as research-creation is grounded in thinking-making-doing. The multiples in the kit invite students to engage with theory and intimate citations through their bodies while connecting the contents to students' lived experiences. Research-creation as an anarchiving practice that seeds does the work of theorizing that is transcorporeal, incipient, and vibrational. The condition of feltness gives the space and accountability for intertextual intimate citational practices to emerge in artistic form. Writing to an activist upends the kinds of citational practice normalized in education. Instead of researching about an activist's life history, students are invited to write personal, intimate letters of appreciation (or not), to ask questions, to respond, and to connect with the activist's work.

One instructor spoke about the kit as a kind of care package: "this beautiful kind of convoluted package that you'll ever get." The instructor spoke about the importance of care packages for international students. Or how, on returning to the United States for school, they would arrive with suitcases filled with food from home—and how the kit engendered similar conditions of care. Care packages are associated with home, cultural identity, and cultural survival, the instructor said. They noted how receiving the kits was very different from getting an Amazon package in which one little book is floating around in a big empty box. There is care in how one packs the kits; the multiples fill the entire space and there is a logic to how each item gets placed. As one instructor put it:

> The fact that you could handle the objects required that they had to think about how they would do that. They had to think about care for the kit which meant they had to think about collective care for each other too. There is a sense of trust and care embedded within the kit. Not only sending the multiples out into the world and allowing people to engage with them, but also how the objects are getting used in different ways. They're getting unfolded, unpacked. Some things are getting diminished, like the gum's getting chewed up. There is a kind of awareness that each person handling those objects has to take care. That is not always something that we're teaching in a classroom when we're looking at artwork through slides.

Articulating care as a politics of touch intensifies radical pedagogy as cocomposition and cotransformation. Touch activates a way of caring that is outside of representation and that figures as a sensorial, affective, haptic, and emotional responsibility. Touch requires us to think about connectedness and the desire for better, more just relations. In relinquishing detached indifference and objectivity, the kits' conditions of feltness necessitate the ways that we experiment with and practice care with others. The politics of interdependence has become of utmost importance, particularly in this time of global crisis. The Care Collective (2020) argues that the solution to the pervasiveness of global carelessness is to radically center care as a priority in the world. What is needed, they contend, is a more interdependent and political mobilization of care that accounts for "the paradoxes, ambivalences, and contradictions inherent in care and caretaking" (21). This requires a feminist, queer, antiracist, and ecosocialist perspective. Maria Puig de la Bellacasa (2017) offers that attending to and being accountable to relations requires an attention to *how* we care. "Care," she writes, "is therefore concomitant to the continuation of life for many living beings in more than human entanglements—not forced upon them by a moral order, and not necessarily a rewarding obligation" (70).

Here I return to the questions I posed in the introduction: *How are relations composed and sustained over time? How are all bodies in relation being accounted for, attuned to, and offered something for their labor of being in relation?* Metis scholar Michelle Murphy (2015, 717) cautions against equating care with positive actions or moral emotions and "argues for the importance of grappling with the non-innocent histories in which the politics of care already circulates." Murphy examines the ways that care is political, in the sense that care can serve settler colonialism and perpetuate inequalities just as much as it can account for particular vital and ethical engagements. Murphy and Puig de la Bellacasa call for an "unsettling" of care. Crucial to such reconceptualizations of care is the recognition that power circulates through care in divergent ways, and that a politics of care must be shifted from seeing care as inherently affirmative and humanistic to something uncomfortable, noninnocent, and complex. Part of this unsettling of care is grappling with capitalism's dependence on caring activities, which neglects those who do the work of caring for others. Not only is the commodification of care services implicated by class, gender, race, and forces of dispossession, the marketization of care (with yoga, self-help books, and so on) further exasperates these asymmetrical power relations. Puig de la Bellacasa (2017, 9) refers to this as "a pervasive order of individualized biopolitical morality." In activating The People's Kitchen Collective's *Kitchen Remedies*, a student sewed small, soft fabric pouches for each student in his class. He brought them to class along with a bag of rice and invited classmates to fill the sacks with rice and then hand-sew them closed. The rice bags were heated up in a microwave and used to sooth body pain or discomfort. This gesture, the instructor commented, created a space in the otherwise institutional classroom for a practice of care, as students massaged the "heating pads" into their necks and backs and even caressed each other. Feltness amplified the need for care in postsecondary institutions and the interdependence between the students.

Keep Queering the Syllabus, by Anthea Black, is a contemporary art fanzine that includes personal snapshots of artists, writers, and cultural producers. The artists here are not historical figures we can only touch at a distance. They are colleagues, mentors, friends, and friends of friends. All continue to share our great queer and trans present with nuance and awareness of the high political stakes of our cultural production.

In their editors' introduction to a special issue of *Social Text*, Nathan Snaza and Julietta Singh (2021) invite us into the "educational undergrowth" where critical, abolitionist, and decolonial practices are dynamic and entangled. Against a dominant conceptualization of education predicated on mastery and quantifiable metrics, and where institutions are understood as bounded entities, the educational undergrowth is porous, agitated, and in a state of unrest. Feltness invokes feelings and affect, touching encounters and proximal liveness alongside agitation. Fulling wool fibers disturbs the helices: agitation as tension and friction, agitation as confrontation, protest, and activism. Agitation as care.

Drawing on the work of Sylvia Wynter, Snaza and Singh argue that the humanist educational project has been built on white supremacy, where the humanization of the white, cis, heteropatriarchal subject is simultaneously the "production of less-than-human and inhuman 'constitutive outsides'" (2021, 2). The educational undergrowth refuses the humanist educational assemblage and is instead directed to "understand the specific kinds of practices, study, and collaboration that happen inside, at the edges of, and below universities, without falling back on an affirmation of the university form as it currently stands" (3). The educational undergrowth gives space to understand how education is entangled with settler colonialism, slavery, climate change, and capitalism and how schools, universities, prisons, and migrant farm labor are also connected—and that, within "the mess of these entanglements, other things (and differently animating affects) sprout, struggle for endurance, and grow" (5). The undergrowth is not a fixed place. It is a condition, an agitation. As Stefano Harney and Fred Moten (2013, 98) make clear, this is a condition of feeling, "hapticality, the capacity to feel through others, for others to feel through you, for you to feel them feeling you." The conditions of feltness, incubated by the *Instant Class Kit*, make possible the potential for the educational undergrowth to attune us to different possibilities of study (Harney and Moten 2013). In the educational undergrowth, Snaza and Singh insist, is a slowing down, a paying attention differently, on "a smaller scale of relation, movement, and collision where things happen without (always or easily) adding up to subjects with identities acting in conscious ways" (2021, 7). Feltness creates such a condition of attentiveness, where the humanist project of education is called into question, momentarily decentered, and undone. The touching encounters conditioned through the kit foreground critical, abolitionist, and decolonial practices.

Rodrigo Hernandez-Gomez's *Listening Exercise* invites students to give a presentation to the class in a language that the majority of the class does not speak. The presentation must be on a noncultural topic of their choice and must be presented without translation. The score is handwritten on the back of colonial postcards. For example, one multiple contains an image of "Statues of Lord Clyde and Sir John Moore" in George Square, Glasgow. As part of his project *Museum without Entrance*, this score references the global abolitionist politics toppling colonial and racist monuments. Large in scale, monuments look down on publics from their lofty pedestals representing inequality, racism, and structural violence. In contrast, Hernandez-Gomez's *Listening Exercise* operates on an intimate scale that enunciates deep entanglements of situated knowledges, cultures, and learning that topple the revering figures of the monument.

An Indigenous student gave a presentation in Cree about her cat named Boots using PowerPoint images and text. There was no explanation or translation, and the instructor noted that most of the class seemed quite captivated by the performance lecture. The instructor commented that, while the class could not fully understand what was being said, there was an embodied interaction with the presentation, an affective witnessing. However, after the presentation, another student asked, "What language was that? Was that cat?" This colonial and racist encounter immediately pried open space in the class to discuss dominant languages and knowledges in education and colonial worldviews. The anger, confusion, laughter, and discomfort set in motion by such a question prompts a widening of attention, or a bewildering of education. Bewilderment, according to Nathan Snaza, is a practice of becoming affectively pushed and pulled in multiple directions, "towards: refusal, failure, and delinquency" (Snaza and Singh 2021, 6). Bewilderment as a political and pedagogical practice recognizes the necessity of becoming lost and as such "may offer us more generative ways of becoming decolonized" (6). In educational spaces, Snaza and Singh remind us, affects such as anger, confusion, boredom, bewilderment, anxiety, and pain circulate, and they are not contained only at the level of the human but are conditioned by the materiality (physical, social, architectural) of institutions. The undergrowth "foreground[s] how the human (and its politics) is suspended in networks of more-than-human affective relation but also approach[es] education—in the university and beyond—through attention to the violence of its neurotypicality and ableist architectures" (7).

In widening attention to the ways that affective assemblages link up and move in classrooms, in institutions, and with the wider human and nonhuman world, *Listening Exercise* not only upsets the master colonial narrative but sets in motion the condition for other bodies, affects, and futurities to imagine a different world. As was related in chapter 4, Stó:lō research-creation scholar Dylan Robinson (2020) refers to settler colonial forms of perception as "hungry listening." This civilizing form of consumption has been imposed on Indigenous people and is passed on intergenerationally. Robinson is specifically referring to music, song, and performance, but I believe his work is informative in grappling with the comment about the performance lecture in Cree. Listening functions to impose rigid categorizations of settler colonial knowledge. What are needed, he contends, are practices of listening differently and responsibly while also critically reflecting on the practice of listening itself. Hungry listening, he writes, "privileges a recognition of palatable narratives of difference . . . content-locating practices that orient the ear toward identifying standardized features and types" (2020, 50). Hungry listening prioritizes familiarity, fit, and recognition. Critical listening, listening-in-relation, requires listening to the "layers of our individual positionalities" (58). Robinson writes, "The foundation of critical listening positionality requires becoming aware of normative listening orientations across a range of gendered and racial formations, and developing self-reflexivity around how these are guided by their own specific forms of hunger, starvation, and drive toward knowledge fixity" (60). This means that what is heard, in the case of the performance lecture in Cree, should not be reduced to the knowable, or to feeling good and comfortable. Not everything needs to be translated to an equivalency. What Hernandez-Gomez's work conditions is an indigestible form of witnessing (Decter 2018). Robinson argues further that this "does not mean that we listen without intentionality, but rather that the work of listening is not predicated on use-value or the drive to accumulate knowledge" (2020, 72). *Listening Exercise* creates space in a classroom for nondominant (non-English) languages to be uttered, but more importantly it asks students to think about their own language and listening formations and biases. Like the relational citation practices, critical listening asks questions about how we come to know, what we don't know, and what we might need to unknow, unlearn, and unhear. This is the work of anarchiving as research-creation and the condition of feltness—the vectors of knowledges—that agitate and interrupt normative habits of learning.

Many instructors spoke about how challenging it is to bring in social justice content or to consider political issues in relation to making art. The kit, they said, spurred complicated conversations that were otherwise absent from the curriculum. Issues related to disability, prison abolition, queer and trans people, Indigenous knowledges, water rights and climate change, and protest movements and activism. These issues, the instructors stated, were absent not because they didn't think they were important, but because it was challenging to engage with students about these topics because of the students' previous experiences or resistance to seeing a relationship between art, education, and politics. Having the physical art in the room broke down some of the perceived hierarchies and asked students to consider: *What are they concerned about? What do they care about? What issues do they want to discuss and think critically about? And how might they do that through their own art?* One instructor shared, "I think sometimes it's really difficult for them to engage in some of these conversations, or to even expose themselves to artworks that they wouldn't necessarily be drawn to. The kit kind of forced them into the uncomfortable position. If they didn't know about a particular issue the multiples encouraged them to do some research or share in conversations with their classmates." As Snaza and Singh (2021, 4) write, "The affective politics of humanism means that no classroom discussion can ever be separated from larger historical-political forces of colonization, racialization, heteropatriarchy, and extractive capitalism." However, Robin DiAngelo and Özlem Sensoy (2014) argue that student resistance to criticality and social justice stems from the persistent neoliberal idea that if we only treat everyone the same inequalities would disappear. In their essay, which serves as an open letter to students, the authors maintain that student resistance to critical thought is based on being unprepared to engage in difficult critical theory, that topics addressed in social justice courses elicit strong feelings and opinions. I would add here that students are ill-equipped to feel uncomfortable. Feelings have become equated with rationalization. With a focus on standardization, education has created conforming and compliant students. The kit multiples pried open curiosity and critical thinking, entangling students' own positionality with the topics and issues addressed in each multiple. By no means was this an easy process, as the performance lecture on Boots the cat attests; rather, in the undergrowth, agitations affirm the urgency of thinking otherwise.

Another instructor noted that they often felt it to be challenging to bring Indigenous content or artists into their teaching out of fear of appropriation. But the BUSH *Manifesto* "just landed in the class, it was right there, and this meant we couldn't not talk about it. Holding the birch bark did something different to how we might address Indigeneity in a first-year studio class." The instructor noted how the presence of the BUSH *Manifesto* meant that they did not need to be the authority on the topic; instead, students themselves took up the manifesto in various ways. Coupled with Hernandez-Gomez's contributions on decolonizing cultural institutions, the inscribed birch bark multiple asked students to think about their own relationship to land and place, land and art institutions.

In other instances, students who identified as queer, trans, or BIPOC saw themselves reflected in the course materials. Anthea Black's *Handbook for*

Queer and Trans Students elicited numerous conversations on what instructors can do to create spaces to support queer and trans students, and to understand how their work is in conversation with the larger art world. One instructor shared that a student had exclaimed, "I just wish one of my teachers would have read this ever." The instructor discussed the affective registers that comment awakened and the resulting threads of conversation that unraveled.

The physicality of the multiples and the kit in the classroom space shifted access and barriers to examining diverse art forms and concepts and "opened possibilities for students to respond to each other and relate in a way that isn't always possible." The kinds of complicated conversations that the performance lecture in Cree instantiated included students negotiating and figuring out how to respond to each other in thoughtful ways while allowing for a diversity of opinions and to engage in difference. Being able to enter into discussions about political, social, and cultural issues through the activation of the multiples became a collaborative process, where the entire class was working through an issue together. "There were so many ways into the kit. So, everyone was bringing either their biases or their excitement, whatever it was, to these objects and the objects were activating all these different ways of living." Snaza and Singh (2021, 7) argue that attending to and practicing in the undergrowth "allows us to better grasp how intrahuman struggles in and over education are always entangled at scales below, around, and beyond the ones usually dominant in educational thought." The feltness—affects, feelings, touching encounters, agitations—conditioned by the kit altered the practice of study and affirmed a pedagogical impulse as collective world-making.

Resolution (Mass of Clarity)
PA SYSTEMS

1 Imagine a dream, desire, goal, aspiration, need, resolution or hope that you have.
2 Sculpt a miniature to represent your idea, it can be literal or not.
3 If you choose, mail your miniature to PA Systems to contribute to the growth of *Resolution (Mass of Clarity)*.

Snaza and Singh (2021) advocate for an undergrowth that isn't necessarily outside of or removed from educational institutions. It can be a condition of community-based activism or artistic practice, but it can also, it needs to, it *must* (as Campt would argue), condition education. For radical pedagogy to flourish we must agitate, destabilize, and unlearn the institution from outside, alongside, and from within. As both Manning (2020) and Loveless (2019) have argued, research-creation is a hybrid practice that "fall[s] out of both the disciplinary and the recognizable" (Manning 2020, 221). But as these scholars also note, there is great risk in research-creation falling sway to the logics of quantifiable capture, to metrics, and identifiable value. I see this in standardized approaches to doctoral comprehensive exams and thesis proposals that desire knowing in advance, rather than seeding speculative middles. I hear this when asked if I might consider adding rubrics and evaluation sheets to the *Instant Class Kit* so that instructors can better assess student engagement. I feel this when presenting my research-creation events and audiences demand to know how the impact of this work can be measured—and assume that it should be. I experience this in trying to place my research-creation work into standardized academic annual merit and progress forms. And I know that while arts-based forms are increasingly being included in classroom practice, the arts, and in particular research-creation, is still very much devalued, or considered suspicious, by the institution.

I opened this chapter with the observation that education has a love affair with capture, representation, legible knowledge systems, and capitalist forms of value. The stories of socially engaged art as research-creation and as conditions of feltness that animate this book, which have been germinating for more than a decade, ask what other forms of thinking-making-doing are possible. I firmly believe that research-creation has much to offer the undergrowth. In attuning ourselves to feltness—touching encounters, transcorporeal relations, sensory modes of knowing, affective forces, and agitated frictive movement— research-creation reorients how we know and develops the kinds of practices needed to unlearn. As Manning (2020, 221) emphatically states, "Research-creation deeply threatens the power/knowledge that holds the academy in place." However, for this to truly happen at the level of the undergrowth we need to break from capture. We can't simply fund and support research-creation practices and admit students into research-creation degrees; we must also resist the expectations placed on students, faculty, and administrators to then continue to evaluate their work using the normative logics of the institution. Imagine that, instead of comprehensive exams, we had students articulate intertextual intimate citations, both text-based and artistic, or write love letters to those whose work inspires them. Instead of critically describing a body of knowledge that is known in advance, how might the qualifying exam ask them to consider *how they know*. As McKittrick (2021) argues, we must move away from who we know and what we know to *how* we know. "Citations are economized," she writes. In Black studies, she argues, and I would add in the undergrowth of research-creation too, citation becomes "a whole new emergence" (27). We must likewise resist demanding students to write proposals based on a proceduralism that determines in advance how the research-creation will unfold. Instead we must encourage our students to embrace the unknown and to undo the structural logics of academic research practices. Research-creation must privilege the idea that we discover something in the process. This does not mean that there isn't some sort of plan, but that the plan should be scored and propositional. It must be allowed to seed and grow. The results of research-creation produce various outcomes, but these can't be determined in advance of the research. Further, if research-creation, as I articulated in the introduction, is a transdisciplinary practice that is hybrid, where the limits of the original disciplines have been transcended to create an entirely new practice, then we must imagine the new kinds of forms that will emerge to share and circulate these new knowledges and practices. In other words, a research-creation dissertation might take the form of a performance lecture, a video installation, and written text of speculative fiction. The function of each is not to translate or interpret one form into another; instead, such oblique or disparate acts are necessary because the research, the knowledges, need to be expressed in different forms and to diverse publics. The evaluation of such work can't be known in advance but must emerge in the midst of its occurrence. This might mean that students themselves become responsible for articulating at least some form of the evaluative process: *What does the work do?* And by *do*, I don't mean impact. *What does it invite us to learn about the world, about how to be in the world in relation?* As a way to imagine radically different futures, research-creation must attune itself to care for the unseen.

In bringing this chapter back through its own intimate citational loop I want to think with Syrus Ware's video *Ancestors, Do You Read Us? (Dispatches from the Future)* (2019). In this multichannel video, Ware imagines a world where racialized people have survived the catastrophic impact of climate change, state violence and policing, and white supremacy. Informed by speculative fiction, and in particular the work of Octavia Butler, the video glitches and loops time, which becomes a portal through which the next generation of racialized activists communicate with us, and their ancestors, and offer us insights into the future where all Black lives matter and thrive. It is 2078 and the great-great-grandchildren of our generation travel back to 2019 to communicate with their ancestors and tell them how to fight, to build new communities and networks of care.

The video is a research-creation practice that explores how we know intergenerationally and through action. It activates an unlearning that ruptures the racialized and colonial logics of the university. It visualizes and names, without representation, through glitches and time loops that undo linear time similarly to the way that McKittrick's slide deck pulses, refusing a narrative about queer, trans, and Black progress. The video queers time and speaks to particular urgencies in our present moment while also making space for an abolitionist vision of our future. *How might unlearning condition the ways we value research-creation? Instead of knowing in advance the procedures, literature review, and methods, how can research-creation make room for speculation, for the practice of thinking-making-doing in the middle of how we know? How could we glitch our way through academic queer time loops?*

As the pandemic closed borders and restricted movement, the circulation of the *Instant Class Kits* came to a sudden halt. They sat, in their worn cardboard boxes, in a corner of my home office for months. And eventually, as we all became more comfortable with virtual modes of delivery, they were opened and workshopped through a number of art galleries and university guest lectures. I also designed and taught a course using the kits' condition of feltness at its core. Andrea Vela Alarcón spent the summer of 2020 creating self-guided workshops, scored activations for one or more of the kit contents. Designed with open-ended questions, possible readings, and activities, the workshops were rendered into PDFs and housed on the research website in conjunction with digital images of the kit contents. And while the kits' tactility is absent from these virtual workshops, they invite participants to think-make-do and so continue to invoke touching encounters. For example, thinking with the multiple *Kitchen Remedies*, participants are asked to share and cook a potato recipe. While collectively cooking over a virtual platform in the isolation of their own home, participants come together to talk about the history of the potato in global colonization, its role in migration, and as a common staple in many cuisines. Cooking, eating, and tasting together, the tactility, affects, and agitation of feltness condition the virtual space. If we believe that the undergrowth of research-creation has the potential to unmake the university, the school, or the classroom in its current form, then we need to continue to dismantle the structures that govern knowledges' capture. In addition to inventing new practices of thinking-making-doing, we need to ensure that we have ways to tune into their feltness that does not return them to the logics of capture. We must not lose sight/cite of the pedagogical impulse.

Chapter Six

Make a Public

Artist publications (e.g., books, zines, broadsheets, posters) have long been a vital part of creative practice. With their capacity for serialization and immediacy, artist publications foregrounded communication and distribution. While there are certainly examples predating the 1960s and 1970s, this became a time of robust proliferation as artists produced artist books, performance documentation, scores, and other intermedia art which could be traded, sold, and reproduced. Technological developments in offset printing, letterpress, risograph, and, later on, digital print-on-demand possibilities all increased the availability, accessibility, and affordability associated with independent publishing. Part of the appeal of artist publications was the tactility of medium and form, and their circulation outside of the white cube of the gallery. For this reason, artist publications contribute to the formation of diverse publics.

This chapter engages with a series of publications produced within a semester-long course at OCAD University, Toronto, titled Pressing Issues and taught by the artist Shannon Gerard. The course is a seminar-studio hybrid course with a syllabus that consists of one score or proposition: *Make a Public*. Each iteration of the course is co-composed between Gerard and the students over the course of the semester. The course blends readings and seminar discussions with field trips, explorations into the field of nanopublishing and artists multiples, and culminates in the students facilitating a publicly engaged community publication project (which typically takes place over a few days). Some form of artist publication, such as broadsheets or newspapers, usually results from the public event. The Latin word for publish, *publicus*, translates to "make a public"; from the middle English, *to publish* was to make something generally known. Playing with the concept *public/ations*, I turn to public pedagogy scholarship to think with the public/ations—publics and printed matter—that emerged in the semester-long course.

In *Art as Social Action*, an edited collection of essays on social practice art and education and a series of lesson plans on how to teach and engage students in social practice, Gregory Sholette (2018, 283) remarks that across all of the lesson plan examples is "student activity that occurs fully outside the classroom." While this statement should come as no surprise to those of us familiar with socially engaged, or social practice art, what strikes me as a missing link here is that while socially engaged art more often than not happens outside of classroom spaces and often in collaboration, or consultation, with community members, there has been little writing done on its relationship to public pedagogy scholarship. As more postsecondary institutions create socially engaged programs and courses, and more scholarship on the teaching of socially engaged art proliferates, it is crucial that different pedagogical theories be explored, including that of public pedagogy. *Art as Social Action* is a unique contribution to teaching socially engaged art, but its emphasis on lesson plans is curriculum-focused. *Wicked Arts Assignments: Practicing Creativity in Contemporary Arts Education* and *The Compound Yellow Manual: Of Prompts, Provocations, Permissions and Parameters for Everyday Practice* offer scores, lesson ideas, and propositions and are similarly concerned with curriculum. In connecting publications, publics, and public pedagogy with socially engaged art, my arguments extend current scholarship on public pedagogy to consider more-than-human public/ations and their role in a radical pedagogy to come. The chapter also turns its attention from the curricula of teaching socially engaged art to consider the kind of interdependent ethics of care that is needed in socially engaged pedagogies, given the nature of moving inside and outside of classrooms while working with diverse publics.

Power UP! The Making of Public/ations

The scene of this research-creation event is Shannon Gerard's class Pressing Issues, an undergraduate course offered through OCAD University's print and publications department, in which Gerard playfully invokes the concept of print-making alongside significant social, political, and community-based or public issues that the students bring to the course. The Pressing Issues course is influenced by Fluxus ideas such as experimentation, chance, propositional scores, antiart and anticapitalism, radical pedagogies, print culture, multiples, and mass production through printmaking. Its main assignment requires students to work together to *Make a Public*, which entails the development of an event or a resource that engages in dialogue with a particular community. The course is structured as a student-led residency in which the class can, per the course description, "come together to conduct research, share knowledge, and work within the field of contemporary publication." The learning is mostly situated outside the classroom and promotes a connection with community partners to develop a large-scale project. For Gerard, publications, with an emphasis on voice and political strategy, is a form of civic and cultural engagement. In this chapter, I take up two iterations of the course that *The Pedagogical Impulse* was involved with (over the course of two different semesters), and I discuss a third iteration as a reference point. Shannon Gerard has been intimately entangled with the decade-long research-creation event chronicled in this book, fabricating an artist residency in the first iteration of the project and designing the *Instant Class Kit* cover design and newspaper publication.

Andrea Vela Alarcón joined the classes as a collaborator on *The Pedagogical Impulse* project and as a research assistant. She was responsible for research undertaken in the context of the Pressing Issues class, which included attending class and taking field notes, talking to students and the instructor informally, and assisting Gerard and the students in the production of the various art projects and events. A culminating interview with Gerard also took place, at the end of each semester. The first class was composed of twelve students, most of whom identified as women, queer, or persons of color, and the second course was made up of fourteen students, ten of whom identified as female, one as nonbinary student, and three as males (two of whom identified as queer)—and the majority of the students were people of color.

I like to think of Gerard's pedagogy as a series of public/ations that are introduced to the students as catalyzing events in the entwined sense of becoming publics and publications. The public/ations are disparately connected and yet fundamentally relational. In the first iteration of the course that we were involved with, some of the public/ations examined included *Blueprint for Counter Education* by Maurice Stein and Larry Miller (1970) and Sister Corita Kent's *Learning by Heart* (Steward and Kent 1992). Students researched and presented on alternative forms of nanopublishing. Gerard adopts the term *nanopublishing* not just to mean a small amount of information communicated in a publication, but also to refer to its size or alternative form and structure. Students were introduced to Fluxkits, small artist zines, books in boxes, texts printed on wooden cutting boards, felted books, publications in tin cans, and a number of other alternative publications. The focus was on form and less about the content of these publications. Another public/ation included visiting the Fluxus archives at OCAD U, which are fairly extensive. Here students experience firsthand Roy Ascott's curricular LP, among other printed and boxed publications. The students also spent time in OCAD U's zine library, one of the most extensive artist publication libraries in the province. Field trips to the ONSITE gallery to see the exhibition Diagrams of Power and guest presentations and walking tours of the city constituted other public/ations.

One of the historical (though recently reprinted) publications that was introduced to the students was the *Blueprint for Counter Education* by Maurice Stein and Larry Miller (1970). It was designed as a portable learning environment, or a radical curriculum, and introduced into the Critical Studies program at California Institute of the Arts (CalArts) in the early 1970s.

The original *Blueprint for Counter Education* (BCE) was a series of posters contained in a box set that map revolutionary thinkers and artists as an interdisciplinary education guide. The posters group together clusters of theoretical, artistic, and intellectual themes, including the names of prominent artists, writers, and scholars. The BCE offers an intermedia approach to curriculum and pedagogy and includes references to political and social justice issues of the time: the war in Vietnam, the rise of mass media, the Civil Rights movement, feminisms, and the events of May 1968 in Paris—all of which challenged university curriculum and hegemonic capitalism. The poster's open-ended entry points are anchored through references to Herbert Marcuse and Marshall McLuhan and their critiques of capitalism, consumer culture, technology, and media. Reproductions of tables of contents from a number of publications appear on the BCE charts. The charts are inspired by blackboard notes and 1960s screen printing designs, which they produced on blueprint paper and Mylar before the book was published. In the Pressing Issues class, the BCE was spread out over the classroom walls and tables, and students spent time studying its pages. Both Gerard and the students acknowledged the lack of current or contemporary references and issues within the BCE itself as an entry point to Fluxus curricular intermedia. In fact, few women are named in the BCE and, as one student noted, the ideologies contained within its form were not reflective of students' understandings of current social-political issues.

For Stein and Miller, the BCE was a visual and diagrammatic way for students to develop radical and critical paths through knowledge and education, much like Maciunas's *Curriculum Plan* board game. The BCE aimed to create curricula with and for the students rather than inserting them into an already predetermined structure. Hovering between Gerard's pedagogical public/ations and the student-directed pathways through the BCE was the artist Corita Kent. One of the few women artists listed on the BCE, Corita Kent was a nun, educator, artist, and activist whose work became a pivotal pathway for the Pressing Issues course. Known for her radical teaching techniques and political screen prints, Kent's artwork of love and peace was popular in the 1960s and 1970s. She belonged to the Immaculate Heart of Mary religious order and taught in the art department of the Immaculate Heart College in Los Angeles from 1938 to 1968. There she developed a radical curriculum and pedagogical practice guided by *relationality, responsibility*, and *hope* (Steward and Kent 1992). In the 1960s her work became increasingly political, taking up issues like poverty, racism, and injustice. In 1968 she left the order and moved to Boston. In many of Kent's screen prints, the phrases *Power up!* and *Handle with Care* appear. Kent's work became a turning point for the Pressing Issues course because she was a woman not often mentioned in the art history canon and because her messages of social justice resonated with the students. Corita Kent's art and pedagogy were embedded in an ethics of care. Through her printmaking and teaching practices, Kent responded to the social struggles of the 1960s. Her most popular art was based on screen printed posters that incorporated bright blocks of color with juxtaposed political messages influenced by 1960s political movements, such as "Power Up," "Get with the action," "Stop the Bombing," and "Love Is Here to Stay." Kent believed that the artist has a responsibility to realize their immense power by fitting things together in a new way.

The semester when *The Pedagogical Impulse* joined this iteration of the Pressing Issues course also happened to be the hundredth anniversary of the birth of Corita Kent, which was going to be celebrated at the Corita Art Center in Los Angeles. As different public/ations began to coalesce around the score *Make a Public*, Gerard received an invitation to travel to the Center, where the students' public engagement would take place at the anniversary event. The students traveled to Los Angeles with Gerard and Vela Alarcón to continue their research in the Corita Kent archives in the Corita Art Center and at the Getty Museum and to participate in the anniversary celebrations as part of their *Make a Public* assignment.[1] For the event, the students conceived of public/ations that would take the form of banner making. Banners were a significant part of Kent's art practice, and the students decided to create the banners at the event with the members of the public and former students who would be in attendance. The banner making process, which involved embroidery, stitching, paint, and fabric markers, was less about the content of the banners and more about the opportunity to share stories with Kent's former students and to learn about the impact she had on their lives. The banner making event created both a dialogic social practice opportunity and marked a space where former Kent students and the Pressing Issues students could stitch and craft their own messages for a future to come. The gathering at the anniversary event, with OCAD U students and former Kent students, created what Lauren Berlant (2011) calls *intimate publics*, people gathering together in a collective response. To culminate the anniversary event activities, the students paraded the banners in a reperformance of the exuberant Immaculate Heart street parades—which were central to Kent's pedagogy—from the Corita Art Center to the campus of the Otis College of Art and Design, a significant art school for social practice.

Although the students had come together in a form of publicness, these activities became further research as they continued to work on their final public/ations. In Los Angeles the students continued their research at the Fluxus archives at the Getty Museum and explored the work of the artist Adrian Piper. Piper was active in the 1960s and continues to be a force in the art world today. Piper is a woman of color, and the students resonated with her work, politics, and aesthetics along with those of Corita Kent. A retrospective of Piper's work was on view at the Hammer Museum in Los Angeles, and the students had the opportunity to engage with her work while on the trip.

While in Los Angeles the students worked with Gerard and Vesna Krstich to curate the selection of *Celebrate People's History* posters that went into the *Instant Class Kit* (MacPhee 2020). The posters bring to publicness moments in the history of social justice such as LGBTQ rights, Black liberation, disability justice, and labor reform. The posters counter dominant history texts and center marginalized and oppressed peoples and stories. A diverse range of artists and activists contributed to the poster series, which are curated by the artist Josh MacPhee. The posters' publicness resides in the collective participation that went into the writing, printing, and visualization of history. More than 125 different designs have been printed with more than 300,000 printed and circulated by the artists' cooperative Justseeds. The posters don't bring together a collection of heroes but rather celebrate social justice struggles to make a more equitable and just world. Fourteen were selected by the Pressing Issues students for inclusion in the *Instant Class Kit*, including posters commemorating the Lesbian Herstory Archives (Carrie Moyer), ADAPT (anonymous), No one is illegal (Jesus Berraza), and ACT UP (ACT UP Philadelphia). These posters are intended to rupture dominant narratives within the curriculum and to provoke alternative ways of understanding and researching the past. Their selections emerged out of the different course public/ations and the students' ongoing conversations regarding 1960s and 1970s activism and its relevance for their lives and communities. According to Rebecca Solnit, these posters further revolutions by keeping them alive: pasted to walls, posters take back the public sphere from corporations and "give it to the radical imagination" (2020, 17). The vitality of street posters, Solnit claims, is "when the walls wake up, they remind us of who we are, where we are . . . that we are not alone, that others have gone before, and hope remains ahead" (18). In an era of eroded public space, protest posters become "small gestures," she contends, that keep alive the power of revolution and hope in the public sphere.

Printmaking is often used as a form of dissent to address social and political issues. From protest posters and zines to leaflets and wheat-pasting, printmaking is often a community activity that, through the making or dissemination process, can enter the public sphere. Because public/ations can be reproduced and are often low cost, they are often understood as an accessible means to voice opposition (Caplow 2009). Metis artist and activist Dylan Miner (2009, 130) writes, "The tactility and expediency of the print is paramount to its capacity to circulate within wide audiences, without being contained by capitalist social relations." Handmade prints in an age of mass digital reproduction, he contends, become an embodied form of resistance. In *Paper Politics: Socially Engaged Printmaking Today* Josh MacPhee (2009), the artist who organizes the *Celebrate People's History* poster series, argues that for many print artists, like Gerard, organizing community public/ations and printmaking is part of social organization and protest. Public/ations insist on an encounter. They want to be used. But they also gesture beyond the text on a page to a more-than, to publics to come. Banner making is a similar form of public/ation that is both community driven and a form of communication. At the Corita Art Center the public's and the students' contributions to the banner included reflections on Corita Kent and her art messages but also contained personal reflections on the world today and its future. Against the idea of the individual genius artist who makes a single valuable art object, printmaking and banner making require techniques available to the many, while also being collective and distributed. When prints, public/ations, and banners circulate, they occupy public space and give voice to political and social issues. Josh MacPhee (2020) maintains that the action of wheat-pasting the *Celebrate People's History* posters on walls in a city space creates small publics as people gather and engage with the work.

Returning to Toronto, the students decided to create a series of three risograph posters contained within a similarly risographed envelope, a format influenced by the *Blueprint for Counter Education*, their research in Los Angeles, and the *Celebrate People's History* posters.[2] However, the students chose references, visuals, and messages from their current lives and from Pressing Issues, and they included art historical references absent from the BCE, for example, to the art of Adrian Piper. Other references and topics included Black Lives Matter, human rights, the right to legal and safe abortion, NO ONE is illegal on stolen land, Nothing about us without us, Coco Fusco, Audre Lorde, #MeToo, bell hooks, Tanya Talaga, Leanne Betasamosake Simpson, and much more. The culminating publication, *Counter with Care*, is a nod to the BCE and to Corita Kent's screen print *Handle with Care*. The publication was assembled in a small edition, and four copies were placed in the *Instant Class Kit*. The *Counter with Care* (CWC) posters publish the concerns and cares of the Pressing Issues students. The CWC gives voice to the issues that the students in the course consider pressing: sex work is work, trans rights, environmentalism. While the CWC points at the *Blueprint for Counter Education* in terms of form, its political citations as relations (Fournier 2021) place it in conversation with political printmaking like the *Celebrate People's History* posters.

While Gerard's score *Make a Public* encourages students to create a project that moves between classroom and community, the public-making is not simply about being outside the classroom in community space. Rather the public/ation is generated by the community-based research-creation that results in a public/ation and its eventual circulation, distribution, and activation. Artists' publications gained momentum in the 1950s and included a diverse array of forms, including newspapers, posters, books, records, and kits. Their ability to be reproduced as a multiple and circulated was essential. Multiples are identical artworks that are produced in small or large numbers with an intent to make art accessible and engage a wider audience. Multiples function in an iterative process, where the ideas of repeatability, circulation, and touch become central components to an art and pedagogical practice. Transversing conventional ideas about the art object and its form, artists' publications moved out of museums and galleries to circulate as counter-publics and question what an equitable, interconnected, and expansive art community could look like and could do. In publishing, the term *circulation* refers to the number of publications that are printed, and therefore the number of readers, but in the case of *Counter with Care* as part of the classroom kits, the circulation became expansive and spread.

Publics to Come

Public pedagogy emerged in educational scholarship to denote processes, forms, and places of learning outside of formal educational institutions such as museums and cultural institutions as well as sites of cultural production like media, film, billboards, and contemporary art (Sandlin, Schultz, and Burdick 2010). Elizabeth Ellsworth (2004, 5) refers to such places of learning as *anomalous*, which she uses to refer to "peculiar, irregular, abnormal or difficult to classify pedagogical phenomena." Anomalous places of learning deviate from dominant educational discourses and practices, rupturing what might be commonly understood as pedagogical. Anomalous places of learning are emergent, iterative, and in the making. Significantly, Ellsworth emphasizes bodies, sensations, and materiality in her conceptualization of anomalous places of learning. Relations, she contends, are imbricated in places of learning and pedagogical events, where pedagogies are in the making rather than predicted.

Problematizing the ways in which public pedagogy is addressed in educational scholarship, Jake Burdick, Jennifer Sandlin, and Michael O'Malley (2014) have called for more complicated conversations regarding methodological and ethical issues in researching public pedagogy and a greater accountability granted to its complexity. Sandlin, O'Malley, and Burdick (2011, 347) use the term *critical public pedagogy* to describe the ways that popular and everyday cultures can be used to "decode and interrupt dominant ideologies of race, class, gender, sexuality, militarism, and neo-liberalism." Problematizing public pedagogy, they draw on the work of Glen Savage (2014), who questions what is meant by the term *public*. He claims that *public* has been used in totalizing ways and operates through a false public-private dichotomy. As a contested space of unequal access, and increasingly neoliberal capitalist entanglements, Savage demands that scholars ask which publics and whose publics they are talking about in their work. As a guiding framework he offers three public distinctions: political publics, popular publics, and concrete publics. Popular publics resonate with Berlant's (2011) notion of intimate publics in that they are self-organizing and are formed around a text, artifact, or, for example, a banner making project at an anniversary event. Intimate publics converge when people come together in collective action or through shared interests. Popular publics or intimate publics are formed through relations that are not given in advance. Intimate publics extend beyond the physically proximate to include the collective, mediated layers of social intimacy and to incorporate the complex, transcorporeal relations between the personal and the collective. Intimate publics are shaped through affects that bring communities together but also create tensions and ambivalence about such togetherness—affects that Berlant (2011) would refer to as "cruel optimism." The politics of intimate publics is the assumption of shared or common sentiments toward something that could potentially mobilize actions but could also supplant universalizing narratives. The popular and intimate publics fostered by the anniversary celebrations at the Corita Art Center brought OCAD U students and former Corita Kent students affectively together for a particular moment, but the publicness of the event didn't alter or intervene into the public sphere.

Concrete publics, Savage offers, are spaces such as galleries, shopping malls, public parks, and other "spatially bounded" entities (2014, 86). Expanding on such spatially bounded informal sites of learning, Savage includes streetscapes as concrete publics made up of road signs, advertising, and public transportation. In concrete publics, care is needed in addressing the complexities of access and spatial inequalities. Writing about the *Celebrate People's History* posters, Josh MacPhee (2020) discusses the ways that these posters intervene into the public sphere, countering the presence of corporate advertising and the state monuments where history is ossified. Through postering, streets—as concrete publics—can become active pedagogical places to come together to witness, discuss, and take action. The posters have not only been pasted on walls; they have been included in exhibitions and reproduced in newspapers and as backdrops in television shows, generating other forms of publicness and public circulation.

Extending this work on publics through affect theory and feminist new materialisms, Sarah E. Truman and I conceptualize the notion of publics as more-than-human (Springgay and Truman 2019d). Publics, we insist, are implicated in different kinds of commons and in relations between humans and nonhumans, affects, ideas, and places. Some of these publics are linked to larger public discourses, while others are activated as fugitive spaces or what might be considered an undercommons (Harney and Moten 2013). As publics to come, the pedagogy does not preexist the pedagogical encounter but rather emerges as different publics and publications come together and interact. In the Pressing Issues examples, publics to come emerge through the making and gathering of the public/ations.

Returning to Burdick, Sandlin, and O'Malley's (2014) consternation about the flattening of public pedagogy, I'm conscious that the Pressing Issues class was part of a university undergraduate program that incorporated public space or informal sites of learning such as the Corita Art Center and the Getty Museum into its curriculum and pedagogy and, given its connection to formal schooling, is not a typical fit within public pedagogy scholarship. However, a crucial part of teaching for Gerard is getting her students to work together on a collaborative publication project either with a public community, or within public space; in doing so, the students have an immediate experience creating a socially engaged art project. This is what Sholette (2018) pointed out about teaching social practice art—that it regularly occurs outside of classrooms. I would argue that, in doing so, there is the potential for different kinds of more-than-human publics to take shape—publics to come. Thinking critically about socially engaged art as research-creation demands that we consider the kinds of publics and public pedagogies that are evented in the process. In socially engaged art as research-creation, public pedagogies bubble over and felt themselves inside and outside of classroom and community spaces, rendering both porous, fluid, and in flux. It's not that art manifests a particular kind of public pedagogy (content) but that the practices or forms of thinking-making-doing socially engaged art as research-creation interrogate publics and publicness as a methodological practice and, in doing so, create possibilities for new, emergent, and iterative publics to seed. This returns me to the necessity of anarchiving. *Counter with Care* as a process of anarchiving keeps the feed-forward mechanism of public/ations moving.

In previous iterations of the Pressing Issues course, students created a newspaper in the town of Port Hope, Ontario, during a creative festival. Wide-ranging questions and prompts were generated by the students alongside the public: *How long have you lived in Port Hope? Tell us a Port Hope legend, folktale, or myth.* Other questions, more focused on agriculture, labor histories, and settler colonialism, included *What happened to the water here? What opportunities exist for artists here?* Participants at the festival could contribute stories about Port Hope by writing on manual typewriters, talking with student facilitators, or drawing—all of which resulted in the public/ation *Report Hope*. Students also researched and visited Molson's Mill, the former site of the OCAD U summer art school, and talked to local residents about the history of the mill. Producing a public/ation on site as a public research-creation event creates space for dialogue with people. A pop-up newspaper studio is a flexible framework that acts as a publication studio, classroom, performance space, and social gathering place. For Gerard it is a manifestation of play, imagination, political agency, and poetic literacy. In the case of Gerard's public/ation, a public becomes an ongoing space of encounter through dialogue, stories, drawings, and performance. Texts themselves don't produce publics, but public/ations as transversally linked and networked vectors of knowledges create publics to come. Public/ation is an activity of becoming or making something public. Erin Manning (2013, 163) argues that there is never *a body*, human or otherwise, but that entities and the environment are "edgings and contourings, forces and intensities." Transcorporeal relations, Ellsworth (2004, 48) writes, create a "membrane" where more-than-human bodies "touch and interpenetrate, flow into and interfuse each other." This is the becoming of public/ations.

Gert Biesta is another scholar who has articulated critical understandings of public pedagogy (Biesta 2012; Biesta 2014). A pedagogy *for* the public is "aimed at the public" (Biesta 2014, 21). The form here, he contends, is that of instruction and the transmission of knowledge. A second iteration is a pedagogy *of* the public, where collective learning is foregrounded. In a third register, public pedagogy can be *in the interest of publicness*, when it "becomes more activist, more experimental, and more demonstrative" (23). It is concerned with the creation of alternative ways of being and doing, while intervening into the public sphere and thereby emphasizing a process of becoming. As a concern for publicness or a "quality of human togetherness," this public pedagogy is iterative (24), a coming-together as an active form of worlding. This shifts public pedagogy from a model predicated on the transmission of knowledge to the *how* of coming together and, in turn, emphasizes accountability and responsibility. Biesta writes, "Things not only *should* be done differently but actually can be done differently" (23).

Pedagogy also manifests in the demonstration of alter-worlds. Examples might include the global protests and toppling of white supremacist monuments, Black Lives Matter reading lists, mutual aid organizing, the *Celebrate People's History* posters, and the *Counter with Care* publication. As Sandlin, Burdick, and Rich (2017) write, public pedagogy considers a "more complex, affective process of relationality and embodiment which extends beyond a focus on a teacher and instead locates the educational moment at the dialogic intersection between multiple subjectivities. This view decouples public pedagogy from its roots in authoritarian views of pedagogy, and perhaps most importantly, allows for the negotiation, rather than the simple transfer, of final meaning" (6). I find resonance here with Irit Rogoff's (2010b) insistence on knowledges that vector as opposed to educational formats (discussed further in chapter 5). Vectors, writes Erin Manning (2020, 196), "move out from known junctures into a wander line that is oriented by a proposition, and in that sense directionally constrained, but is at the same time open-ended in way that invites new takings-form on the fly." Rather than thinking of a gallery or a public art performance as public pedagogy simply because it takes place in "public" space and instructs us about something, Rogoff, Biesta, and MacPhee gesture toward the knowledges and actions that assemble and intervene when public/ations come together in different and open ways and thus constitute publics to come. In a new materialist or posthumanist framework, Biesta's human togetherness can be extended to incorporate more-than-human entanglements. Publics to come take place both at the level of the students coming together with others to create public/ations and in the circulation and dissemination of the publications, creating more-than-human publics to come.

Building a Wetter Orchid

The Pedagogical Impulse teamed up with Shannon Gerard the following year for another iteration of Pressing Issues. The course was designed around the *Instant Class Kit*, but the syllabus still retained the score *Make a Public*. For Gerard the kit functions as a public/ation that circulates and intervenes into different publics. Students engaged with all of the multiples in the kit, including the cwc posters created by their peers. However, the focus turned toward a series of broadsheets and stencils in the kit by Mare Liberum (Jean Barberis, Ben Cohen, Dylan Gauthier, Arthur Poisson, Sunita Prasad, Kendra Sullivan, and Stephan von Muehien). The broadsheets provide step-by-step instructions to fabricate three vessels: a dory, a punt, and a kayak. Following radical design practices and DIY principles, Mare Liberum has designed a number of watercrafts as platforms for art, inquiry, and environmental activism. *Mare liberum* is Latin for "freedom of the seas." Launching boats in local waterways, participants are invited to use the crafts to engage and explore local history, water and climate issues, processes of gentrification, and human-nature ecologies.

Before discussing the public/ations resulting from this iteration of the course, I'd like to provide some historical context surrounding the history of Fluxus and Roy Ascott's tenure at the Ontario College of Art (oca, now ocad u) in the 1970s (which I introduced in chapter 3). In 1972 the oca instructor Frank Ogden sailed with a dozen students from Toronto to Nassau, Bahamas, on *The Voyage of the Wet Orchid*. As a floating school, Ogden's voyage was highly controversial and fraught with potential to harm and lack of care for the students on board.[3] Upon completion of the course, Ogden printed diplomas on paper bags, a gesture further complicating or resisting institutional knowledge. The Pressing Issues students were introduced to this historical project through the OCAD U archives, alongside other Fluxus-type work from the 1960s and 1970s. Creating their own public/ation *Building a Wetter Orchid* over the course of a semester, the class departed significantly from Ogden's voyage and engaged with queer, feminist, and Indigenous scholarship on land, water protection, and climate change. Field trips included exploring Toronto's lakeshore, which was underwater at the time of the Toronto Purchase (Treaty 13) and remains the unceded territory of the Wendat, the Haudenosaunee, and the Anishinaabe peoples, including the Mississauga of the Credit First Nation. OCAD U is situated between the Humber and Don Rivers and Lake Ontario, all significant water trade routes and all implicated in the violence of settler colonialism. Students had opportunity to explore Toronto's inaugural Biennale of Art and, in particular, the curatorial project *The Shoreline Dilemma*, and to learn from Elder Duke Redbird's houseboat and meeting center. Research-creation inquiry was also guided by the Blackwood Gallery's exhibition and publication *The Work of Wind Air Land Sea*, and in particular Tania Willard's essay on land-based art practices and her "BUSH Manifesto" in the *Instant Class Kit*. The students connected with Dylan Gauthier, a founding member of Mare Liberum, on boat-building as environmental activism. Over the course of the semester, students responded to diverse research-creation processes through nanopublishing, making small-scale vessels from Mare Liberum's broadsheets out of recycled cardboard; printed protest posters overlaid on maps of Toronto and Ontario waterways; broadsheets and zines on water issues and water rights, climate change, and the Beaufort Scale; and a full-size punt out of wood and fiberglass. Each nanopublication was printed in an edition for each member of the class and housed inside a brown paper bag (a nod to Ogden's diplomas), printed with a white orchid on one side and on the other side a text explaining the context of the publication. One of these paper bag public/ations was inserted into the *Instant Class Kit* before being put back into circulation. As a kit within a kit, or a public/ation within a public/ation, and as a practice of anarchiving, *Building a Wetter Orchid* further extends and mobilizes publishing and printmaking as radical public pedagogies. Dylan Gauthier asks, in the Mare Liberum broadsheet, how one can make art about water when its scale is so vast and complex. One response, he suggests, is that the sea is impossible to sense or reproduce through traditional singular forms. It requires a research-creation approach that recognizes within it an incompleteness of knowing and the impossibility of bringing parts into a complete whole. The nanopublishing and research-creation of the *Building a Wetter Orchid* public/ation reside in a similar incompleteness and unlearning; they are public/ations to come.

In the conventional hubris of doing research, knowledge mobilization is described as the dissemination of research results. There is an assumption that the activities of doing research and the use of research are separate acts, suggesting a linear, procedural method: gather research results; analyze; and communicate results. One example might be: examine Fluxus materials in the archives; synthesize and collate that information; share the results and findings of that information through various forms including but not limited to academic papers. But the *Instant Class Kit*, the cwc, and the *Building a Wetter Orchid* muddle this procedural approach. In research-creation all of these various stages often occur simultaneously, or at the very least they trouble the relationship between results and knowledge mobilization as linear. For example, in the germination of the public/ations, not only are knowledges being gathered into a publication form and new publics being shaped: the circulation of the public/ations is happening in a similar unfolding spatiotemporal moment. The pop-up studio with typewriters is not merely a place of extracting research data but becomes what Ellsworth (2004) calls a membrane across which publics and public pedagogies can emerge and flow. As this work is being done, public/ations are already emerging that circulate and entwine themselves with future publics to come, or as Ellsworth puts it: "A staged public event becomes pedagogical and pedagogy becomes a public event when, together, they create a space between that reforms both the self and the other, the self and its lived relations with others" (48). Anarchiving is in constant formation, resisting the distinctions between researchers and users, and public pedagogies are felted into every iterative turn. As Manning (2020, 93) notes, anarchiving's "work is to proliferate, to make felt, for future reuptaking, germs of experience excluded from the occasion's taking form, it cannot be approached the same way twice." Anarchiving's movement is multidirectional. Seeded by a score, *Make a Public*, each iteration anarchives something different, a more-than of the proposition.

Public/ations as an Ethics of Care

If socially engaged art is enacted outside of classroom spaces and, in some instances, with diverse publics, and if public pedagogy is concerned with the emergence of publics to come, then it follows that we need to ask complex questions about what it means to come together in the interest of publicness. In the introduction, I posed these questions, which I repeat here: *How are relations composed and sustained over time? How are all bodies in relation being accounted for, attuned to, and offered something for their contribution to or labor of being in relation?* These are questions that I have returned to over and over throughout this book, not with any definitive answers but with a commitment and responsibility to the idea that an ethics of care must shape our work. This is why care as a concept repeats and felts its way through so many chapters. Opening space for the production of intimacy demands that we are response-able to the formation of relations. Intimacy stems from an awareness of the efforts it takes to cultivate relatedness in difference. The artist Pamela Matharu contends that intimacy is about holding space for relations, for things to come and for future worldings (Matharu and Goodden 2020).

Moreover, as O'Malley, Sandlin, and Burdick (2020) contend, doing the work *outside* of institutions must also alter the ways we do our work *inside* of the classroom. In other words, to return to Sholette's remarks that most socially engaged pedagogy occurs outside of the classroom, one must also ask critical questions about how the publicness of socially engaged work is actually transforming and interrupting the pedagogical encounter. When learning happens in communities and with communities there is a risk that socially engaged projects recenter whiteness and mobilize settler colonial logics of knowledge production and value. Further, outside can't be reified as learning par excellence unless it is interrupting the status quo of learning everywhere. The binary of outside or inside education requires intimate agitation. Engaging with communities outside of conventional classroom spaces necessitates that we make visible the structures of power and aim to cultivate horizontal relations grounded in care. This requires that we become accountable to the *how* of the pedagogical relation, to the coming together of bodies, human or otherwise. An ethics of care in the interest of publics to come must not be equated with positive actions or morality but needs to grapple with the noninnocent histories in which care circulates. As I have noted in previous discussions, care can serve settler colonialism and perpetuate inequalities, in as much as it can account for particular vital and ethical engagements. Writing about trans care, Hil Malatino (2020) argues that we need to interrogate the ways that care conventionally invokes family and kinships that are embedded in whiteness, domesticity, and cis-heteronormativity. As Julie McLeod (2017) and Alexis Shotwell (2016) contend, the anxiety of living in precarious times requires new modes of caring that neither idealize it nor depoliticize it. Socially engaged art as research-creation in the context of public pedagogy must become accountable to an ethics and politics of care.

Such an attention to care would expand Biesta's public pedagogy in the interest of a publicness that creates new ways of being and doing—a demonstration of alter-worlds—by making *how* we care central to this project. Biesta's togetherness requires an accountability and responsibility to caring across difference.

In addressing collaboration in the introduction, I quoted Astrida Neimanis (2012, 216), whose words regarding togetherness I feel are worth repeating here: "To collaborate is a doing-in-common, more than a being-in-common."

If, as Sholette (2018) observes, the teaching of socially engaged art requires students moving outside of the classroom to develop projects in situ and with diverse publics, then we need to ask complex questions about socially engaged arts' public pedagogy. Too often, the publicness of socially engaged art is articulated as ameliorative, transformative, and inclusive (Springgay 2014). While the public/ations created in the Pressing Issues courses attended to care at the level of content and curriculum—climate change and water rights, Black Lives Matter, trans rights, and so on—the form (methods) of the pedagogical encounters did not unsettle care. How the students came together (or didn't, in some cases) was rarely interrogated, nor was the form altered to create more just caring practices. For example, not all of the students, even though the funding for the trip was covered by the grant, were able to travel to Los Angeles. Some students could not take time off work, while others did not have the luxury of crossing international borders easily. In these details, questions of interdependent care did not shape the form of the project, just the content: there was an overriding assumption in the ameliorative possibilities of coming together as a form of publicness through a field trip but little accountability to the unequal access different students had to participating in this event. The lack of care further manifested in students' final contributions to the *Counter with Care* poster series, as those who had not been able to travel to Los Angeles didn't have the same lived experiences or connections to the content that shaped the publications.

As the Care Collective (2020, 45) asks, "How do we create the kind of caring communities that make our lives better, happier, and even in some cases, possible?" This is a fundamental question to ask of education. *What infrastructures, mutual aid, and spaces are needed to create caring communities inside and outside of schooling? How can socially engaged art as research-creation become a mode of care? How can public pedagogy become a form of care? And, how can caring become artful?* When we think of experiential education and community-engaged teaching, which is at the heart of teaching socially engaged art as research-creation, questions about the role that artists play in enacting care need to be asked. Public pedagogy in the interest of publics to come must privilege transcorporeal relations predicated on accountability, responsibility, and holding space for difference. Our becomings and worldings are entangled with what we touch and what touches us. Touching encounters demands that we care in and for the pedagogical event.

Susan Jahoda and Caroline Woolard's contribution to the *Instant Class Kit*, their *Making and Being* cards and booklet, shows one possible way to foreground an ethics of care in pedagogy. The book and cards offer discussion topics, activities, and writing exercises that examine collaboration, contemplation, and social-political analysis, including asset mapping, individual and group agreements, labor conditions, artist payments, student debt, support systems, and so on. In the project they ask: What if ways of being were integral to spaces of learning? Pedagogy must not only be concerned with form and content but must become accountable to the conditions that a pedagogical encounter creates. Centering an ethics of care as a fundamental condition of public/ations means public pedagogy becomes feltness.

Loveless (2019) contends that research-creation creates public forms of research. It would seem paramount then to practice an attention to publics to come as an ethics of care. As art schools proliferate programs and courses on socially engaged art and research-creation, and as issues of community engagement and publics become central in the work that we do, it is crucial that we become accountable to how we care in the act of forming socially engaged projects, and not just at the level of content. Perhaps the score *Make a Public* should become *Make a Caring Public*, or *Redefine Caring Relations*. Public/ations have the capacity and, in fact, the responsibility to approach public pedagogy differently, to make space for interdependent caring relations. If, as Loveless (2019, 102) claims, "form makes worlds" and research-creation is part of reshaping and recalibrating academic and artistic work, then socially engaged art as research-creation has a responsibility to center care actions in the pedagogical event and in our becoming publics.

Chapter Seven

Pedagogical
Impulses

A number of years ago, when I was first teaching at the Ontario Institute for Studies in Education (OISE), University of Toronto, during the early conceptualizations of my research-creation activities entangled with the Pedagogical Turn, I decided that I wanted to bring my curatorial practice into the university and my teaching. Before entering graduate school for my PhD, I worked as a curator at a small, publicly funded gallery in Ontario, the Latcham Gallery, where I first started thinking with and writing about contemporary queer feminist textile arts, embodied pedagogies, and social justice. It wasn't that I wanted to curate gallery-style exhibitions for the corridors or foyer spaces of the institution, but rather that I wanted to think of the work I do as an academic-artist through a curatorial-artistic framework: how to make one's office-work-classroom into a work of art. Part of what I wanted to do was to shift the ways in which we approached reading and studying in the academy—as something solitary and typically assigned in course work—to a practice of intimacy. To that extent I wanted to alter the function of my university office from a place where a faculty member held office hours, consulted students, and answered emails to a place of intimate relations between people, books, journals, performance ephemera, art objects (artist publications, prints, banners, buttons, badges, and small sculptural forms) that could be handled, borrowed, and sometimes altered.

Many of the artist contributions that reside in my office are pieces that have been gifted to me, or that I have collected, by many of the artists I write about in this book and with whom I have a long history of collaboration. Among the many are Shannon Gerard's *Keener Badges* and *Plants You Can't Kill*, Emelia-Amalia's artist publications on feminist citation and collaboration, posters by Justseeds artists, pennants by Marty Tremonte and Dylan Miner, and a divining rod by Aubyn O'Grady. The eighty-foot yellow-orange braided net from *Walls to the Ball* graced a corner, and banners from Hazel Meyer's *Muscle Panic* hung on a large expanse of wall. There were always stashes of red wool and felt making supplies. Part studio in orientation, part reading nook, and part gallery, my office became an important place to conceptualize radical pedagogy as feltness. There was a tea cart with an assortment of mugs, pots, kettle, and tea, and my students and research assistants had a key, taking up residence in the space even when I was not on campus.

In composing this space over the years, I have been partially informed by other similar office-curatorial-art spaces, although I have never visited any of these locations. The *Museum of Walking* at the University of Arizona is an archive, library, and resource center founded by Angela Ellsworth that is accountable to situated knowledges in relation to land through the act of walking. *The Bookcase and Micro-Museum and Library*, by Kirsty Robertson, at Western University, was an eight-month pop-up cabinet of curiosities organized by color to encourage a different form of browsing and study. Another example, by Jorge Lucero, at the University of Illinois Urbana-Champaign, is THEJORGELUCEROSTUDYCOLLECTION, an art library and ephemera archive that is open for study one hour per week to the public as a practice of institutional nearness. Lucero (2018, 82) writes of the study collection, "As an artist who thinks of pedagogy as material, I open the space once a week to the public in order to see if collecting, installation, and contemplation is a means to connect with people over long periods of time. The space has no rules of engagement other than that visitors must visit. How many times and to what level of engagement a visit is made is purposefully indeterminate."

All of these projects, in different ways, intervene into formal museum collection and display practices, while also questioning, interrupting, and remaking the behaviors, uses, and relations of educational institutional spaces, prioritizing intimacy and radical relatedness. Lucero (2018) considers his study collection a space of contemplation but also a critical space of questioning, interrogating, play, collage, and the absurd.

These office interventions are interdependent with other socially engaged art as research-creation practices that take place within educational spaces. Aubyn O'Grady, the program director at the Yukon School of Visual Art (SOVA) and a doctoral candidate at OISE, is composing a practice around the history of the school, its pedagogical innovations, and its relationship to the Tr'ondëk Hwëch'in First Nation in Dawson City, who are partners in the governance of the school. Using the concept of gold-as-mediator, the research-creation project will tune, receive, and transmit the stories of SOVA by way of AM radio waves. Research-creation enables O'Grady to broadcast, transmit, and complicate *currere*, the living curriculum of SOVA, and imagine a speculative future for the school. Jorge Lucero's work is similarly impressive and influential in my thinking. His ongoing project *Conceptual Art and Teaching* is interested in the flexibility of teaching as conceptual art and the teacher as a conceptual artist.[1] Having been artists in residence for the *Pedagogical Impulse*, Hannah Jickling and Reed Reed moved to Vancouver where they taught at the Emily Carr University of Art and Design. There they designed a series of courses on socially engaged art for university students that took up residency in a Vancouver elementary school, continuing to create sweets—bubble gum, candy bars, and other edibles—and pushing the concept of children as tastemakers and artists. Craig Morrison, founder and teacher at the Toronto District School Board's secondary school the Oasis Skateboard Factory, centers youth agency and BIPOC knowledges in his research-creation practices with youth. The school's curriculum and pedagogy, which Morrison has named "push pedagogy," is centered through the making of skateboards, SK8 brands and designs, and the entrepreneurial skills necessary to market and sell creative work.

These research-creation initiatives attest to the ongoing pedagogical impulses in socially engaged art. They are also, I would argue, reminders that while the university or education at large is in a moment of deep crisis, it is also a site of profound change in the undergrowth (Snaza and Singh 2021). And while Lucero, Morrison, and O'Grady might conceptualize and theorize their own practices differently from my own, I believe there is deep synergy between their work and what I call radical pedagogy as feltness. Furthermore, these artist-scholars agitate the boundaries between art and life by undertaking socially engaged art as research-creation with children, youth, families, students, teachers, community members, and nonhuman materials as acts of intimate relations. Their work pulses. These vibrations, as Campt (2017) notes, are not always audible. As a hum, or a haptic register, it becomes a movement of the undergrowth, casting off new vectors, anarchives, and helices. These impulses, I would add, extend to the ever-expanding research-creation programs across Canada, including the new iArts (Integrated Arts) undergraduate degree at McMaster University. As I discussed in the introduction, those of us working at Canadian universities in research-creation understand how complicit research-creation can be with the neoliberal logics of the colonial university. I also noted the ways in which research-creation can erase Indigenous and Black artistic and research practices that have been doing the work of refusal for far longer than the term *research-creation* has existed. However, the vibratory hum of increased research-creation degrees, programs, schools, departments, publications, exhibitions, performances, and public works suggests that careful attention to radical pedagogies of feltness are crucial if research-creation might possibly remake education. Not only should research-creation proliferate, it should be accountable to social justice and equity, to different articulations of value, to radical relations and publics to come as an ethics of care. This means we can't simply "teach" research-creation or facilitate research-creation theses; rather, we must interrogate the how of research-creation and the how of our coming together. Research-creation must also make space for, and hold space for, students who find themselves excluded from education. This means that the kinds of knowledges that shape socially engaged art as research-creation must constantly be made anew. It cannot become a sedimented act.

One of the challenges of doing this kind of work inside of institutions is formulating how to talk about the outcomes and impact of research-creation when the hum is not always discernable, when haptics, touching encounters, and feltness refuse capture and measurement. But what if we were to see these pedagogical impulses, these vectors, as felted tentacles of impact, their urgencies and relations evidence of an entangled knot of interdependence. As the above examples attest to, and the various projects threaded throughout the chapters of this book demonstrate, the hum of art as pedagogy is much louder than we might realize. Pedagogy matters. What these pedagogical impulses expose is the material, affective, and transcorporeal co-compositions of knowledge and art-research form-taking. This is a radical pedagogy that materializes immanent modes of transversal transformations and which emerges from relations of touching encounters.

I opened the introduction to this book with a description of the *Upside Down and Backwards* residency and the color bar compositions fabricated on the banks of the Don River. I return to it in this final chapter, to think with conditions of feltness as coming-to-form, or form-worldings. This coming-to-form entangles human and more-than-human bodies, matter, and pedagogies as endless, yet also mutating, iterative gestures. On another field trip as part of the residency, the classes walked to a different section of the Don River, to the now gentrified Brickworks Park. The Evergreen Brickworks Park (commonly referred to as the Brickworks) is a corporate landscape urbanism project that has repurposed an old brick factory in Toronto into a space with hiking and biking trails, a weekly farmers' market, an upscale café, a restaurant, and a "green" shop and garden center. The park supports a children's garden and programming and, in the winter, there is a public skating rink. Buildings on the site can be rented for corporate events and weddings.

At the Brickworks, the students walked with Elinor Whidden's *Rearview Walking Sticks* (on loan from the artist). The *Rearview Walking Sticks* are made from large tree branches and discarded car rearview mirrors. The walking sticks playfully suggest the ability to see behind oneself on a path. As a walking stick they imply usefulness, but they ultimately became ridiculous or burdensome as the students maneuvered between looking forward and reflecting back in space and time—not to mention the fact that the sticks were twice the height of the students. The paths in the Brickworks are human-made wooden boardwalks and well-groomed gravel paths, and so carrying a large walking stick seemed to be a misplaced walking behavior, a detail further emphasizing the students' own unbelonging on the paths of a gentrified park in the Canadian landscape.

The students also used round mirrors, roughly the size of an average child's head, and digital cameras to stage a series of exposures. Students placed the mirrors in front of their faces and a partner photographed their portrait—but with a reflection of land, sky, or park object (e.g., a brick wall or lily pad) in the mirror. The results produced a series of student portraits in which their faces became intertwined with place, entangling them with the landscape. Juice boxes were covered in reflective, mirrored paper and used to create additional compositions. The various research-creation projects invented different possibilities of existence: rather than figuring racially and ethnically diverse school children as "out of place" or unbelonging in nature, the research-creation interventions enabled them to reimagine a different future for themselves, one in which they are part of the spatiotemporality of the Canadian landscape—or, more importantly, of their local park and neighborhood. In a final gesture connecting students with place and home, the students had been asked to position the rainbow color bars in upper-floor balconies of the apartment buildings where they lived, which faced the Brickworks park. On top of a hill in the park, and using telescopes, the children could see their homes and the queer constellation of rainbow color bars, a kind of proximal or touching encounter between home, school, river, and landscape. While the residency sought to rupture settler colonial and normalized canons of landscape art in the elementary school curriculum, it also seeded the conditions of radical pedagogy as feltness. This residency, like the other exemplifications throughout the book, are attuned to the *how* of research-creation: a how that is emergent, iterative, and form-taking. Against the idea that art is subjective and, as such, able to be anything at all, Lucero (2018) ponders whether a more direct definition is plausible, suggesting that art occurs when an artist tests pliability. This is an articulation of how, not what. For research-creation, pliability renders thinking-making-doing elastic, in flux, a score. Pliability also infers a future tense, a public to come, but so too it invokes touch, agitation, and movement. This is how I conceive of pedagogical impulses: mutations, transformations, and entanglements. Instead of a Pedagogical Turn, what if we thought of this impulse as a vector, a multiplicity that is ever evolving and mutating, like the *Endless Paintings?*

I have claimed throughout this book that feltness—conceptualized as touching encounters, as feelings and affects, and as friction and agitation—conditions radical pedagogy that is attuned to social justice and an ethics of care. Disrupting the values and tastes normalized through educational institutions and art, socially engaged art as research-creation is concerned with a future and with publics to come, that must. As anomalous, as intertextual intimacies, imponderable, open, ordinary, and scored, radical pedagogy as feltness seeds and germinates future anarchives and transversal entanglements between art, research, and pedagogy.

Socially engaged art as research-creation is collaborative, and many interlocutors are knotted throughout this book. Part of collaborating is generosity and capaciousness; to the teachers who opened their classrooms to me and my research team over many months and sometimes repeatedly, I am forever grateful. The students in K–12 schools and in postsecondary classes with whom I have had the privilege to think-make-do remind me of the necessity of humor and play in research-creation. Perhaps everyone needs a little bit of poo humor and butter dancing in their lives. There are many thoughts in these pages that owe a debt to my graduate students over the last decade and to many colleagues. Research-creation emerges out of the middle space of know-ing and not knowing, learning and unlearning, where pliable curiosity felts its way into something else altogether. It cannot be replicated. I figured out how to practice research-creation as feltness in the midst of these many projects, and I am still making space as I embark on new projects and events to know research-creation differently through each new impulse.

INTRODUCTION

1   For a robust discussion on research-creation in relation to other arts-based or artistic research practices see Natalie Loveless's book *How to Make Art at the End of the World* (2019).

2   The Pedagogical or Educational Turn emerged in the 1990s as a research-informed art practice concerned with questions about education.

3   The artist Joseph Beuys, whose practice is loosely connected to socially engaged art, often used felt as a material. However, his work is not a reference for my own felting practice. He typically used grey industrial felt, while I am interested in the handmade process of felting wool and human hair and draw on feminist textile art practices.

4   CARFAC is Canadian Artist Representation/Le Front des artistes canadiens, a non-profit association for visual artists. Among their many mandates is supporting economic and legal rights for artists. They publish an annual fee schedule that publicly funded museums and galleries must follow. I use CARFAC rates to pay artists.

5   Grant funds would pay for the cost of a substitute teacher so that the regular classroom teacher could meet with the artists or research team. This was, and remains, a significant part of my research-creation practice. Teachers work tirelessly; to contribute to and participate in the projects, their labor needs to be acknowledged and rewarded. I did not want meetings or planning sessions to happen after school hours, and I wanted to consider their paid work as vital to the projects.

6   Rather than limit the kinds of research possible, SSHRC funds enable the research-creation to flourish because funding makes possible such large-scale projects. SSHRC prioritizes paying students, artists, and community collaborators and supports highly speculative proposals. There are no expectations by the funders to produce particular kinds of outcomes nor final reports, and research-creation is a grant category in the SSHRC funding taxonomy.

7   Photodocumentation with students is governed by institutional ethics. In many cases this included both University of Toronto ethics and Toronto District School Board ethics. In photographing students, parental or guardian consent is required. The consent process incorporated a multipronged approach. All students could participate in

the project regardless of consent. Parents or guardians and students could consent to the following: (1) documentation of student artwork only for research purposes, not to be published; (2) documentation of student artwork for research purposes, with publication allowed; (3) documentation of student artwork that could include images of the students, only for research purposes and not to be published; (4) documentation of student artwork that could include images of the students, for research purposes and with publication allowed; (5) no documentation of any kind. Class photos were given to us by the teachers, with student names labeled. We further annotated this photo based on the consent forms submitted. At the end of each research day, as the digital images were uploaded to a hard drive, my lead research assistant would move images into folders marked by the first four categories described above. Any images that fell into category number 5 were destroyed. Images that were later curated for the research website had to be selected from folders 2 and 4, while folders 1 and 3 could be used for reflections and discussion among the artists, teachers, and research team. Obtaining consent to use photodocumentation is complicated but not impossible if you follow such labor-intensive and consensual processes. Names of schools have been given pseudonyms per ethics guidelines, and students and teachers are not named in the research. Artists could choose to have their identities included in documentation.

ONE. BITTER CHOCOLATE IS FOR ADULTS!

1   As mentioned in the introduction's note 7, for ethical reasons, schools discussed in this book have been assigned pseudonyms.

2   This is the website for the National Bitter Melon Council. You can find more information on their project here: Andi Sutton, "The National Bitter Melon Council," March 2021, http://www.andisutton.net/post-is-a-post/.

3   Both of the school-based residencies started from the proposition *trade*. However, based on student input and different school contexts, the two residencies became unique. However, both residencies commenced with a socially engaged activity that got students thinking about value and its relationship to trade and commerce. Students were introduced to the artist David Hammons and the work *Bliz-aard Ball Sale* (1983). In this artwork Hammons sold snowballs on a street corner in Cooper Square in New York City's East Village. The snowballs were of varying sizes and were laid out on a colorful woven mat. Having been introduced to this artwork, and after engaging in a series of classroom discussions on trade and value, the students gathered outside the schools to make their own snowballs in small groups. In both instances it was an unusual winter in Toronto and there was very little snow on the ground. The artists hauled snow, which they collected from local ice rinks, in large Ikea bags to the schoolyard. In groups the students made snowballs according to the kind of value and trade they wanted to create. After they had made their snowballs, and with an adult supervisor, the students moved through the school neighborhood and traded or sold their snowballs to strangers. Some groups made their snowballs quickly, amassing as many as they could with the intended value of a snowball fight with a group of

strangers. One group made more tightly packed, fairly round snowballs, which they traded for pieces of contraband chewing gum. One student spent a long time making a perfect heart-shaped snowball, which she sold for twenty-five dollars to a young man entering the subway. The proceeds from the snowball sale went to an end-of-residency pizza party.

4   This grade-six teacher had come to the chocolate residency open house and trade fair and subsequently expected to host an identical residency in his class. While the initial activity in both schools was the sale of snowballs, the socially engaged art as research-creation took different directions. I mention this to emphasize that research-creation can't be procedural or predictive. It emerges in the middle of the research event.

TWO. IMPONDERABLE CURRICULA

1   Noteworthy, as discussed previously, is a pseudonym.

2   Steveni's authorship of the APG (later renamed O+I) and her pivotal role in negotiating placements and developing the international profile of the APG have been overshadowed in historical records and art publications by attention to the work of her former husband and partner, John Latham.

3   The School Resource Officers program was launched in 2008, one year after the fifteen-year-old grade-nine student Jordan Manners was shot and killed at C. W. Jeffreys Collegiate in the Toronto District School Board (TDSB). The program drew sharp criticism from activists, particularly those affiliated with Black Lives Matter, and was dismantled in 2017. Noteworthy occupies the same geographic and demographic area in the TDSB as C. W. Jeffreys (the northwest quadrant of the city) and was selected to maintain a police presence on site; out of 110 schools in the TDSB, 45 kept uniformed officers on site.

4   The Ontario Safe Schools Act, known by many as the "zero tolerance" policy, was officially adopted in 2000. It takes a hardline approach to behavior, discipline, and safety and enables principals and teachers to suspend students for up to twenty days. Most significant is the involvement of uniformed police in school suspensions and expulsions. Critics of zero tolerance note the disproportionate impact on Black and Indigenous students, students of color, and students with disabilities. In 2012, when we first started working at Noteworthy Secondary School (we continued working there until 2014), there was a heavy police presence and the school was very much governed by the zero tolerance policy.

THREE. FLUXUS AND THE EVENT SCORE

1   This publication was funded by the Carnegie Corporation of New York and included five essays, including proposals from Maciunas and Watts. It also collected quotations and interview excerpts from a wide range of art educators, artists, scholars, and college students.

2 Barbara Steveni's *I Am an Archive* is a mobile, performative examination of APG archives in situ. I was introduced to the project by Steveni, and documentation can be found here: https://en.contextishalfthework.net/ (accessed March 2021).

3 Other artists affiliated with Fluxus included Philip Corner, Robert Filliou, Alison Knowles, Arthur Köpcke, Shigeko Kubota, George Maciunas, Jackson Mac Low, Shiomi Mieko, Yoko Ono, Nam June Paik, Ben Patterson, Dieter Roth, Takako Saito, Tomas Schmit, Daniel Spoerri, Ben Vautier, and Wolf Vostell.

4 Quotes in this section come from recorded conversations with the participants.

5 The Dish with One Spoon Treaty is an agreement between the Anishinaabe, Mississauga, and Haudenosaunee that binds them to share and protect the land that is now considered an area of southern Ontario.

FIVE. CONDITIONS OF FELTNESS

1 The kits' circulation was brought to an abrupt halt as the world responded to the pandemic and institutions closed their doors. For months they sat in a corner of my home office begging to be opened and handled. Over the course of the summer Andrea Vela Alarcón, an artist and activist and my research assistant, created a series of self-guided workshops to activate the contents of the kits in an online form. These self-guided workshops bring together two or more multiples through a series of propositional questions and activities that educators might do with their students. As online PDFs accessed through the research website, the kits' circulation can continue in this moment of provincial, national, and global lockdown.

SIX. MAKE A PUBLIC

1 Funding for the trip came from the print and publications department at OCAD U, fundraising efforts by the students, and my SSHRC grant.

2 The risograph is a stencil duplicator technology created in the 1980s. Its capacity to print a large volume of materials resembles that of a photocopier, but its layered functioning is similar to the screen printing process. In the past decade it has become a popular and affordable medium for artists to reproduce their work.

3 The condition of the boat was reported to be poor and the students spent most of the trip doing repairs to keep it running. There was little organization on the part of Ogden, who abandoned the project and the students once they arrived in Nassau.

SEVEN. PEDAGOGICAL IMPULSES

1 Lucero's *Conceptual Art and Teaching* is documented on his website. You can find more information here: https://www.jorgelucero.com/cat-about-1/ (accessed March 2021).

Ahmed, Sara. 2004. *The Cultural Politics of Emotion*. New York: Routledge.

Ahmed, Sara. 2010. "Happy Objects." In *The Affect Theory Reader*, edited by Melissa Gregg and Gregory J. Seigworth, 29–51. Durham, NC: Duke University Press.

Ahmed, Sara. 2014. *Willful Subjects*. Durham, NC: Duke University Press.

Ahmed, Sara. 2019. *What's the Use?* Durham, NC: Duke University Press.

Alaimo, Stacy. 2010. *Bodily Natures: Science, Environment, and the Material Self*. Bloomington: Indiana University Press.

Alaimo, Stacy. 2016. *Exposed: Environmental Politics and Pleasures in Posthuman Times*. Minneapolis: University of Minnesota Press.

Allen, Felicity. 2011. *Education*. Cambridge, MA: MIT Press.

Aoki, Ted. 1993. "Legitimizing Lived Curriculum: Towards a Curricular Landscape of Multiplicity." *Journal of Curriculum and Supervision* 8, no. 3: 255–68.

Apple, Michael W. 1979. *Ideology and Curriculum*. London: Routledge.

Barad, Karen. 2007. *Meeting the Universe Half Way: Quantum Physics and the Entanglement of Matter and Meaning*. Durham, NC: Duke University Press.

Barad, Karen. 2012. "On Touching: The Inhuman That Therefore I Am." *differences: A Journal of Feminist Cultural Studies* 23, no. 3: 206–23.

Berlant, Lauren. 2011. *Cruel Optimism*. Durham, NC: Duke University Press.

Berlant, Lauren, and Kathleen Stewart. 2019. *The Hundreds*. Durham, NC: Duke University Press.

Bertelsen, Lone, and Andrew Murphie. 2010. "An Ethics of Everyday Infinities and Powers: Felix Guattari on Affect and the Refrain." In *The Affect Theory Reader*, edited by Melissa Gregg and Gregory J. Seigworth, 138–57. Durham, NC: Duke University Press.

Biesta, Gert. 2012. "Becoming Public: Public Pedagogy, Citizenship and the Public Sphere." *Social and Cultural Geography* 13, no. 7: 683–97.

Biesta, Gert. 2014. "Making Pedagogy Public: For the Public, of the Public or in the Interest of Publicness." In *Problematizing Public Pedagogy*, edited by Jake Burdick, Jennifer A. Sandlin, and Michael P. O'Malley, 15–25. New York: Routledge.

Bishop, Claire. 2012. *Artificial Hells: Participatory Art and the Politics of Spectatorship*. New York: Verso.

Bishop, Claire. 2013. "Follow-Up Interview: Claire Bishop, Art Historian." In *What We Made: Conversations on Art and Social Cooperation,* edited by Tom Finkelpearl, 179–218. Durham, NC: Duke University Press.

Bishop, Claire. 2014. *Radical Museology: Or What's Contemporary in Museums of Contemporary Art?* Cologne: Walther König.

Bishop, Claire, and Nikki Columbus. 2020. "Free Your Mind: A Speculative Review of #newMoMA." *n + 1,* January 7. https://nplusonemag.com/online-only/paper -monument/free-your-mind/.

Black, Anthea, and Nicole Burisch, eds. 2021. *The New Politics of the Handmade.* New York: Bloomsbury Visual Arts.

Blackman, Lisa. 2015. "Affective Politics, Debility and Hearing Voices: Towards a Feminist Politics of Ordinary Suffering." *Feminist Review* 3, no. 1: 25–41.

Blackman, Lisa. 2017. "'Loving the Alien': A Post-Post-Human Manifesto." *Subjectivity* 10, no. 1: 13–25.

Blaise, Mindy. 2014. "Interfering with Gendered Development: A Timely Intervention." *International Journal of Early Childhood* 46, no. 3: 317–26.

Boetzkes, Amanda. 2019. *Plastic Capitalism: Contemporary Art and the Drive to Waste.* Cambridge, MA: MIT Press.

Bruguera, Tania. 2019. "Notes on Political Timing Specificity." *Artforum* 57, no. 9 (May). Accessed March 1, 2021. https://www.artforum.com/print/201905/notes-on-political -timing-specificity-79513/.

Bruguera, Tania. 2020. *Tania Bruguera in Conversation with Claire Bishop.* New York: Fundación Cisneros.

Burdick, Jake, Jennifer A. Sandlin, and Michael P. O'Malley, eds. 2014. *Problematizing Public Pedagogy.* New York: Routledge.

Cahill, Susan. 2012. *The Games of Art: The Art of Games; Exhibition Essay.* St. John's, NF: Eastern Edge Art Gallery.

Campt, Tina. 2017. *Listening to Images.* Durham, NC: Duke University Press.

Caplow, Deborah. 2009. "Political Art and Printmaking: A Brief and Partial History." In *Paper Politics: Socially Engaged Printmaking Today,* edited by Josh MacPhee, 12–19. Oakland, CA: PM Press.

Capper, Emily. 2016. *Allan Kaprow and the Dialectics of Instruction, 1947–1968.* PhD diss., University of Chicago.

Care Collective. 2020. *The Care Manifesto: The Politics of Interdependence.* New York: Verso.

Chapman, Owen. 2020. "Foreword." In *Knowings and Knots: Methodologies and Ecologies in Research-Creation,* edited by Natalie Loveless, xv–xxvii. Edmonton: University of Alberta Press.

Chen, Mel Y. 2012. *Animacies: Biopolitics, Racial Mattering, and Queer Affect.* Durham, NC: Duke University Press.

Choi, Alvis. 2017. "Introduction." *Bodies as Archives: QTBIPOC Art and Performance in Toronto. Marvellous Grounds,* no. 2. Accessed January 1, 2019. http://marvellousgrounds .com/blog/issue-2-qtbipoc-art-and-performance-introduction/.

Classen, Constance. 1993. *Worlds of Sense: Exploring the Senses in History and across Cultures.* New York: Routledge.

Clough, Patricia. 2008. "The Affective Turn: Political Economy, Biomedia, and Bodies." *Theory, Culture and Society* 25, no. 1: 1–22.

Couillard, Paul. 2020. "From No-ing to Knowing, from Naughts to Knots." In *Knowings and Knots: Methodologies and Ecologies in Research-Creation*, edited by Natalie Loveless, 43–74. Edmonton: University of Alberta Press.

Cutler, Randy L. 2020. "Open Wide: Figuring Digestion as Research-Creation." In *Knowings and Knots: Methodologies and Ecologies in Research-Creation*, edited by Natalie Loveless, 3–28. Edmonton: University of Alberta Press.

Cvetkovich, Ann. 2003. *An Archive of Feelings: Trauma, Sexuality, and Lesbian Public Cultures*. Durham, NC: Duke University Press.

Decter, Leah. 2018. *Performing Memoration: Integrative Artistic Strategies for Unsettling from a White Settler Perspective*. PhD diss., Queens University, Kingston, ON.

Deleuze, Gilles, and Félix Guattari. 1987. *A Thousand Plateaus: Capitalism and Schizophrenia*. Minneapolis: University of Minnesota Press.

Deleuze, Gilles, and Félix Guattari. 1994. *What Is Philosophy?* New York: Columbia University Press.

De Robertis, Carolina. 2017. *Radical Hope: Letters of Love and Hope in Dangerous Times*. New York: Vintage.

Derrida, Jacques. 1995. "Archive Fever: A Freudian Impression." Translated by Eric Prenowitz. *Diacritics* 25, no. 2: 9–63.

Dewhurst, Marit, and Keonna Hendrick. 2017. "Identifying and Transforming Racism in the Museum." *Journal of Museum Education* 42, no. 2: 102–7.

DiAngelo, Robin, and Özlem Sensoy. 2014. "Leaning In: A Student's Guide to Engaging Constructively with Social Justice Content." *Radical Pedagogy* 11, no. 1: article 2.

Drobnick, Jim. 1999. "Recipes for the Cube: Aromatic and Edible Practices in Contemporary Art." In *Foodculture: Tasking Identities and Geographies in Art*, edited by Barbara Fischer, 69–80. Toronto, ON: YYZ Books.

Drobnick, Jim. 2016. "Germaine Koh: Post-performativity and Incidental Aesthetics." In *Caught in the Act, Vol. 2: Performance by Canadian Women*, edited by Johanna Householder and Tanya Mars, 270–81. Toronto, ON: YYZ Books.

Dyment, Dave, and Gregory Elgstrand, eds. 2012. *One for Me and One to Share: Artists' Multiples and Editions*. Toronto, ON: YYZBOOKS.

Ellsworth, Elizabeth. 2004. *Places of Learning: Media, Architecture, Pedagogy*. New York: Routledge.

Farley, Lisa. 2018. *Childhood beyond Pathology: A Psychoanalytic Study of Development and Diagnosis*. Albany: State University of New York Press.

Filliou, Robert. [1970] 2014. *Lehren un Lernen aus Auffuehrungskuenste/Teaching and Learning as Performance Art*. Cologne/New York: Koenig. Facsimile edition, Occasional Papers.

Finkelpearl, Tom. 2013. *What We Made: Conversations on Art and Social Cooperation*. Durham, NC: Duke University Press.

Fisher, Jennifer. 1999. "Performing Taste." In *Foodculture: Tasking Identities and Geographies in Art*, edited by Barbara Fischer, 29–48. Toronto, ON: YYZBOOKS.

Fournier, Lauren. 2021. *Autotheory as Feminist Practice in Art, Writing, and Criticism*. Cambridge, MA: MIT Press.

Friedman, Ken, ed. 1998. *The Fluxus Reader*. London: Academy Editions.

Garneau, David. 2013. "Extra-rational Aesthetic Action and Cultural Decolonization." *FUSE Magazine* 36, no. 4: 15–16.

Gaztambide-Fernández, Ruben A. 2013. "Why the Arts Don't Do Anything: Toward a New Vision for Cultural Production in Education." *Harvard Educational Review* 83, no. 1: 211–36.

Gerling, Max. 2019. "Excrementalisms: Revaluing What We Have Only Ever Known as Waste." *Food, Culture and Society* 22, no. 5: 622–38.

Gordon, Bonnie, Lani Hanna, Jen Hoyer, and Vero Ordaz. 2016. "Archives, Education, and Access: Learning at Interference Archive." *Radical Teacher* 105: 54–60.

Graham, Janna. 2010. "Between a Pedagogical Turn and a Hard Place: Thinking with Conditions." In *Curating and the Educational Turn*, edited by Paul O'Neill and Mick Wilson, 124–39. London: Open Editions.

Graham, Janna, Valeria Graziano, and Susan Kelly. 2016. "The Educational Turn in Art: Rewriting the Hidden Curriculum." *Performance Research* 21, no. 6: 29–35.

Greetham, David. 1999. "Who's In, Who's Out: The Cultural Poetics of Archival Exclusion." *Studies in the Literary Imagination* 32, no. 1, 1–28.

Grumet, Madeleine, and William Pinar. [1976] 2014. *Toward a Poor Curriculum*. 3rd ed. Troy, NY: Educator's International Press.

Guattari, Félix. 1984. "Transversality." In *Molecular Revolution: Psychiatry and Politics*, translated by Rosemary Sheed. Middlesex, UK: Penguin.

Guattari, Félix. 1995. *Chaosmosis: An Ethico-aesthetic Paradigm*. Bloomington: Indiana University Press.

Haiven, Max. 2018. *Art after Money, Money after Art: Creative Strategies against Financialization*. Toronto, ON: Pluto Press.

Halberstam, Jack. 2011. *The Queer Art of Failure*. Durham, NC: Duke University Press.

Halberstam, Jack. 2013. "The Wild Beyond with and for the Undercommons." In *The Undercommons: Fugitive Planning and Black Study*, edited by Stefano Harney and Fred Moten, 2–12. New York: Minor Compositions.

Haraway, Donna J. 2008. *When Species Meet*. Minneapolis: University of Minnesota Press.

Haraway, Donna J. 2016. *Staying with the Trouble: Making Kin in the Chthulucene*. Durham, NC: Duke University Press.

Haritaworn, Jin, Ghaida Moussa, and Syrus Ware. 2019. "Introduction." In *Marvellous Grounds: Queer of Colour Histories of Toronto*, edited by Jin Haritaworn, Ghaida Moussa, and Syrus Ware 1–20. Toronto, ON: Between the Lines.

Harney, Stefano, and Fred Moten. 2013. *The Undercommons: Fugitive Planning and Black Study*. New York: Minor Compositions.

Harren, Natilee. 2016. "Fluxus and the Transitional Commodity." *Art Journal* 75, no. 1: 44–69.

Harren, Natilee. 2020. *Fluxus Forms: Scores, Multiples, and the Eternal Network*. Chicago: Chicago University Press.

Harren, Natilee. Forthcoming. "Proposals for Intermedia Art Education: Robert Watts's Experimental Workshop at the University of California, Santa Cruz, 1968–69." In *Intermedia, Terra Foundation Essays* Vol. 6, edited by Ursula Frohne. Chicago: Terra Foundation for American Art.

Hatch, Ryan, Sonya Sternlieb, and Julia Gordon. 2019. "Sugar Ecologies: Their Metabolic and Racial Effects." *Food, Culture and Society* 22, no. 5: 595–607.

Hawkins, Gay, and Stephen Muecke. 2003. *Culture and Waste.* New York: Rowman and Littlefield.

Hecker, Sharon. 2019. "Luciano Fabro: Bitter Sweets for Nadezhda Mandelstam." In *The Taste of Art: Cooking, Food, and Counterculture in Contemporary Practices,* edited by Silvia Bottinelli and Margherita D'Ayala Valva, 121–42. Fayetteville: University of Arkansas Press.

Heijnen, Emiel, and Melissa Bremmer, eds. 2020. *Wicked Arts Assignments: Practicing Creativity in Contemporary Arts Education.* Amsterdam: Valiz.

Helguera, Pablo. 2010. *Education for Socially Engaged Art.* New York: Jorge Pinto Books.

Hennessy, Kate, and Trudy Lynn Smith. 2018. "Fugitives: Anarchival Materiality on the Archives." *public: Art/Culture/Ideas* 57: 128–44. Toronto, ON: York University.

Higgins, Dick. 1998. "Theory and Reception." In *The Fluxus Reader,* edited by Ken Friedman, 217–36. London: Academy Editions.

Higgins, Hannah. 2002. *Fluxus Experience.* Berkeley: University of California Press.

Hird, Myra. 2017. "Proliferation, Extinction, and an Anthropocene Aesthetic." In *Posthumous Life: Theorizing beyond the Posthuman,* edited by Jami Weinstein and Claire Colebrook, 251–69. New York: Columbia University Press.

Holert, Tom. 2020. *Knowledge beside Itself: Contemporary Art's Epistemic Politics.* Berlin: Sternburg Press.

Howes, David. 2004. *Empire of the Senses: The Sensual Culture Reader.* New York: Routledge.

Hudek, Antony. 2010. *The Incidental Person Exhibition Essay.* New York: Apexart.

Hudson, Audrey, Awad Ibrahim, and Karyn Recollet, eds. 2019. *In This Together: Blackness, Indigeneity, and Hip-Hop.* New York: DIO Press.

Iversen, Margaret, ed. 2010. *Chance: Documents in Contemporary Art.* London: Whitechapel Gallery.

Jackson, Shannon. 2011. *Social Works: Performing Art, Supporting Publics.* New York: Routledge.

Jickling, Hannah, and Reed Reed, eds. 2017. *Multiple Elementary.* Toronto, ON: YYZBOOKS.

Jickling, Hannah, and Reed Reed. 2019. "Big Rock Candy Mountain." Interview by Marina Roy. Canadianart, January 29. Accessed March 1, 2020. https://canadianart.ca/reviews/big-rock-candy-mountain/.

Johnson, Emily, and Karyn Recollet. 2020. "Kin-dling and Other Radical Relationalities." *Artlink* 40, no. 2: n.p.

Kaprow, Allan. [1966] 2010. "Assemblage, Environments and Happenings." In *Chance: Documents in Contemporary Art,* edited by Margaret Iversen, 52–57. London: Whitechapel Gallery.

Kaprow, Allan. [1972] 1993. "Education of the Un-artist Part II." In *Essays on the Blurring of Art and Life,* edited by Allan Kaprow, 110–26. Berkeley: University of California Press.

Kaprow, Allan. 1994. "Success and Failure When Art Changes." In *Mapping the Terrain: New Genre Public Art,* edited by Suzanne Lacy, 152–58. San Francisco, CA: Bay Press.

Kashmere, Brett. 2018. "Neither/Nor: Other Cinema as an Archives and an Anti-archives." *Public* 57: 14–26.

Kelley, Lindsay. 2019. "Everyday Militarisms in the Kitchen: Tasting History." Accessed March 8, 2022. https://sei.sydney.edu.au/opinion/everyday-militarisms-kitchen-tasting-history/.

Kester, Grant. 2004. *Conversation Pieces: Community and Communication in Modern Art.* Berkeley: University of California Press.

Khanna, Neetu. 2020. *The Visceral Logics of Decolonization.* Durham, NC: Duke University Press.

Kinnunen, Tania, and Marjo Kolehmainen. 2019. "Touch and Affect: Analyzing the Archive of Touch Biographies." *Body and Society* 25, no. 1: 29–56.

Krauss, Annette. 2013. "Documenting Secrets." *The Pedagogical Impulse.* Accessed March 1, 2020. https://thepedagogicalimpulse.com/documenting-secrets/.

La Berge, Leigh C. 2019. *Wages against Artwork: Decommodified Labor and the Claims of Socially Engaged Art.* Durham, NC: Duke University Press.

Langlois, Justin. 2021. "Invisible Hospitalities of the Art School." *Public* 61: 196–207.

Lara, Ali, Wen Liu, Colin P. Ashley, Akemi Nishida, Rachel Leibert, and Michelle Billies. 2017. "Affect and Subjectivity." *Subjectivity* 10, no. 1: 30–43.

Lather, Patti, and Elizabeth A. St. Pierre. 2013. "Post-qualitative Research." *International Journal of Qualitative Studies in Education* 26, no. 6: 629–33.

Loveless, Natalie. n.d. "Action a Day." Accessed January 1, 2020. https://www.justpowers.ca/projects/action-a-day-performance-project/.

Loveless, Natalie. 2015. "Towards a Manifesto on Research-Creation." RACAR: *Revue d'art canadienne/Canadian Art Review* 40, no. 1: 52–54.

Loveless, Natalie. 2019. *How to Make Art at the End of the World.* Durham, NC: Duke University Press.

Loveless, Natalie, ed. 2020. *Knowings and Knots: Methodologies and Ecologies in Research-Creation.* Edmonton: University of Alberta Press.

Lowry, Glen. 2015. "Props to Bad Artists: On Research-Creation and a Cultural Politics of University-Based Art." RACAR: *Revue d'art canadienne/Canadian Art Review* 40, no. 1: 42–46.

Lucero, Jorge. 2011. *Ways of Being: Conceptual Art Modes-of-Operation for Pedagogy as Contemporary Art Practice.* PhD diss., Pennsylvania State University.

Lucero, Jorge. 2018. "Wallowing in Weird Passions: A Conversation on Art, Collecting, and Studying with Jorge Lucero and Tyson Lewis." *Visual Arts Research* 44, no. 1: 76–88.

Lucero, Jorge. 2020. *Teacher as Artist-in-Residence: The Most Radical Form of Expression to Ever Exist.* Washington, DC: The John F. Kennedy Center for the Performing Arts.

Lucero, Jorge, and Laura Shaeffer, eds. 2020. *The Compound Yellow Manual: Of Prompts, Provocations, Permissions and Parameters for Everyday Practice.* Chicago: Hyde Park Art Center.

Maciunas, George. 1963. *Fluxus Manifesto.* New York: Museum of Modern Art.

McLuhan, Marshall. 1964. *Understanding Media: The Extensions of Man.* Cambridge, MA: MIT Press.

Maclure, Maggie. 2013. "The Wonder of Data." *Cultural Studies/Critical Methodologies* 13, no. 4: 228–32.

MacPhee, Josh, ed. 2009. *Paper Politics: Socially Engaged Printmaking Today.* Oakland, CA: PM Press.

MacPhee, Josh, ed. 2020. *Celebrate People's History: The Poster Book of Resistance and Revolution.* New York: Feminist Press at CUNY.

Malatino, Hil. 2020. *Trans Care.* Minneapolis: University of Minnesota Press.

Mann, Anna, Annemarie Mol, Priya P. Satalkar, Amalinda Savirani, Nasima Selim, Malini Sur, and Emily Yates-Doerr. 2017. "Mixing Methods, Tasting Fingers: Notes on an Ethnographic Experiment." *HAU: Journal of Ethnographic Theory* 1, no. 1: 221–43.

Manning, Erin. 2007. *Politics of Touch: Sense, Movement, Sovereignty.* Minneapolis: University of Minnesota Press.

Manning, Erin. 2013. *Always More Than One: Individuation's Dance.* Durham, NC: Duke University Press.

Manning, Erin. 2016. *The Minor Gesture.* Durham, NC: Duke University Press.

Manning, Erin. 2020. *For a Pragmatics of the Useless.* Durham, NC: Duke University Press.

Manning, Erin, and Brian Massumi. 2014. *Thought in the Act: Passages in the Ecology of Experience.* Minneapolis: University of Minnesota Press.

Martin, Aryn, Natasha Myers, and Ana Viseu. 2015. "The Politics of Care in Technoscience." *Social Studies of Science* 45, no. 5: 625–41.

Massumi, Brian. 2016. "Working Principles." In *The Go-To How-To Book of Anarchiving*, edited by Andrew Murphie, 6–8. Montreal: SenseLab. Accessed March 1, 2021. http://senselab.ca/wp2/wp-content/uploads/2016/12/Go-To-How-To-Book-of-Anarchiving-landscape-Digital-Distribution.pdf.

Matharu, Pamila, and Sky Goodden. 2020. "Communing with (Art) Ancestors." *c Magazine* 144: 16–22.

McKittrick, Katherine. 2021. *Dear Science and Other Stories.* Durham, NC: Duke University Press.

McLeod, Julie. 2017. "Reframing Responsibility in an Era of Responsibilisation: Education, Feminist Ethics." *Discourse: Studies in the Cultural Politics of Education* 38, no. 1: 43–56.

Mereweather, Charles. 2006. *The Archive.* Cambridge, MA: MIT Press.

Miller, Janet. 2005. *Sounds of Silence Breaking: Women, Autobiography, Curriculum.* New York: Peter Lang.

Miner, Dylan. 2009. "Existence Section." In *Paper Politics: Socially Engaged Printmaking Today,* edited by Josh MacPhee, 130–31. Oakland, CA: PM Press.

Mirzoeff, Nicholas. 2016. "It's Not the Anthropocene, It's the White Supremacy Scene: Or, the Geological Color Line." In *After Extinction,* edited by Richard Grusin, chap. 6. Minneapolis: University of Minnesota Press. Kindle.

Mishra Tarc, Aparna. 2015. *Literacy of the Other: Renarrating Humanity.* Albany: State University of New York Press.

Mohamed, Maandeeq. 2018. "Somehow I Found You: On Black Archival Practices." *c Magazine* 137. https://cmagazine.com/issues/137/somehow-i-found-you-on-black-archival-practices.

Mol, Annemarie. 2008. "I Eat an Apple: On Theorizing Subjectivities." *Subjectivity* 22: 28–37.

Moten, Fred, and Stefano Harney. 2004. "The University and the Undercommons: Seven Theses." *Social Text* 22, no. 2: 101–15.

Murphy, Michelle. 2015. "Unsettling Care: Troubling Transnational Itineraries of Affect in Feminist Health Practices." *Social Studies of Science* 45, no. 5: 717–37.

Nash, Jennifer. 2019. *Black Feminism Reimagined: After Intersectionality*. Durham, NC: Duke University Press.

Neimanis, Astrida. 2012. "On Collaboration (For Barbara Godard)." *Nordic Journal of Feminist and Gender Research* 20, no. 3: 215–21.

Ng, Wendy, Syrus M. Ware, and Alyssa Greenberg. 2017. "Activating Diversity and Inclusion: A Blueprint for Museum Educators as Allies and Change Makers." *Journal of Museum Education* 42, no. 2: 142–54.

Nishida, Akemi. 2017. "Relationality through Differences: Disability, Affective Relationality, and the U.S. Public Healthcare Assemblage." *Subjectivities* 10, no. 1: 89–103.

O'Malley, Michael, Jennifer Sandlin, and Jake Burdick. 2020. "Public Pedagogy Theories, Methodologies, and Ethics." In *Oxford Research Encyclopedia of Education*, n.p. DOI 10.1093/acrefore/9780190264093.013.1131. Oxford: Oxford University Press.

Parker, Roszika. 1984. *The Subversive Stitch: Embroidery and the Making of the Feminine*. London: Bloomsbury.

Philpot, Clive. 2011. "Fluxus: Magazine, Manifestos, Multum in Parvo." George Maciunas Foundation. Accessed March 1, 2021. http://georgemaciunas.com/essays-2/fluxus -magazines-manifestos-multum-in-parvo-by-clive-phillapot/.

Piepzna-Samarasinha, Leah L. 2018. *Care Work: Dreaming Disability Justice*. Vancouver, BC: Arsenal Pulp Press.

Podesva, Kristina L. 2007. "A Pedagogical Turn: Brief Notes on Education as Art." *Fillip* 6. Accessed August 1, 2010. https://fillip.ca/content/a-pedagogical-turn/.

Probyn, Elspeth. 2000. *Carnal Appetites: Food, Sex, Identities*. London: Routledge.

Probyn, Elspeth. 2016. *Eating the Ocean*. Durham, NC: Duke University Press.

Puar, Jasbir. 2012. "'I Would Rather Be a Cyborg Than a Goddess': Becoming-Intersectional in Assemblage Theory." *philoSOPHIA* 2, no. 1: 49–66.

Puig de la Bellacasa, Maria. 2017. *Matters of Care: Speculative Ethics in More Than Human Worlds*. Minneapolis: University of Minnesota Press.

Rajan-Rankin, Sweta. 2021. "Material Intimacies and Black Hair Practice: Touch, Texture, Resistance. *Nordic Journal of Feminist and Gender Research* 29, no. 3: 152–64.

Recollet, Karyn. 2018. "Kinstillatory Gathering." *c Magazine* 136: 49–52.

Reed, Reed, Hannah Jickling, Loree Lawrence, Syrus Ware, and Pamila Matharu. 2012. "Doing Horizontal Work in Vertical Structures." *The Pedagogical Impulse*. Accessed March 1, 2021. https://thepedagogicalimpulse.com/doing-horizontal-work-in-vertical -structures/.

Robinson, Dylan. 2017. "Public Writing, Sovereign Reading: Indigenous Language Art in Public Space." *art journal* (Summer): 85–99.

Robinson, Dylan. 2020. *Hungry Listening: Resonant Theory for Indigenous Sound Studies*. Minneapolis: University of Minnesota Press.

Rogoff, Irit. 2000. *Terra Infirma: Geography's Visual Culture*. London: Routledge.

Rogoff, Irit. 2008. "Turning." *e-flux* 00. Accessed August 1, 2010. https://www.e-flux.com/journal/00/68470/turning/.

Rogoff, Irit. 2010a. "Free." *e-flux* 14. Accessed January 1, 2021. https://www.e-flux.com/journal/14/61311/free/.

Rogoff, Irit. 2010b. "Practicing Research: Singularising Knowledge." *MAkuZine: Journal of Artistic Research* 9. Accessed January 1, 2021. https://research.gold.ac.uk/id/eprint/20621/1/MAkuZine%209%20-%20Practising%20Research%20Singularising%20Knowledge%20IR%20only.pdf.

Roy, Parama. 2010. *Alimentary Tracks: Appetites, Aversions, and the Postcolonial*. Durham, NC: Duke University Press.

Sandlin, Jennifer A., Brian Schultz, and Jake Burdick. 2010. *Handbook of Public Pedagogy: Education and Learning beyond Schooling*. New York: Routledge.

Sandlin, Jennifer A., Jake Burdick, and Emma Rich. 2017. "Problematizing Public Engagement within Public Pedagogy Research and Practice." *Discourse: Studies in the Cultural Politics of Education* 38, no. 6: 823–35.

Sandlin, Jennifer A., Michael P. O'Malley, and Jake Burdick. 2011. "Mapping the Complexity of Public Pedagogy Scholarship: 1894–2010." *Review of Educational Research* 81, no. 3: 338–75.

Sarbanes, Janet. 2012. "A Community of Artists: Radical Pedagogy at CalArts, 1969–72." East of Borneo. June 5, 2014. Accessed March 2021. https://eastofborneo.org/articles/a-community-of-artists-radical-pedagogy-at-calarts-1969-72/.

Savage, Glenn. 2014. "Chasing the Phantoms of Public Pedagogy: Political, Popular and Concrete Publics." In *Problematising Public Pedagogy*, edited by Jake Burdick, Jennifer A. Sandlin, and Michael P. O'Malley, 79–90. New York: Routledge.

Schmidt-Burkhardt, Astrit, ed. 2003. *Maciunas' Learning Machines: From Art History to a Chronology of Fluxus*. Berlin: Vice Versa.

Schröter, Jens. 2012. "Four Models of Intermediality." In *Travels in Intermediality*, edited by Bernd Herzogenrath, 15–36. Hanover, NH: Dartmouth College Press.

Sekula, Allan. 1986. "The Body and the Archive." *October* 39: 3–64.

Shange, Savannah. 2019. *Progressive Dystopia: Abolition, Antiblackness, and Schooling in San Francisco*. Durham, NC: Duke University Press.

Sholette, Gregory. 2018. "Dewy, Beuys, Cage, and the Vulnerable yet Utterly Unremarkable Heresy of Socially Engaged Art Education (SEAE)." In *Art as Social Action*, edited by Gregory Sholette, Chloe Bass, and Social Practice Queens, 279–94. New York: Allworth Press.

Sholtz, Janae. 2018. "Fluxus Affects of Indeterminacy." In *The Dark Precursor: Deleuze and Artistic Research*, edited by Paulo de Assis and Paolo Giudici. Ithaca, NY: Cornell University Press.

Shotwell, Alexis. 2016. *Against Purity: Living Ethically in Compromised Times*. Minneapolis: University of Minnesota Press.

Simpson, Leanne. 2014. "Land as Pedagogy: Nishnaabeg Intelligence and Rebellious Transformation." *Decolonization: Indigeneity, Education and Society* 3, no. 3: 1–25.

Singh, Julietta. 2018b. *No Archive Will Restore You*. Lexington, KY: Punctum Books.

Singh, Julietta. 2018a. *Undoing Mastery: Dehumanism and Decolonial Entanglements.* Durham, NC: Duke University Press.

Smith, Owen F. 1993. "Fluxus: A Brief History and Other Fictions." In *In the Spirit of Fluxus: Essays,* edited by Janet Jenkins, Joan Rothfuss, and Elizabeth Armstrong, 22–37. Minneapolis, MN: Walker Art Center.

Smith, Owen F. 2005. "Teaching and Learning about Fluxus: Thoughts, Observations, and Suggestions from the Front Lines." *Visible Language* 39, no. 3: 218–34.

Snaza, Nathan, and John Weaver. 2015. *Posthumanism and Educational Research.* New York: Routledge.

Snaza, Nathan, and Julietta Singh. 2021. "Dehumanist Education and the Colonial University." *Social Text* 39, no. 1: 1–19.

Solnit, Rebecca. 2020. "Foreword." In *Celebrate People's History: The Poster Book of Resistance and Revolution,* edited by Josh MacPhee, 17–20. New York: Feminist Press at CUNY.

Sonu, Debbie, and Jeremy Benson. 2016. "The Quasi-Human Child: How Normative Conceptions of Childhood Enabled Neoliberal School Reform in the United States." *Curriculum Inquiry* 45, no. 3: 230–47.

Springgay, Stephanie. 2008. *Body Knowledge and Curriculum: Pedagogies of Touch in Youth and Visual Culture.* New York: Peter Lang.

Springgay, Stephanie. 2012. "The Chinatown Foray as Sensational Pedagogy." *Curriculum Inquiry* 41: 636–56.

Springgay, Stephanie. 2014. "How to Be an Artist by Night: Critical Public Pedagogy and Double Ontology." In *Problematizing Public Pedagogy Handbook,* edited by Jennifer A. Sandlin, Michael P. O'Malley, and Jake Burdick, 133–48. New York: Routledge.

Springgay, Stephanie. 2019. "How to Write as Felt: Touching Transmaterialities and More-Than-Human Intimacies." *Studies in Educational Philosophy* 38: 57–69.

Springgay, Stephanie, and Sarah E. Truman. 2016. "Stone Walks: Inhuman Animacies and Queer Archives of Feeling." *Discourse: Studies in the Cultural Politics of Education* 38, no. 6: 1–13.

Springgay, Stephanie, and Sarah E. Truman. 2017. "A Transmaterial Approach to Walking Methodologies: Embodiment, Affect, and a Sonic Art Performance." *Body and Society* 23, no. 4: 27–58.

Springgay, Stephanie, and Sarah E. Truman. 2018. *Walking Methodologies in a More-Than-Human World: WalkingLab.* New York: Routledge.

Springgay, Stephanie, and Sarah E. Truman. 2019a. "Counterfuturisms and Speculative Temporalities: Walking Research-Creation in Schools." *International Journal of Qualitative Studies in Education* 32, no. 6: 547–59.

Springgay, Stephanie, and Sarah E. Truman. 2019b. "Walking Research-Creation: QTBI-POC Temporalities and World Makings." *MAI: Feminism and Visual Culture,* May 16. https://maifeminism.com/walking-research-creation-qtbipoc-temporalities-and-world-makings/.

Springgay, Stephanie, and Sarah E. Truman. 2019c. "Research-Creation Walking Methodologies and an Unsettling of Time." *International Review of Qualitative Research* 12, no. 1: 85–93.

Springgay, Stephanie, and Sarah E. Truman. 2019d. "Walking in/as Publics: Editors. Introduction to the Special Issue WalkingLab." *Journal of Public Pedagogy* 4: 1–12. http://www.publicpedagogies.org/wp-content/uploads/2019/11/01-Springgay.pdf.

Stein, Maurice, and Larry Miller. 1970. *Blueprint for Counter Education*. Los Angeles: Inventory Press.

Steward, Jan, and Corita Kent. 1992. *Learning by Heart*. New York: Bantam Books.

Stewart, Kathleen. 2007. *Ordinary Affects*. Durham, NC: Duke University Press.

Stoler, Ann L. 2002. "Colonial Archives and the Arts of Governance." *Archival Science* 2, nos. 1–2: 87–109.

Styres, Sandra. 2019. "Literacies of Land: Decolonizing Narratives, Storying, and Literature." In *Indigenous and Decolonizing Studies in Education: Mapping the Long View*, edited by Linda T. Smith, Eve Tuck, and K. Wayne Yang, 24–35. New York: Routledge.

Thompson, Cheryl. 2018. "Searching for Black Voices in Canada's Archives: The Invisibility of a 'Visible' Minority." *PUBLIC: Art/Culture/Ideas* 57: 88–95. Toronto, ON: York University.

Thompson, Chris. 2011. *Felt: Fluxus, Joseph Beuys, and the Dalai Lama*. Minneapolis: University of Minnesota Press.

Tompkins, Kyla. 2012. *Racial Indigestion: Eating Bodies in the 19th Century*. New York: New York University Press.

Truman, Sarah E. 2020. "The Intimacies of Doing Research-Creation." In conversation with Natalie Loveless, Erin Manning, Natasha Myers, and Stephanie Springgay. In *Knowings and Knots: Methodologies and Ecologies in Research-Creation*, edited by Natalie Loveless, 221–51. Edmonton: University of Alberta Press.

Truman, Sarah E., and Stephanie Springgay. 2015. "The Primacy of Movement in Research-Creation: New Materialist Approaches to Art Research and Pedagogy." In *Art's Teachings, Teaching's Art: Philosophical, Critical, and Educational Musings*, edited by Megan Laverty and Tyson Lewis, 151–64. New York: Springer.

Truman, Sarah E., and Stephanie Springgay. 2019. "Queer Walking Tours and the Affect Contours of Place." *Cultural Geographies* 26, no. 4: 527–34.

Tsing, Anna. 2015. *The Mushroom at the End of the World*. Princeton, NJ: Princeton University Press.

Tuck, Eve. 2009. "Suspending Damage: A Letter to Communities." *Harvard Educational Review* 79, no. 3: 409–27.

Tuck, Eve, and Marcia McKenzie. 2015. *Place in Research*. New York: Routledge.

Ware, Syrus. 2017. "All Power to All People? Black LGBTTI2QQ Activism, Remembrance, and Archiving in Toronto." *TSQ: Transgender Studies Quarterly* 4, no. 2: 170–80.

Ware, Syrus, 2019. "Organizing on the Corner: Trans Women of Colour and Sex Worker Activism in Toronto in the 1980s and 1990s." Interview with Monica Forrester and Chanelle Gallant. In *Marvellous Grounds: Queer of Colour Histories of Toronto*, edited by Jin Haritaworn, Ghaida Moussa, and Syrus Ware, 32–46. Toronto, ON: Between the Lines.

Ware, Syrus. 2020a. "*Crip Times* Episode 1: The Syrus Marcus Ware Episode." *Bodies in Translation*, November 16. Accessed December 1, 2020. https://bodiesintranslation.ca /crip-times-episode-1-the-syrus-marcus-ware/.

Ware, Syrus. 2020b. "Power to All People: Black LGBTTI2QQ Activism, Remembrance, and Archiving in Toronto." In *Until We Are Free: Reflections on Black Lives Matter in Canada*, edited by Rodney Diverlus, Sandy Hudson, and Syrus Ware, 279–94. Regina, SK: University of Regina Press.

Watts, Robert. 1970. "The Artist as Teacher." In *The Arts on Campus: The Necessity for Change*, edited by James Ackerman and Margaret Mahoney, 51–62. Greenwich, CT: New York Graphic Society.

Weheliye, Alexander. 2014. *Habeas Viscus: Racializing Assemblages, Biopolitics, and Black Feminist Theories of the Human*. Durham, NC: Duke University Press.

Willard, Tania. 2018. "The BUSH Manifesto." *c Magazine* 136: 6–7.

Willard, Tania. 2019. "Strong Breeze Cmes'ekst." In *The Work of Wind: Air, Land, Sea*, edited by Christine Shaw and Etienne Turpin, 188–210. Berlin: K. Verlag.

Wilson, Elizabeth. 2015. *Gut Feminism*. Durham, NC: Duke University Press.

Wolfe, Morris. 2001. *Five Turbulent Years*. Toronto, ON: Grub Street Books.

Page references with n refer to notes; page references with P refer to plate numbers.

worldings, future. *See* future worldings

Wynter, Sylvia, 145

Your Lupines or Your Life: about, 45–49; *Abject Awards,* 45, 47–49, 53–54, P.24–P.27; aesthetic taste and art, 46–47; artist-residencies, 45–46, 180n3; contemporary art, 47, 180n3; found posters, 46, P.22–P.23; funeral flowers, 45, 47–49, P.24–P.27; garbage, 46, P.21; key questions, 51; as radical pedagogy, 53–54; research-creation, 181n4 (Ch. 1); snowball sales, 180n3, 181n4 (Ch. 1); socially engaged art, 49–54, 180n3; students (Gr. 6), 45–46; trade, 180n3, 181n4 (Ch. 1)

youth. *See* children and youth

zines: *Instant Class Kit,* 113; *Keep Queering the Syllabus,* 121, 141, 144–45, P.49; as multiples, 92–93, 101–2, 113; OCAD U's archives, 156; syllabi, 92–93, 101–2; transformations over time, 140. *See also* multiples; public/ations